Sister, Survivor

Finding Your Survivor Spirit

--------------------2nd Edition--------------------

Ayngel "BOSHEMIA" Overson

www.Sister-Survivor.com

*If you would like a copy of the full color version of the book go
to Sister-Survivor.com for details on the free PDF.*

Copyright © 2013 by Ayngel "Boshemia" Overson

Boshemia's Bohemia
PO Box 134
Nucla, CO 81424
www.boshemiasbohemia.com

Ordering Information:
Quantity sales. Special discounts are available on quantity purchases by corporations, associations, and others. For details, contact the publisher at the address above.
Orders by U.S. trade bookstores and wholesalers. Please contact Boshemia's Bohemia:
Tel: (970) 864-7557 or visit www.boshemiasbohemia.com

Printed in the United States of America

ISBN#: 978-0984552603

Credits...

Cover art created by © Vasilis Akoinoglou |
Dreamstime.com

Cover design by Dzines18.

Technical adviser on the book Kaitomono.

Chapter separation images used with the gracious permission of Elizabeth Alraune and Cedonaah. Please visit
cedonaah.blogspot.com to find out more about her
healing artwork.

Line art is public domain. Z-Most fonts. Why use the
odd little things? T adore them! he Z-Most fonts were
drawn by Hindmost – and fonted by Zillah 2003. You
can download the fonts at www.fonts2u.com (search Z-
Most there are a lot!)

Roll Call from print or media sources and most were
found at:
http://www.aswaterspassingby.org/notablesurvivors.ht
ml

To My Dearest Elizabeth,
**(And the things we aren't supposed to
talk about...)**

Contents

"My mission in life is not merely to survive, but to thrive; and to do so with some passion, some compassion, some humor, and some style."

~Maya Angelou

Beyond Simply Living...

The question has been asked: when a plane crashes on the border of a country in the east and a country in the west, in which place should the Survivors be buried? The answer? Survivors aren't the people who need to be buried. Those, we call victims.

To survive...

To remain alive, to exist;

To persevere despite hardships or trauma.

To remain functional after damage or injury;

...

To outlive, or to live longer than;

To endure or live through...

On the outside, there is very little to distinguish one abuse Survivor from the next. But inside is where things really matter. Some may see the victim of abuse as weak but many of the bravest people I have ever known were Survivors.

Your Survivor Spirit is there to keep you alive, and it will, even in the most unthinkable circumstances. What happened to make you a Survivor can range from bad, to worse, to "Oh my God!"

Throughout this book, you will find the names of famous people who have somehow survived the unthinkable. Movie stars, famous authors, sports celebrities and more... so different, yet so similar.

They had their secrets, but they kept going. They had their sorrows, but they kept going. They had their pain, but they kept going. They are still here, because they keep going.

The only difference you will find between the helpless and hopeless victim of circumstances and the Oprah Winfreys of this world is simple, the victims gave up and the Survivors kept going.

There is no magic gift or divine blessing that allows one person to live a life of happiness while the other is doomed to a life of sorrow.

The word Survivor finds its origins in the Latin word supervivere, from the root word vivere, which means "to live." Super brings vivere to a place above simply living; it brings it beyond. To survive is to live through your experiences.

You are a born fighter, and you are still here for a reason.

Too many people muddle through life without ever really living at all. They are passive participants in their own lives, blown about by the winds and whims of others.

Many of our stories begin in abusive homes... But they do not have to end there..

There is no secret formula, or magic trick. A Survivor just keeps going long after the victim has given up.

I have no doubt that life exists after death, but I do have some real questions about life before death. There is more to life than simply living. To survive is to break free and rise above.

Your story is still being written even now. Every day is a new page. But who is holding the pen? Survivors keep moving toward the light at the end of the tunnel. Just one step more, always one step more.

The nature of the Survivor is to face the darkness head-on, moving around it, through it, and beyond it. You can make it through some mighty dark times, but tough times were never meant to be permanent.

Nobody was born to be a victim.

If you weren't a Survivor you wouldn't still be here, but here you are. You had your secrets, but you kept going. You had your sorrows, but you kept going. You had your pain, but you kept going. You are still here, and still you keep going.

Every cycle has a beginning, but how it ends is entirely up to you.

The woman who was a child abuse victim, can easily become a teen sexual assault victim. As an adult, she may become a battered housewife, and later in life, a victim of elder abuse. She may never know anything else.

I was four years old the first time I was molested. Before the age of twelve, eight different pedophiles had their hands on me. People who loved you hurt you; that's just how it was in my world.

The abuse was still there inside of the hyperactive child who longed to be a superhero. It was still there inside of the teenager who traded her body for the closest thing to love she knew. It was still there inside of the woman who was afraid to leave her own children alone with a babysitter. It is still there now. There is no way for me to make those experiences go away.

I entered adulthood with the idea that love was supposed to hurt, and would confirm this fact over and over in my life. People have always been quick to see the damage that is visible, but they never seemed to ask, "Why?"

After my divorce and a subsequent date rape, I realized that it was about time that someone started asking those questions. I had become responsible for the lives of three other human beings, and I owed it to them to stop the cycle for good.

Looking back there was clearly a pattern running through my life. There were a lot of abusers in my past, but the only common denominator was me. In my mind that meant there was something wrong with me, but the more questions I asked of my family, the bigger the picture became.

I had always understood that my mother was different, although I was too young to understand why. I knew that we were closer on one level than most parents and children were, but there were times when the distance between us seemed immeasurable.

My mother and I had a hot and cold relationship: too close, too far, too dependent, too independent. I would later be able to describe my first marriage the very same way.

The Dance of the Survivor.

I grew up watching my mother endure one painful relationship after another. She had her own battles with drugs and alcohol, and frequent bouts of depression, but those were just on the surface. Inside my mother was a Survivor - just like me.

3

I later discovered that my mother was molested by several family members beginning at a very young age. Some of the abuses that she suffered were horrific. She had grown up watching her father abuse her mother, and there was nobody around to show her anything different.

It is any wonder that her adult relationships were often tumultuous and painful? Like me, abuse was her normal.

My mother and her siblings grew up dirt poor while my grandfather conducted a very open affair in full view of their small town neighbors. He and his mistress had a child together several years before my grandmother finally found the courage to divorce him.

It wasn't easy.

My grandfather beat my grandmother when she tried to leave. He once left her so severely bruised that she was afraid to go to work the next day. Even after the divorce, he stalked her, tampered with her vehicles and threatened other men who spoke to her.

> If abuse has become your normal then something has to change. Stop looking outside of yourself for the solution. You will never find it there.
>
> That something that needs to change in your life is not someone else, it is You.

My grandmother raised her children as a divorcee in a small town in the 60's. People were not always kind to her, or to her children. Despite that, she raised five happy and healthy children who have seen much success in their personal and professional lives.

She did what she had to do for her children.

Stepping back another generation, my great-grandmother grew tired of her husband's drunken beatings and risked it all. My great-grandfather blacked out drunk one night and woke up on a Greyhound bus destined for California. It took a great deal of courage for her raise five children as a single mother at the end of the Great Depression, but what other choice did she have?

I am a fourth generation divorcee. A fourth generation codependent. I am a fourth generation victim of abuse.

More importantly I am a fourth generation SURVIVOR.

What can I say? It's a family tradition.

You and I have never met, but we are part of a family just the same. We are a family joined not by blood, but by spirit. We share something far more intimate than ancestry or genetics. We have secrets.

Upon first glance, it hardly seems we have anything in common at all.

But we are a family. We are here with you in spirit always.

We are men. We are women. We are young, and we are old. We've all lived our own unique stories, from our own unique backgrounds, and cultures. We all have different skin colors and economic status. On the surface, it hardly seems we have anything in common at all, but what we have in common is deep within.

Your Survivor Spirit has probably gotten you into trouble once or twice, and has more than likely saved you a few times as well. It's okay if you don't see it yet, many people can't, but it's inside of each of us just waiting for its opportunity to be voiced.

As the worst parts of the abuse fade away you will find yourself left with the real you. It is the You that you were always meant to be.

While your secrets have separated you from so many others, they are what connect you to the family of Survivors.

Surviving abuse takes courage. Surviving abuse takes tenacity. Surviving abuse takes guts. You don't need a hero to save you. You are perfectly capable of rescuing yourself, if given half a chance.

Many women have come before you, many men as well. If you aren't sure that you have the strength of your own to use, it's okay, you can borrow some of theirs for a while.

Like any journey worth taking, there will be ups and there will be downs, but don't worry, you aren't alone. There are support groups both online and off, no matter what your situation or comfort level. If you reach out your hand you will find someone willing to help.

There are many of us Survivors in the world. Far too many. You belong to a different kind of family now, a safe family, a family with some of the strongest roots you will ever encounter.

We all come with an inborn Survivor Spirit, and with it comes the strength to help you stand up for yourself, assert your rights, heal yourself, and even create positive changes in the world around you. It is that spirit that has kept you going all this time and it keeps you going even now.

Even those parts of you that have been picked on, kicked around, ridiculed, and criticized are part of your unique Survivor Spirit. That stubbornness that people sometimes complain about? That part of you that doesn't seem to know when to quit?

It is just waiting for you to use it. It always has been.

So little sets the Survivor apart from the rest of the world, but set them apart it does.

Survivors of Note...

Abraham Lincoln
President of the U.S.
Domestic Violence

Ludwig van Beethoven
Composer
Child Abuse

Maya Angelou
Author, Poet
Underage Rape

Oprah Winfrey
Media Mogul
Incest

Victoria Beckham (Posh Spice)
Singer
Bullying Survivor

"When the Japanese
mend broken ob-
jects, they ag-
grandize the dam-
age by filling the
cracks with gold.
They believe that
when something's
suffered damage
and has a history
it becomes more
beautiful."

~Barbara Bloom

Fingerprints In The Clay

When people share their stories of abuse, they often lay it bare before you as if it were a broken thing, scarred and hideous. Do they expect horror? Disgust? Disbelief? Pity? Judgment? Blame?

Yes.

And far worse.

Abuse can so easily become an invisible barrier between yourself and the world at large, setting you apart, casting you out. Victims have faced rejection in the past that can make something as simple as telling the truth a terrifying experience.

There are no explanations, no ways to make sense of abuse.

If someone loves you then they place value on you, or at least that's how it was supposed to be. So what of the abuse Survivor? Were they abused because they were not worthy of better treatment?

No. No. No. NO.

Some have suffered unimaginable abuse at the hands of other human beings. Humans don't need a reason to be horrible to each other. Yet most of us still operate under the delusion that bad things only happen to you if you really, really deserve it.

Though you may feel as if it were something unique about you that caused your abuse, it takes no special qualities or talents to become a victim. Simply being in the wrong place with the wrong person at the wrong time is enough in most cases.

What happens does not unhappen.

When someone gains access to your most vulnerable self and violates your trust, your life can feel like shards of pottery scattered on the floor. Cracks be damned, the past has now become a part of who you are, but it is only a piece. Abuse doesn't go away; it's always there, but it doesn't have to rule your life.

Years ago, my mother and I were hired to handle an estate sale for an elderly woman who had passed away. New to the Ebay business, we had no idea of the scope of the project in front of us.

Heavy lidded trunks, button-up baby shoes, and brass bed sets filled every room of the woman's home. The sheer variety of depression glass alone was overwhelming. We didn't have much experience with antiques at the time, but we oohed and ahhed at each new discovery.

> Every crease, every line spoke to me...
>
> ✵
>
> Among those fingerprints I found not defects, but a strange sort of perfection.

Somewhere in the midst of the butter crocks and canning jars from the kitchen we found a plain brown bottle made of earthen clay. It seemed so out of place among the other items, so much so that at first we mistook it for junk. I tried to make out the only obvious marking, a smudged craftsman's stamp of a lion pressed near the neck but found little else in the way of identification.

On closer inspection I noticed something unusual towards the bottom. Several fingerprints were barely visible beneath the glaze. We only found one similar bottle in our research, which just gave us a general age and little more. Just a slight change in my perspective, and I suddenly saw the bottle in a very different light. Those "defects" were left by fingers placed in wet clay over 100 years ago.

Among those fingerprints I no longer found defects, but a strange sort of perfection. Every crease, every line now spoke to me of a time when items were hand-formed and hand-finished, when individuality still counted for something.

Humans can be as impressionable as clay, especially within their most intimate relationships. Each person who has ever touched your life has left some sort of mark behind. Like that wet earth, you are shaped and formed by events that are sometimes beyond your control. A fingerprint here, a stamp there, and now and then a crack.

In life, even the tiniest of pieces can be put back together by a patient and loving hand. And there is only one person who knows which pieces fit where. A bottle is only a bottle, and that is all it will ever be. It was created to fill a temporary need, and once met there were no aspirations to become something bigger, something better... something happier.

When I allowed myself to see the bottle for what it really was, I no longer saw the imperfections and flaws, but a mark of individuality. I had to learn to look at myself the very same way. It's okay to see yourself as you truly are; it isn't as horrible as you think, I promise you. Those fingerprints are part of your value.

You aren't trash, but nobody else is going to see your value until you do. No, you aren't perfect, nobody is, but you are the only person in the world who can be a perfect YOU.

Once you figure it out other people will catch on.

Find that part of you that is authentic, the person you were truly meant to be. Not the person you are told to be, not the person others wish you were, but your true self.

You have the ability to be far more than what you appear to be. Even if you are emptied of purpose right now, you can be refilled. Look beyond what has always been. The bottle only became precious to me when I took the time to get to know it and discover its rich history. You owe yourself that same respect.

Every once in a while, even the most predictable person can surprise you. The real trick is finding a way to surprise yourself. There is value in being you, but it will not be apparent until you choose to see it. You really do have something to offer the world that nobody else can, and that something is simply *you*.

You have already put a lot time into imagining your life with the abuse. You have to spend even more time doing the opposite.

Before now your creativity has gone towards continuing the patterns you are used to. It's easy to start thinking that darkness is all there is to life. The bad can become so overpowering that it blocks out those parts of your life that are good.

Eating, sleeping, and anxiety disorders develop. Addictions are formed. Depression can build, which can lead to self-mutilation and suicide attempts. When you cast back through your mind, through the bulk of your memories, and all you find is negative, then depression is a pretty logical outcome.

It is hard to take control of your mind when you can't see the good stuff. If your mind is stuck in a bad place then you might react with anger or even tears. And yet, if that same situation happened when you are having a good day the same that incident could slide by almost without notice.

Bad moods aren't just for full moons. They can become your whole life. It's like you are trying to see the good parts of your life through a layer of mud. Some bad moods just never end, but then again, it depends on what we feed it.

Being imperfect is a wonderful way to determine your own humanity.

The one person who most needs to see how uniquely magnificent you are, is you.

In the happiest of lives some rain still must fall. Your life is never going to come to a place where your "happily ever after" has arrived. Even fairy tales don't work that smoothly.

You can't take the bad out of the good, and you can't take the good out of the bad, either. There will be ups and there will be downs, but most of all there will be middles. The middle is where true contentment is found. You may be at the bottom of the pit, but look up. It's not too late.

My life began as a cool, clear glass of water, but through the years I had collected so much muck and mud that seeing through all of it was almost impossible. Water that is tainted may settle for a time, but all it takes is a small disturbance to send it all spinning out of control again. People kept telling me to fix it, but how do you take the water out of the mud?

Inconceivable!

I couldn't take them out or make the bad things go away. Neither can you. Nobody can. What we can do is dilute it. We can take that glass of cloudy water and pour it in a bucket full of clean water. We can take that bucket and pour it into a bathtub. We can drain that bathtub into a lake. We can follow that lake all the way to the ocean.

You can't take away from your experiences, but you can always add to them.

My negative mindset had almost totally blocked some of my pleasant memories from view, but I was the one who was keeping things stirred up. Wherever you allow your mind to dwell you will find yourself dwelling as well, so you have to make an effort to choose that place wisely. You can't strain the bad stuff out of the water, but you can drown it out.

When I stopped being afraid of the bad memories that might pop up, good memories began to surface as well–times of laughter, times of comfort, and times of hope. Mother and daughter sexual abuse Survivors are bound to have some intimacy issues, and we did, but we got over it. Even though we weren't a traditional family, there has always been love.

Bad stuff happened in my childhood, but there was still far more good than bad.

My childhood is also where my mother taught me the proper usage of a Walmart toy aisle. To this day we can entertain ourselves in the toy department for hours. We figured out how to rap using sound bites from talking books, and what fun it is to set off a whole shelves of bouncing tigers. We touch every toy and pull every string.

My grandmother has pretended not to know us out of sheer embarrassment.

I remember the pain my mother went through when I was growing up, and I remember my own pain as well. Those are such small parts of the whole though. My childhood had moments of abuse, but there was so much more.

My mother taught me how to create my own happiness. I remember being very lonely as a child, but I also fondly remember my mother and her amazing breakfasts over open camp fires in the summer. There were ice cream sundae parties that lead to whipped cream fights in the kitchen, and chocolate syrup in our hair.

My mom and I had some amazing times together.

My kids wonder why their mother will walk through the store singing "All You Need is Love" without shame today. It's because my own mother took fun to a whole new level. My kids and I love to sing, and we aren't hurting anybody.

Yes, we get strange looks but it's fun!

I always wanted the mother daughter relationship that I saw in the movies, but the movies aren't real. Our relationship has always been intense, and strange, and wonderful. I don't always understand the dynamic between us but I accept it.

I have learned so much from her.

My mother was the person who taught me to love words in the first place.

Taking control of your own mind is not about getting rid of all of the bad stuff; that's impossible, instead you must dilute it with good whenever you get a chance. When life is calm and things are good, stop and record those moments in your brain so that you can use them when you need them most. Store your happiness up within you, no matter how small it may seem. It adds up.

Your life began as a cool clear glass of water. Over the years it has collected a lot of muck and mud.

❀

Water that is tainted may settle for a time, but all it takes is a small disturbance to send it all spinning out of control again.

Stop trying to make your relationships into what you think they should be and start asking yourself why they are there. If you have to force it to work, it's because it was never meant to work in the first place.

Hope can sustain you through just about anything. It won't make your problems magically go away, and it won't make other people change into something they are not, but it can keep you afloat long after others have gone down with the ship.

Sometimes large parts of our lives are covered in a veil of darkness, the abuse was particularly horrific, the pain incredibly intense. Maybe there is very little happiness in your past worth holding on to. It happens.

That does not mean you can't create new memories.

Sometimes the best things I can find to be joyful about are a snippet of a song in my head, or a handful of Milk Duds waiting on my nightstand–small victories, but victories just the same. The scope of the miracle involved doesn't stop me from doing a tushie dance in celebration anyhow.

While many will tell you to stop living in the past, I won't. I know how very hard that can be. That decision rests only with you.

You may have faced things in your past that left you wondering if you even wanted life to go on at all, but life has gone on and will continue to go on. It doesn't matter if you choose to move along with it or not.

Time is relative, and the only person who can decide exactly how much time it will take for you to reach the next step is you. When we are ready to let go and move on from our hurt, we do.

All or none, life will go on.

Underage Rape Survivors

Billie Holiday
Jazz Singer/Songwriter

Elizabeth I
Queen of England

Fantasia Barrino
Singer

Fiona Apple
Musician

Mary Karr
Author

"I've never known a normal day in my life, and Lord willing, I never will."

~ Me

Where Do Boshemia's Come From?

A local group church people has shunned me. When I asked why, I was told it was because I dressed Goth. I'm not Goth. I'm not anything. I'm just me.

And I really like black.

A friend of mine who fancied himself the next H.P. Lovecraft once asked my mother what had happened to make me so strange. She laughed and told him that she blamed it all on Stephen King. (A bit unfair to the master of horror I think.)

I always wanted to be a good girl, I was just never very good at it. Being named Angel is kind of like being the preacher's kid. It comes with a whole lot of expectations behind it. You either find a way to live up to it, or you just try to live it down.

My mother always told me that the name Angel came to her in a dream. As if I was sent here for a special purpose of some sort. My life has been quite the opposite of my mother's intentions though.

To be fair, my grandmother warned her that naming me Angel was destined to end in disaster. "She'll be the biggest devil on the block..."

Yeah, about that....

My life has been a bit of a mess, but my family and I have just found our own version of peace amongst the chaos. I finally found a place where I am perfectly content just being me, living in my own little writer's bubble. I've never known a normal day in my life, and lord willing I never will. It has taken me a long time to learn to love myself warts and all, and my past is just another part of that whole. It's time to bring those skeletons out of the closet and make them dance!

So, Where do Boshemia's come from anyway?

Born in Germany, my parents returned to the U.S. when I was 7 months old. My young parents divorced when I was two, and I went to live with my grandparents while my mother went into the Air Force to build a future for us.

My earliest memories take place on 88 acres of Colorado pastureland. My mother was a hippie, and a lot of people blamed her for my free spirit. Or maybe it was running through freshly irrigated hay fields barefoot and naked in a world where nobody really cared. I still have a lot of that little girl inside of me today, perhaps even more now than I was allowed to have in my child-hood.

I was four years old the night the family found me sitting in the kitchen sink using the kitchen sprayer to wash myself off. I'd wet the bed again, and every-one thought it was so adorable that I had crawled into the sink to clean myself off rather than wake up an adult to help me.

At four years old I already had a very big secret. Late one night I had asked a house guest for help, but something had happened. A bad thing. I didn't like the things that he had done to me, or the way they made me feel so. I never wanted to trust a big person to touch me in those places again. Everyone was so proud of me for growing up. I had just grown wise.

It happened again at the dairy, and then in other places at other times. It just kept happening and I had no idea why. When I was alone with men, they sometimes put their hands on me that's just the way it was. I learned not to trust people who were kind to me. At four years old I understood that nobody does anything for you without expecting something in return.

By the time I was twelve, seven different men had left their marks upon my life. The last person who molested me was a female. In a strange way I learned to trust people who treated me like shit over those who were kind. At least they were honest up front.

And over the years the free spirit within me slowly died away.

I still ran around barefoot, but I didn't dance naked in the rain anymore. I couldn't stand being naked at all, and I still can't. I still can't sleep without something covering my body. I need a barrier between myself and the world to feel safe. And I have a very hard time trusting people enough to allow them to get close to me.

The people who hurt me weren't creepy neighborhood strangers. They were all friends. Family members. Daycare providers. People I loved and trusted. People that I thought loved and trusted me.

In my world, the sexualization of a child was not shocking, simply normal. Sex was just something that one person did with another. I thought that everybody had been through the things that I had.

My mother had also been molested, but I didn't know or understand what that did to her ability to open up to me. She didn't know that I had been molested either. It was just a subject that never came up. If we had to deal with the other's problems, it meant dealing with our own, and neither of us were ready for that.

My whole life I have watched women sacrificing their *self* on the altar of love again and again until there was no SELF left to give.

They didn't have to, but they have never known anything else. It became our normal.

My mother didn't talk about abuse, and my grandmother didn't either. So neither did I. I was holding in a lot of secrets by the time my teen years rolled around.

She was distant, never really able to bond with me fully. I, in turn, was a deeply troubled child hungry for attention. And my young mother was often unable to handle me. I began drinking before puberty, smoked cigarettes, and got caught stealing.

I was a bona fide wild child, but nobody knew why.

To this day, when I begin to feel like my world is crumbling out of control, my first instinct is to return to those old self-destructive behaviors. To seek unhealthy attention. To demean myself. To punish myself. To deny myself. To rebel against what is good for me and return to the comfortably painful patterns of past relationships.

To return to what was normal for me.

In my eyes, I held no worth other than what I could do for others. My life has been a constant search for approval

My mother had deemed me completely uncontrollable by then (a perspective that still hasn't changed). There were problems at school, problems at home, and there was nowhere to turn for either of us. I was busted shoplifting, and then for larceny. I was ditching school almost every day.

But love was always my drug of choice.

My reactions to abuse were abnormal in polite society, but they were my normal. Your reactions to abuse have probably been very normal for you as well. I put myself through hell looking for Mr. Right, but I was really looking for someone who was just as dysfunctional as I was.

The moment one relationship fell apart I was out searching for another long before the tears had dried. I went through relationships like tissues, only I was the one being used and thrown away. I tried to drown my pain in drugs and alcohol, and attempted suicide several times. I wanted someone else to give me value.

It doesn't take much for one Survivor to recognize another, you just look for the cracks.

So many people in my life had told me that I was broken, and I believed them. I over-thought every decision I ever made, and kicked myself for every mistake. I was tired of living with the word victim stamped across my forehead, and as my children grew I began to think that it might be genetic.

A lot of people told me that my kids would be just like I had been, or worse. The very thought terrified the hell right out of me.

To this day, my kids still have to remind me to take the safety helmet off and let them live. I hovered over my children nearly every waking hour of their lives, and yes, I checked on them while they were sleeping.

I couldn't stand the thought of that cycle repeating in their lives and I desperately sought a way to prevent it.

After what seemed to be a lifetime of defeat I finally surrendered my stubborn pride. I went looking for help and I found it.

I went to our local advocacy center, the San Miguel Resource Center (SMRC), to talk about the rape. We ended up talking about my entire life. Frequent changes of caregiver... Twenty-two different schools...

I didn't call the things that had happened in my life abuse back then, I didn't know that's what it was. I had to learn to redefine a lot of words, and even learn a whole new vocabulary while working with the SMRC. I discovered new ways to define the experiences I had always simply thought of as "normal:" domestic violence, emotional abuse, neglect, and a childhood full of sexual abuse.

They had to help me redefine normal.

The SMRC helps victims recognize, escape, and recover from abuse. The advocates know what we need because many of them have already been there themselves. When you have a journey to make, it always helps to have a guide familiar with the path.

Angela Goforth was my angel in the process. While most of the world stands at the top of the long dark staircase and shouts at you to join them, advocates offer you their hand and help you with the tougher steps. She encouraged me to look beyond my experiences, to find out what I was really capable of.

> I kept looking in the mirror trying to locate the invisible tattoo that only abusers could see.
>
> ⬒
>
> The one that said VICTIM.
>
> It seemed like everybody but me could see it.

I found support from their 24-hour hotline, met with an advocate for one-on-one guidance and began participating in different classes and events.

I was even able to do for others what the SMRC had done for me. At the age of 36, I became a Colorado Certified Victims Advocate. Sometimes we speak for those who can't speak for themselves, sometimes we are the voices of those who are not yet strong enough to use their own but most of the time we are tour guides.

As an advocate, I began connecting victims with the resources they needed to better their own lives and helping them navigate the complex system, but much of the time I was just a voice on the other end of the phone when someone needed to talk.

Sometimes that's all it takes.

In 2009, I was named the Domestic Violence & Sexual Assault Advocate of the Year for the work I had done with Survivors locally, and on the Internet as Boshemia.

In my spare time I started on a very special book that would talk about the many lessons that I had learned (and am still learning) along the way from Victim, to Survivor, to Thriver. That original concept, the idea of the positive traits that Survivors often possess only began with a few ideas, and a title, "Sister, Survivor."

My alter ego, Boshemia was anxious to get my writing out of the closet and into the light for her own reasons I suppose, but in time I had plenty of reasons of my own. Ed was in an accident, and I was sick. The doctors said that Ed had to find a new career, and that I would never work again. We were broke and had four kids to feed.

Desperation is an excellent motivator.

My diagnosis still varies depending on the doctor, but in short (take a deep breath anyway) repeated trauma beginning at a young age caused chronic post traumatic stress disorder presenting as ADHD. My body stayed in hyper drive for long periods of time and crashed causing a bipolar state, eventually resulting in adrenal fatigue causing bouts of chronic fatigue and Fibromyalgia symptoms.

Even shorter? PTSD.

Like a car with the gas pedal stuck to the floor, I cycled like that for nearly forty years. I kept going until I couldn't go anymore and then collapsed. I was constantly

Left untreated over the long term post traumatic stress disorder disrupts our proper stress response and weakens our adrenals. Weakened adrenals can give us the symptoms many Survivors experience...

These symptoms are sometimes mislabeled as fibromyalgia, chronic fatigue syndrome, attention deficit disorder, and bipolar depression.

tired, but utterly unable to truly rest. My body, mind, and sometimes even my spirit were exhausted but I had too much adrenaline to stop. More studies are coming out every day saying that these all may be manifestations of the same thing. Our body's natural reaction to trauma gone into hyper-drive.

After a time, our brains can be wired to react in certain ways, and continue to do so long after the dangers have passed. Life is fine, but we are still in fight or flight mode. It can keep our relationships in turmoil. It can affect our work, and our families; it can even destroy our lives.

PTSD is a very real part of the Survivor's life. It is a very real part of my life. It affected my ability to trust and form relationships, it affected my ability to care for my children, and sometimes it kept me from simply functioning like a normal human being.

I couldn't just make it go away. I had to learn to live around it. I had to learn to live through it.

They talk more about PTSD now than ever before, but it is still deeply misunderstood. It took me getting sick and nearly dying to understand the relationship between stress and the adrenals. My body was in constant overdrive and I just didn't have the tools to stop it.

I do now.

The doctors said that I would never be able to work a traditional job again, but Boshemia kept reminding me that I still had my writing.

Hidden in notebooks and file folders, and tucked away on dusty old hard drives I had the beginnings of a career. It wasn't much, but it was there. I tried to tell her that my writing wasn't for *them*, it was for me. I was happy hiding it away. It was my secret guilty pleasure nothing more.

Boshemia didn't care.

I was a hermit. I just wanted to live the quiet, lonely, isolated life of a writer, the one that everybody warned me about. But, once Boshemia took control all hope of ever attaining that was lost.

Boshemia was just a name I made up to blame my writing on, a feminization of the word Bohemian. At first hiding behind her gave me courage, but she took on a life of her own.

"Just write," she told me, but that wasn't enough. She wanted me to write publicly, and the next thing I knew she had me writing a book. Then there were talent shows, public speaking gigs, movies. It won't be long before she has me headed off to Mordor with some Hobbits to dispose of a ring.

And I slowly stepped out of the writers closet with the help of the online website Squidoo. At first, they say that you should write what you know, and I know Survivors. I was cautious in the beginning, afraid of the people out there who could hurt me but as I heard from other Survivors like me, my confidence grew.

I talk about a lot of things that people aren't supposed to talk about, and I talk about them in very different ways. I've been called a freak my whole life, and it hasn't been easy. I have lived in shame all of these years just because I knew I was different.

And the crew from Reel Thing actually liked that about me.

Uranium Drive-In became a voice for my hometown. I got to advocate for a town that I believe with all my heart is worth saving, despite the pain that I have seen here, it a a wonderful place full of wonderful people.

I doubt my small role in the movie will change anybody's minds about uranium mills or mining, but it will change their minds about each other. It will make a connection, I have already seen it beginning. Locally, this movie could bring jobs in that may save 1200 people.

Personally, it could launch a career. From standing up for abuse victims, to standing up for a whole community my voice now has the potential to be heard worldwide.

Weird.

And people still call me a freak like it's a bad thing.

I'm finally okay with that. I am what I am and I embrace it. It took me almost forty years to realize that they don't make movies about normal people...

I'm am far from a perfect Angel.

Despite all of the teasing I have had about my name not matching my personality over the years, the name Angel has nothing to do with perfection or innocence.

Its true meaning is messenger of God.

I don't know about the speaking for deities part, but I have spent most of my life studying the Survivor Spirit in one form or another, trying to figure out what it was that other people had that I did not. It turns out that I had it too, I just had to figure out how to use my powers for good instead of evil.

Something had to change to stop that cycle for good. That something was ME. I am a fourth generation abuse Survivor, I was blessed with so many strong women in my own life to learn from.

If there is a message somewhere in my mess of a life it is this...

From Victim,

To Survivor,

To Thriver...

Roll Call...

Elizabeth Barrett Browning
Poet
Abuse Survivor

Marilyn VanDerber Atler
Former Miss America
Incest

Kenny Lattimore
R&B Musician
Child Sexual Abuse Survivor

Don Lemon
CNN Anchor
Child Sexual Abuse

Janice Mirikitani
Poet
Incest Survivor

"When you stay in a situation like that, you're trapped in negative energy. I believe that if you'll just stand up and go, life will open up for you. Something just motivates you to keep moving."

~Tina Turner

Going Back Home Again, & Again...

You may not realize it yet, but you are looking for the abusers in your life as much as they are looking for you. It isn't just parents and lovers, no. Bosses, landlords, neighborhood nuisances... they seem to find you wherever you go. Once you reveal yourself as a doormat, word gets around.

It may not be normal, but somehow it has become your normal. If you grew up in an abusive home, you were wired for victimhood from the start.

You keep trying to go home over and over.

When you grow up feeling unloved or unwanted, you begin to believe you really are those things. When you think of yourself as trash, it shouldn't come as a shock when others follow suit. It shouldn't, but somehow it always does.

Our local physician's assistant, Ken Jenks, explains it this way: When a man makes a trek to the river to get water every day, he eventually wears a path. At first there is only a slight disturbance in his path. Some grass pressed down, a few bare spots. As his trips continue, the path begins to deepen and widen. After awhile other villagers begin to use it as well. Then other travelers begin to use it as well. Then, the next thing you know a man buys the land nearby and builds an inn. You become so accustomed to having those pathways inhabited that you hardly notice people taking liberties at all.

You may even begin to abuse those same paths yourself. We all have pathways in our brains, and the more those pathways are abused by one person the easier they become for other people to access and use...and the more open you are to allowing them to be used.

Some victims leave after the first sign of violence, but the majority stay as long as they can keep believing. For years and years it can go on, the cycle repeating and building.

Words like normal, love, self, and communication take on totally different meanings in the Survivor's world. Those faulty definitions become so ingrained in the brain that they are still hanging around today, years or even a lifetime later.

You have to recognize and define abuse for yourself, and for your own purposes. At the back of this book you will find a list complied by Dr. Irene Matiatos from DrIrene.com to help you determine if you have suffered abuse.

If it is abuse, call it by its rightful name. Don't move in and make yourself at home with it, but call it what it is. If your experiences have hurt you then you have earned the right to call it abuse - regardless of what the world chooses to call it.

> They are right, it's all in our head, and our bodies, and our spirits.
>
> PTSD might not be real to anybody else, but it is very real to me.

The sooner you accept that change is not in the abusers agenda, the better. Be realistic about it, don't fall into the fantasy. You can't make them change. Nobody else can either. You don't need more words, you need to see action, and you need to see it long-term.

When it comes to getting what the abuser wants versus giving you what you need, the abuser always wins. Oh, they are good at making promises, and they really do seem sincere, but they rarely keep them for long. If an abuser doesn't change the core of who they are then they will continue to do what makes them feel good, when it feels good doing it.

So when does a woman finally leave her abuser?

When she is ready, and not a moment before. Only the victim knows which straw will be the last. They rarely know when that time will be until it finally happens. Always keep some spare money, a change of clothes for you and your kids, and copies of important documents accessible.

We all left when we could stand no more, but it is amazing how much we went through to get there. Yes, you can keep hoping. Nobody is stopping you. Sometimes that hope is all that you have left to hold on to. If you truly believe that your abuser is going to change then I can't say anything to take that hope away from you. Nobody can. Hold onto it, because you are going to need it.

Things can get a lot worse than where you are now.

Little Tina's sharecropper parents had been trapped in an unhappy marriage by pregnancy. They went away to work and left her with her grandmother. It was a strict environment where she often felt trapped. When Young Tina met Ike Turner she thought she had found a way out.

It didn't take long for his actions to grow violent. He hit her with the heel of a shoe once, and another time he beat her in her face and ribs with a shoe stretcher. She says he would walk around biting his lip like he was working himself up, and she knew what was coming. He intentionally gave her black eyes, like he wanted her bruises to be seen.

Tina Turner knew it wasn't love that powered her husband's fists, but she didn't know how to escape. She didn't have anywhere to go if she did.

Why do we stay?

The fear of being alone, of isolation. The fear of losing what little support you have. The fear of the unknown. The fear that you don't have the ability to make good decisions. The fear that nobody will listen. The fear that you aren't sure if you will be able to care for yourself or your children. The fear that you are afraid to reach out for help because things might get worse.

Maybe you are afraid of everything, and maybe, just maybe, you are afraid of nothing.

On rare occasions abusers do get help. They work hard to learn healthy relationship skills. They learn to live in a balanced world that doesn't revolve around them. They utilize Group Therapy, Alcoholics Anonymous, and learn to manage their anger. It isn't a process that takes weeks or months, but a lifetime.

You have a responsibility to keep yourself safe first, and if you have children that responsibility is doubled. Ignoring abuse in the hopes that it will go away can have deadly consequences. Over 1,000 women are killed every year by intimate partners. Men are only slightly safer, at just over 400 per year.

In 1976 Ike beat Tina Turner one last time, and she promised herself that she would die before she went back. "I was just happy when I started to like myself—when I divorced and took control of my life."

Escaping from Ike with just 36 cents to her name, Tina began a new life. She cleaned houses for a while and started singing in smaller venues. She released her solo album, *Private Dancer* in 1984, which went on to sell more than 10 million copies. Three Grammys and a number one hit later, she is still filling stadiums at the age of 70.

Nobody knows what would have happened to Tina if she'd stayed with Ike. She didn't wait around to find out. The chances that he would kill her grew each time he hit her. Tina's advice: "For anyone who's in an abusive relationship...Go."

That is the Survivor Spirit talking, ignore it at your peril. If it isn't already present, physical harm becomes more and more likely with each repeat of the pattern.

Once you reveal yourself as a doormat, word gets around. You keep trying to go home over and over.

When you are abused, your brain makes connections between things that were never meant to be linked. Love and pain. Love and sorrow. Love and regret. Love and rejection.

You don't have to constantly scramble to earn love.

There is plenty of love to go around if you know where to look for it. A relationship where people love and respect one another really does exist. To get there, something has to change.

You can't meet Mister Right as long as Mr. Wrong is filling up his place in your life. Millions of Survivors who have come before you have walked away from abuse for good, and so will you.

Where will you be two weeks from now? Two years? Ten?

If you have placed your life on hold waiting for that magic moment to arrive when you finally see the end of the abuse, the wait is over. You have many places to go, and you can't waste your time in the world of the victim anymore.

As long as you go on thinking that you have to take whatever you can get however you can get it, somebody else is going to benefit. Happy and healthy relationships with other human beings aren't a fairy tale, but you aren't going to find them digging around in the scraps.

Your abuse is in your past. Even if only a day has gone by since you escaped your abuse, it is one more day of surviving that you did not have before. You are older, you are smarter, and you are stronger. One more day of growing. One more day of becoming.

Each day is another step away from the abuse you have suffered, but are you just moving away from the bad or are you actively moving towards the good?

There is no global shortage of love. Functional relationships offer love that is not dependent upon someone else's behavior, or mood, or the cycles of the moon. Love is just love. If you truly want to change your life for the better then something has to actually...you know...

Change.

Roll Call

Rain Pryor
Actress
Child Physical Abuse/Teenage Sexual Abuse

Gwen Moore
U.S. Congresswoman
Child Sexual Abuse, Rape & Domestic Violence

Mary J. Blige
Singer
Emotional Abuse/Child Rape/Childhood Domestic Violence

Meat Loaf
Singer
Physical and Emotional Abuse/Bullying

Marlee Matlin
Actress
Child Sexual Abuse & Domestic Violence

"Maybe the answer is that there isn't one. Maybe the answer is that there isn't JUST one."

~Elizabeth Alraune

But We Don't Talk About It

I grew up with a lot of secrets. I remember trying to reach out to the Big People, struggling to find a way to tell them of all of the horrible visions that were stuck in my head. I don't know how many times I got up my nerve to tell someone, but the conversation always got cut short. Maybe it was the look on their face or the way their voice changed, but something about the way they reacted stopped me in my tracks.

When I was a young mother my friend and fellow writer, Susan Graybeal, warned me about the trials of teaching preschoolers the differences between boys and girls. She believed that her children should know the proper names for body parts. So, for that reasonwhen they asked she told them the truth. "Boys have a penis and girls have a vagina."

The lesson appeared to go well, until they went to the grocery store later and her daughter decided to share her wonderful new lesson with a passerby. Susan then had to explain to her daughter that some things were private and we did not discuss them in public. That evening, much to her mother's horror, her daughter leaned over and whispered to her father, "You have a penis, but we don't talk about it."

Susan's little girl changed absolutely nothing with her observation about differences in body parts, but it sure did make people uncomfortable. Susan was never one to shy away from things that needed to be talked about, and her daughters have grown up much the same way. If only we could all speak with such candor about the things that are on our mind. Perhaps not in the grocery store, and maybe not at the dinner table - but some information is just too important to be left to be unsaid.

You can't blame her daughter for being confused. There are a lot of things we still aren't supposed to talk about, even as adults. As I grew up I realized that people had a way of skirting things that they aren't ready to deal with. They can't help it. Their mind sees the danger coming and slaps up a detour sign before they have time to realize what's up. "Nothing to see here. Move along. Just move along now."

People don't like to talk about things that they are uncomfortable with, so they usually don't.

I remember wondering why the Big People would say that someone is "expecting," or "in the family way" rather than just saying that they were pregnant. Or how they would tell me that someone had "passed" instead of just telling me that they died. And being "sick" could mean anything from the flu, to depression, to cancer.

> "It seems to me that in all ways we have to discover what is best for us. I really don't think there is any one-sized-fits all answer for anything. And the times that we try to have one can be detrimental to those who that one size doesn't fit – and never will fit."
>
> ~Elizabeth Alraune
>
> Relatetocancer.com

My irritation with the things we aren't supposed to talk about has never gone away.

When I think about some of the things I have had to face in my life I am thankful for the many friends who have been there to see me through. To just let me talk about anything and everything. Politics, sex, religion. Nothing with a true friend is off the table. The last thing we need is a friend with the "please stop telling me this," face.

'Tis why I love my JoLoPe so.

She is one of my most trusted confidants. Known to the world as JoLoPe aka Elizabeth Alraune. To my knowledge I have never made her make the "Please Stop!" face. Naturally, she is one of my favorite people to turn to when it comes to the power of words.

Elizabeth was there in some form almost every step of the way during the creation of this book. She served as my sounding board, and often as my inspiration for whole new chapters. She could possibly even identify the conversations that led to them. Our discussions on labeling, defining words, letting go, and acceptance -- they are all here in some form or another.

We talk about words a lot. Elizabeth's career in hypnosis and position as talk host of the World of Perspective Radio show mean that she is perhaps more aware of the power of words than most. Words can too easily become labels, and labels have the potential to define you, limit you, and constrict you. There can also be a freedom in labels , as they can help to define whole new realities.

> *"If you think about it, even the one-size-fits-all item doesn't. I even now see advertising that says 'one size fits most.' Apparently someone took issue with the fact that the label wasn't accurate - as it did not include them. The thing is, most labels aren't accurate. They're an approximation, based on a what a person perceives to be the truth. That is why so many times we will see a disclaimer attached; your results may vary."*
>
> *~Elizabeth Alraune*
>
> *Relatetocancer.com*

And sometimes what we don't talk about can be even more important than what we do.

Early in my friendship with her, Elizabeth and I were discussing my position as a victim's advocate, and I referred to myself as an abuse survivor. Elizabeth and I have tackled some pretty tough subjects in our friendship, but something in her reaction stopped me and made me really think about how I felt about the word Survivor for the first time ever. What did the label Survivor really mean to me?

I didn't know that that moment was the beginning of this book until many years later, but it was.

I have spent a lot of time trying to communicate the wonder that the Survivor Spirit holds for me to others. Reactions are always mixed. While there are some negative aspects to be certain, I wouldn't change my status for the world. It's something that I have unintentionally studied my entire life. It was clear that Elizabeth did not view the idea of Survivor Pride the same way that I did.

But her experiences with the word were very different than mine.

Somewhere between the second draft of this book and the final my friend

Elizabeth got sick, and it wasn't just the flu. She was the third loved one that was diagnosed with cancer in a very short period of time and I found myself asking, why them? If bad things really do only happen to bad people then why choose three of the kindest people I knew?

Elizabeth didn't want chemotherapy, but after a hysterectomy and what she was told, she felt she had little choice. We talked almost daily during that time, sharing the good, the bad and the ugly of her strange, new experience. She blogged about it on her website and shared videos she made, but there were still so many things that she wasn't ready to give a public voice to yet.

Elizabeth and I are not exactly the same people that we were when we met. It has been a few years, and we have grown and changed, and we have taken very different paths than we first thought we would. Who knew either of our lives would take the directions that they have.

Elizabeth kept going because she had to. The mantra of every Survivor is that we do what we have to do. As dark and scary as cancer may be, it isn't like it offers you any other options. I felt powerless to help. Sometimes we all run out of positive, and Elizabeth did a time or two. Sometimes I ran out with her. Sometimes we all have to give up – even if it is just for a few moments.

Advocacy is a lot easier with abuse Survivors than friends with cancer, and for the record it is never easy. Elizabeth and I have very common experiences that society would rather we didn't talk about. We have both become determined to keep talking about it until that veil of silence goes away.

I clearly remember the discomfort in an adult's voice when I talked about things I shouldn't. I always thought that voice meant that someone was in trouble, and in my experience that person was usually me. Each time I tried to confess, I would stop. If they pressed, it was so much easier to tell them that a friend had told me something and I was just being curious. Sometimes I played it off as a joke.

There are too many people out there just like us who are going through their darkest moments alone. We both know exactly what it is like to feel so alone. Nobody should ever have to be.

So, we will keep talking.

I remember the day a man she knew discussed doing an event with her that could help her financially. She was so excited about the opportunity, but slowly things changed and her role in the speaking gig was minimized significantly. One of the final times, after speaking with a committee of others, the man came to her and said that they didn't think she should talk about cancer because frankly...it was a bummer.

No doubt cancer is a bummer. If it is uncomfortable for someone else to hear about it, then imagine how it is for anyone living with it. That's exactly what Elizabeth has been saying. I thought so when I had cervical cancer. I thought so when my nephew Josh was diagnosed with melanoma at 19. I thought so when my Uncle Larry was diagnosed with prostate cancer. And I thought so when my children's grandfather died from lung cancer. According to Seer-.Cancer.Gov 1 in 2 people will be diagnosed with cancer during their lifetime.

The day Elizabeth was told that cancer was a bummer, I saw that righteous anger come pouring forth. She wasn't as upset about the changing events as much as feeling as if there were things she should not be talking about. I could hear how determined she was to talk about what she had been through without censorship someday. She dreamed of helping others find their voice too.

> "I am who and how I am. Period. It is all I ever will be right this very moment. It is all I can be. It makes zero sense for me to sit here and try to figure out what a 'better' version of me would be like."
>
> ~Elizabeth Alraune
>
> Relatetocancer.com

Elizabeth continues to blog. She continues to create as Cedonaah, her artistic, alter-ego. She continues to do what she can. Sometimes she gets quiet, and I worry about her a bit. There are sometimes long periods where our blogs are our only real conversation.

She has such a powerful voice on her blog that what she is going through is difficult to hear, even for me. She can't get out of bed some days, her back constantly hurts, and she is never certain of anything. Her fears and concerns about what is next and how she will go about getting there aren't easy to share, but she shares them so openly.

Throughout her experience, it seemed that people wanted to see the bright side of her journey. They wanted to hear her Survivor story - without the ugly parts that she had to go through to get there. So often we view our heroes this way. We only see the good stuff. Sometimes it is the way they want us to see them. At other times, it is how we choose to see them, because seeing someone we care about struggling is so painful.

We don't see the moments when they are alone in the middle of the night clutching their knees to their chest and wondering if they are going to see to-morrow.

The cancer had gone away for awhile, so it seemed that most of her problems should have gone with it. Work did not magically rebuild itself, the bills re-mained unpaid. I was blessed to have a husband to help me through my toughest times, Elizabeth had to do much of it on her own.

And cancer doesn't always accept its eviction quietly.

Elizabeth had remained cancer free for five months when she was told that there were signs it had returned. The second time she heard the news was even more difficult in some ways than the first for her. She already knew what she would be facing, and she already knew what it would do to her ability to function. She still had not recovered physically, fin-ancially, or emotionally from the first round of treatment and here she was facing the possibility of doing it all over again.

"Maybe all the hiccups and blips and upsets and frustrations of life are exactly as they are meant to be. Maybe I am exactly how I am meant to be today in the same way that I was exactly who I was meant to be 10 years ago today. Maybe it is time we stopped buying into the idea that we need to be someone else, somewhere else, something else."

~Elizabeth Alraune

Relatetocancer.com

Survivor experiences come in all shapes and sizes. Sometimes it is through ill-ness and sometimes it is abuse, but a Survivor is a Survivor no matter how they come to be one.

Many people were working hard to keep Elizabeth positive, telling her that she shouldn't say this, or that she shouldn't feel that way. So many people were telling her to cheer up, to look on the bright side, and not be negative. I tried really hard not to be one of them. I tried to respect her boundaries large and small and did my best to help keep her looking forward.

I still do.

I've only been able to watch from -the outside as this new person develops within Elizabeth. Some days she is joyous, others she falls flat on her face. There are times when she is prepared to fight on, and times when she just wants to surrender. There are times when she feels loved and supported, and times when she feels utterly alone. There are days when she is weak, and days when she is incredibly strong.

If being a Survivor required always being positive, none of us would make it. Sometimes you have to curl up in a little ball and wallow in your own misery. Sometimes you have nothing else left. The majority of what we deal with happens in private.

But we shouldn't have to.

When you spend night after night holding yourself in the dark wondering if you are going to die, life can be a pretty scary place. I've been there. Sometimes all you can do is cry, but you do what you have to do to just keep going one step further.

Way too many people do the "ugly" in private, and put a smile on in public.

Back when my grandmother was young, people didn't talk about abuse openly. Much of what she went through, she suffered in private. Even when her bruises were visible, even when my grandfather and his mistress had a child together, most people in our small town thought that it was none of their business. My grandmother didn't talk about the things people had done to her either. Now and then she still surprises me with a revelation, and I have been listening to those same stories my whole life.

I have never once heard my grandmother refer to herself as a Survivor, but I have never heard her call herself a victim either. Things happened, she moved on. The end. More than that she learned from it, and I learned from her example.

I label myself as a Survivor with no small amount of pride.

I've never understood why admitting that I was molested makes people squirm the way they do, and have found that many of Elizabeth's experiences with cancer have been no different. No one affected by these types of things should have to talk about it only in private or whisper about it in public. It isn't as if the person affected is the only one who has ever faced illness or abuse, and the person certainly will not be the last.

In the process of addressing the things that the world would prefer be left un-addressed, I have learned to redefine a lot of words. What I think they mean is not always the same thing as what everybody else thinks. While I have become comfortable talking about my past in a very open and honest manner, the in-formation is not always something others want to hear about.

I see the journey from victim to Survivor as a process of becoming. It isn't the hardship that we face, it is the person that comes out of the other side of that process. Whether we face it pretty, or whether we face it ugly, whether we feel weak, whether we are strong – We are Survivors always. It doesn't matter how we get there, only that we do.

Elizabeth has a very different view of the word Survivor than I do, and it was difficult for me to absorb at first. No matter what comes my way, I already know that I can survive it. I have already been through much worse. Even at my weakest moments, I am still a Survivor.

The fact that we have very similar views on many topics had me taken off guard when she reacted the way she did when I first called her one. If I couldn't convince her of the value in the word, would I convince anyone? I think deep down, I just feared that it meant she wasn't claiming survivorship, and that this world could lose her far too soon. So I focused on what I did feel shining brightly. Every day I reach out for her light, the spirit of joy, love and peace that I have come to know within her.

> *"Maybe if we live more fully here and now we will choose exactly what we need to to be ex-actly who we need to be in the next moment, too. Maybe life has everything to do with truly embracing this moment and engaging ourselves in it - not in trying to figure out how to make our next moment's self better."*
>
> *~Elizabeth Alraune*
>
> *Relatetocancer.com*

JoLoPe = Joy, Love, and Peace

I don't know that she was always aware of it, but it was there. There is this righteous passion that comes showing through when someone sees that what happened to them was not okay. They see that they were treated in ways that are unacceptable. They become determined to change things, no matter who or what gets in their way.

I heard it on her worst days when she just wanted to give up. I heard it on her best when she knew exactly what was ahead. I heard it as she allowed herself to accept the things she never thought she would have to accept.

I heard it when she got pissed.

Elizabeth started talking about finding ways to help others avoid the hell she went through. She knew that nobody should ever have to face the things that she has had to alone. If she needed help, then she knows that others need it as well. Today she is determined to become that person. She is determined to talk about her experiences without shame and without censorship.

We both feel it is important to speak so that other people don't have to suffer in the same ways we did.

While I was writing this book, I vaguely described a vision I had in my head of a woman becoming a tree to Elizabeth. This woman had her feet rooted in the ground, with her arms - as branches - raised to the sky. A few hours later Elizabeth returned with the perfect Survivor Tree Nymph. She had incorporated everything I had envisioned, even details I had neglected to ask for. The image she came up with has the essence of a Survivor. Our roots may be in the darkness, but our branches are ever reaching toward the light.

It is a bit odd to have a friendship based on the things that we aren't supposed to talk about I suppose but what are friends for? There is no doubt in my mind that Elizabeth is ever reaching.

"When a tree sways in the wind the weak branches fall off. The branches left behind help to keep a tree strong and help it keep its balance when it gets swayed again."
~*Elizabeth Alraune*

To Donate to Elizabeth's ongoing expense fund please visit http://www.gofundme.com/rioj8

Roll Call

Chevy Chase
Actor/Comedian
Child Abuse

Erin Gray
Actress
Child Abuse

Greg Lemond
Pro Cyclist
Child Sexual Abuse

Rosie Perez
Actress
Child Sexual Abuse

Sandra Dee
Actress
Child Sexual Abuse

"For what does it profit us if we have a neat, polite, charming young- ster who could watch people suffer and not be moved to take action?

~Haim G. Ginott

A Victim Nor A Bully Be

I entered my first marriage a very broken individual, it should be no surprise that I left that marriage even more broken. We both did. We had both crossed the lines we had sworn we never would. We did things we aren't proud of, and our children saw it.

We were playing out ancient scripts within our brains. Family traditions of how we treated others and how we expected to be treated ourselves were in play from day one.

We were passing those scripts on to our own children, just as they had been passed on to us. We hit our children when we were angry with them. We threw their things across the room. We teased them and hurt their feelings. We called them names. When other people did those things to us, we didn't like it, but that didn't stop us from doing them to our own children.

It doesn't matter how deep your hurts lie. If you are using that hurt to control others then you have stepped out of the role of victim and into the role of abuser.

Which begs the ultimate question. What is our goal as parents?

In disciplining my children, was I also raising them to accept the circumstances life throws their way without question?

I didn't want my children to become the fifth generation to come from a broken home, but I didn't want them to have to live with abuse in the process.

I had no desire to deny them the power to defend themselves when need be, but I did not want to raise little bullies either. There had to be something in between...A child without discipline is nobody's joy and everybody's misery. Parents are supposed to discipline their children; it isn't a point that is worth debating. I just took issue with the "traditional" methods: hitting, screaming, insulting, controlling. None of these things fit into my view of the world I wanted my adult children to live in.

We can become abusers far more easily than any of us care to admit: guilt-trips, emotional manipulation, blaming, refusing to take no for an answer, damaging other peoples property.

Child psychologist and concentration camp Survivor Haim G. Ginott often spoke of the difference between those who are human and those who are humane. In the book *Liberated Parents, Liberated Children,* the doctor was leading a parenting group formed by the books authors Adele Faber and Elaine Mazlish. During one meeting he asked the women what their major goals as parents were, and one woman replied,

> "To produce children who are, among other things, brilliant, polite, charming, neat, and well-adjusted, of course."

Of course! Who wouldn't want these things? Dr. Ginott responded to the mother...

> "It seems to me that our large goal is to find ways to help our children become humane and strong. For what does it profit us if we have a neat, polite, charming youngster who could watch people suffer and not be moved to take action?
>
> What have we accomplished if we have reared a child who is brilliant—at the top of their class—but who uses his intellect to manipulate others? And do we really want children who are so well-adjusted that they adjust to an unjust situation? The Germans adjusted only too well to the orders of the Nazis to exterminate millions of their fellow man.
>
> Understand me: I'm not opposed to a child being polite or neat or learned. The crucial question for me is: What methods have been used to accomplish these ends? If the methods used are insults, attacks, and threats, then we can be very sure that

*we have also taught this child to insult, to attack, to threaten,
and to comply when threatened.*

*If, on the other hand, we use methods that are humane, then
we've taught something much more important than a series of
isolated virtues. We've shown the child how to be a person—a
mensch, a human being who can conduct his life with
strength and dignity."*

To be human takes nothing more than the act of reproduction, but he thought to be humane was to show both intellectual and moral progress. To illustrate this concept he used the Yiddish word, "mensch."

Any parent can teach their child to be controlled by making their decisions for them, forcing them to comply with your will, and pressuring them to reach for the goals you see fit for them.

> According to Leo Rosten, author of The Joys of Yiddish, to teach a child to be "a real mensch," is to help them become someone to admire and emulate, someone of noble character. It is for us to instill in our children nothing less than character, righteousness, dignity, a sense of what is right, responsibility, and decorum.
>
> Whew...and I have a hard time getting them to pick up after themselves.

Eventually other people will come along and influence your children, people who might have a stronger influence on them than you do. Everyone they meet will leave some sort of impression. A child that is easily manipulated by a parent softens so much easier under outside pressure.

If you could protect them from all outside influences then that might not be so bad; but you could also end up raising an Adolf Eichmann. The man who once said "I will leap into my grave laughing because the feeling that I have five million human beings on my conscience is for me a source of extraordinary satisfaction."

Sixteen years later, during his trial for war crimes, Eichmann testified that: "I never did anything, great or small, without obtaining in advance express instructions from Adolf Hitler or any of my superiors. In the end he said that he was just a "transmitter" with very little power."

He was a another man who was just "following orders."

Those who have lived with abuse often struggle with a burning need for approval. No matter where I moved, it seemed that the "bad kids" were so much easier to win approval from than the popular or accepted crowds. If you can't live up to people's expectations, the next best thing is to seek out those with lower expectations.

Teaching our children to make good decisions is a responsibility that we can't afford to skip out on. Good decision-making should be taught in homes, and in schools, and in churches, and on street corners. Not how to make the correct decision mind you, or the right decision even...but simply how to make good decisions for themselves and their future. For their friends and neighbors. For the planet.

Everyone's journey in life begins and ends the same. What you do in between those two points is your path, and yours alone. Princes can become beggars and beggars can become kings. Hard working, well behaved and yes, even loving young boys can become Nazis.

As long as you are willing to accept abuse as a part of your life it will continue to be a part of your reality, whether you are the one being abused or the one abusing others.

The line has to be drawn somewhere.

If you are going to teach your child to stop abuse, it begins with you. In *"Teacher and Child: A Book for Parents and Teachers,"* Dr. Haim G. Ginott said:

> I am a Survivor of a concentration camp. My eyes saw what no person should witness. Gas chambers built by learned engineers. Children poisoned by educated physicians. Infants killed by trained nurses. Women and babies shot and burned by high school and college graduates.

> So I am suspicious of education. My request is: help your students become more human. Your efforts must never produce learned monsters, skilled psychopaths, or educated Eichmanns. Reading, writing, and arithmetic are important only if they serve to make our children more human.

My own abuse taught me that I do not own my children. I do not own their bodies. I do not own their minds. The moment that fact dawned on me my whole parenting method changed. I stepped away from what had always been and looked at where we were all headed. I was never raising children in the first place. I was raising adults and I was only given 18 years to do it in–adults that will go out into the world and live for another 60 years–or more.

If I am hitting my children then I am teaching them that the proper way to deal with frustrations is to strike out at another person. I am teaching them that it is okay to hit. I am also teaching them that it is okay to be hit. I am giving them permission to continue the cycle of abuse.

Besides, if I couldn't control myself with my children then what is the point of being a mother?

It doesn't matter if you are the mother, the child, or the cousin twice-removed; if you are finding excuses for your abuse then you are continuing the cycle. Getting your needs met at the expense of another person is an abuse of power no matter who you are.

I expect my children to respect the rights of others, and I've marched them into the principal's office more than once for failing to do so. I also expect other people to respect my children's rights.

Harming another person should never be acceptable. If the cycle of abuse is going to stop with you, it goes both ways. If you are still using abusive behaviors to get what you want then you are making it okay. You are telling other people in your life that it is acceptable.

There is no way to take action against another person without placing a mirror in front of your own face.

During my first marriage my kids saw violence. My kids saw hate. Then a few years into my second, there was a spanking that went overboard. My husband left bruises on my son's backside. I had to report it to police or I could lose my kids, and when I did they still threatened to press charges on me.

I left Ed that night. We split up for 18 months. He sobered up and I worked on my own baggage. When we got back together, our family made a promise to one another. We would go forward together on level ground. If we were going to repair our home and our family, we had to start with the basics. It began in such small ways. We banned teasing and name calling in our home, parents, children, and even guests included.

I was done with violence, done with control, done with having my decisions made for me. I had no idea how to build a healthy relationship, none of us did.

So we started at the beginning.

I expect my children to speak to me in a respectful manner, therefore I choose to speak to them in kind. I get many frowns. Other parents lecture me on the need to control my children, to show authority, to guide them. That I could do all of those things and still offer it without violence seems to be a totally foreign concept.

My husband and I came back together, and we all agreed to leave the abuse behind. We promised that from that day on we would be a team, and we would work together to make a non-violent home. We would figure out how to do things without power struggles. When I told Ed that name calling hurt my feelings and people yelling made me feel unsafe, he didn't always understand it, but he tried to respect it.

> Your reality is not what you experience, but rather how you experience it.
>
> ⊜
>
> Stop waiting for change to come into your life and be the change you want to see.

Whenever possible, words should be respectful towards yourself and towards others. Leaving the dignity of both parties intact does not come naturally to those who live in abusive homes. I have always cautioned them about the power of words. When we are angry, when our feelings are hurt, when we are frustrated, or even tired, our words can and will do damage. Perhaps it is just being the children of a writer. The kids took the new rules to heart. Even as I corrected their words, they corrected mine. We discovered how easy it is to insult another human being. My kids picked it up much faster than I did.

Sometimes that damage can last a very long time.

Rather than fighting and name calling, we promised that we would all get a chance to make our feelings known without demeaning or insulting the other person. When one of us hurts another person's feelings, we don't have to excuse it or try to convince the other person that it was okay. We just need to say that we are sorry. We make mistakes, but we can always "rephrase," try again and again until we get it right.

People think that my refusal to hit my children is the same thing as a lack of discipline, but it takes a lot more disciple to restrain yourself than to strike out.

Instead of spankings my children get "the lecture": a lengthy conversation that covered what we did, who was responsible for our actions, and exactly how we were going to fix it. A report was usually required, detailing what they should have done in the situation or what they would do if the situation came up again. To this day my children will tell you that I was stricter with them than many of their friends' parents were.

If they did something that would be considered a crime in the adult world, they were treated as such. We had full mock trials, witnesses called, and interrogations. Once we had the proof we needed we delivered sentencing, just like a court would. What other parents called grounding, we called "jail time," doing community service, paying for restoration. My kids' friends thought we were the meanest parents ever.

It made more sense to me to discipline them in ways that would help them grow. Instead of hitting and forgetting we focused on what went wrong and how to make it right again. I accepted their mistakes, but I also expected them to learn from them.

Sometimes we still blow up. People still yell. Feelings still get hurt. But then someone says, "That hurt my feelings," and the other person is expected to say, "I'm sorry." I've fought with in-laws, stepparents, educators, and youth group leaders to be sure that these rules are followed.

They are human beings. And deserve to be treated as such.

I have always approached my parenting differently because my own childhood was different. Compliance with the will of others has never been something I was particularly interested in.

Our children need to understand above all that life is not just a series of days, but a series of decisions, one link of the chain fading into another. A cup of coffee at a new place can lead to a date, a date can lead to a bar, a bar can lead to a casual fling, and unplanned sex is all too easily followed by an unplanned pregnancy.

At least three lives are forever changed. Because of coffee?

It happens every day.

Once the consequences are set in motion, it is already too late. We will be forced to live with the consequences of our decisions whether we like it or not, but they are a lot easier to live with if we learn to make decisions consciously.

Everyone you meet will affect your walk, no doubt, but you and you alone are responsible for your own path and where it ultimately leads you. Every choice you make alters the path ahead of you whether you choose to recognize its impact or not.

New twists and turns in the path ahead of you are forming right now based on the decisions you are making today. Repeating old patterns, creating new ones. Once you have discovered that you are repeating past cycles in your life, you are left with another decision before you: will you continue as things have been, or will you reinvent your life?

As long as you think that abuse is acceptable then it will continue to be acceptable no matter how many times you change your situation. When you enter into a new relationship without understanding those old destructive ways of thinking then you are training your new partner in much the same way you were trained. The cycle continues.

Controlling a child is not the same as parenting them...

The truly successful parent raises children who are capable of controlling themselves.

You find a new, better person, and yet somehow the relationship dynamic stays the same. The problem is that while you can change partners every six months or every six years, until you change yourself those old scripts are going to keep replaying themselves.

Someone somewhere taught you that abuse was okay. You can't change your family and you can't change the past, but you can change the future. Take a look at the list in the back of this book again, only this time ask yourself if you have been guilty of those same behaviors. Chances are you have. We all have.

Give yourself and the world a break.

Once upon a time you knew without a doubt that your life belonged to you. You knew that abuse was not an unavoidable part of life, that your body belonged to you, that your feelings belonged to you. You knew it then and you know it now. You may have tucked those feelings deep inside, but you knew that abuse wasn't the way things were supposed to be.

Being a bully is no better than being a victim, in the end someone else is still in control.

Survivors Turned Activist

Alice Walker
Author
Abuse Survivor

Lauren Book
Author/Founder LaurensKids.org
Child Sexual Abuse Survivor

Marie Waldrep
Poet
Incest/Domestic Violence Survivor

Rachel Lloyd
Author
Child Sexual Abuse, Commercial Sexual Exploitation,
Rape & Domestic Violence Survivor

Tori Amos
Musician/Creator of Rape, Abuse and Incest National Network
(RAINN) - Rape Survivor

"Our dependency makes slaves out of us, especially if this dependency is a dependency of your self-esteem. If you need encouragement, praise, pats on the back from everybody, then you make everybody your judge."

~Fritz Perls

Waiting For Permission To Heal

Our modern society is full of quick-fix products that don't really fix anything. Day after day you are shown shiny new things guaranteed to change your life with the least amount of effort possible. There are pills, books, gimmicks, and promises.

A few years ago when my family owned our second hand store, we finally had to put a ban on any and all exercise equipment. We had plenty of like-new, still in the box, all parts included items. Plenty of people bought them but they all discovered the same thing. Buying it and placing it neatly in the corner did nothing for their health or fitness. The commercials made it look so easy but there was still work involved.

Americans have been blinded by the hope of change without effort.

We keep buying the products and they keep selling them. None of these things are really change. Change requires stepping outside of our comfort zones, and that is where the journey usually stops. Humans don't like leaving their comfort zones.

I know, I know. It's scary out there.

If there was a way to get through this without facing your fears, believe me, I would tell you. Change isn't easy. It takes time, it takes effort, and it even hurts a little now and then. If you have been in a dark place for a very long time, change is not going to be comfortable.

Many people wait for an outward sign before they begin the healing process. They wait for their abuser to see the error of their ways and make amends, for someone to come along and offer their support and guidance, for the legal system to right the wrongs, for the gods to exact divine vengeance...

They wait, and they wait, and they wait.

Those who do rely on the justice system to handle their abusers often find long, lengthy legal battles with no real benefit when it is all said and done. Abusers are master manipulators, and their slimy slithering is legendary in police stations, courtrooms, and anywhere else they need to wiggle out of responsibility for something. They drag it out as long as they can. They play the victim. They use the system to their advantage.

A confidential study of male sex offenders conducted by Emory University found that they had molested an average of 52 female victims each, while those who had molested boys admitted to an average of 150 victims. Only 3% of those crimes were ever detected. In the end, nineteen out of twenty sexual assailants will inevitably walk free, and only one in seventeen will ever spend a day in jail.

They are not entitled to everything they have labeled as "mine," but nobody has ever bothered to tell them that. There is no victim like an abuser caught.

If they want something they will get it. Homes, money, spouses, children, pets. Even the smallest victories will come with large price tags. They giveth and they taketh away because they are the center of their universe.

It really should stop somewhere, don't you think?

If you have called the police on them, or blasted out an email to their friends list, or keyed their car, then you have already given them more time and energy than they deserved. Every time you strike out at an abuser, you are just validating their belief that *they* are the victim.

If you are counting on the justice system as being your path to healing then you will find that it is more system than justice. By no means am I saying that you should avoid prosecuting your abuser, especially if they pose a danger to others. If they belong behind bars, and you have the means to help them find their way there, then do so. But please don't hold your breath.

My ex-husband and I hadn't even been separated two months when I found a handsome young man at a party who swept me off my feet then left me crumbled in a ball next to the bed sobbing. My "near rape" was stopped from becoming a "completed sexual assault" only by the people who heard me screaming and pulled him off of me. I threw myself in the corner and prayed the ground would split open to swallow me whole. But it didn't.

I cried myself to sleep that night and tried to forget the whole thing. I didn't talk about what had happened for a very long time. I called it the bad thing, told people it had been a rough night, but I couldn't tell them what had really happened.

I couldn't use the right word.

We live in an area with 1200 people, and I still had to look the witnesses in the eye. Sometimes I saw the guy who raped me around town, but most of the time it was easier to just hide in my home. In the end I had no choice but to go on.

> You have been looking to the wrong sources for your empowerment.
>
> ⬤
>
> Stop concentrating your energy on fixing your relationships, your family, your children, and your employers, and instead focus on fixing your relationship with yourself.

Then another girl's name came out as one of the guy's victims.

By then I had waited three years to come forward. This girl was the first person I told the entire story to and hers was very similar to mine. We started talking, and eventually so did the other victims. Another girl's name came out and then another until we had a list of twelve.

Only three of us filed reports.

The rape investigation was hell on all of us, it lasted three long years but it went nowhere. Not a single rape charge was ever filed. In a small town there is nowhere to go when things get bad. We were on our own. We were hiding in our homes, afraid to go anywhere alone. Eventually, the other girls left.

I am still here.

Cops, judges, district attorneys, and just about everybody else we turned to for help laughed in our faces.

The man who raped us denied the allegations to authorities, but he tried his best to shut us up. He chased our vehicles down country back-roads. He went to the places we worked and watched us. He hung out across the street from our homes watching our children play in their yards. He struck up conversations with our companions. He was everywhere we were it seemed.

Desperate, I turned to the local court.

The woman I spoke to said I didn't have enough grounds for a protection order because an act of violence must have occurred. I responded, horrified, "How do you define rape in non-violent terms?"

She laughed awkwardly and said, "You know what I mean..."

No... I still don't.

It was upsetting she explained, but nothing she felt the judge would need to waste a piece of paper on. My request was denied three times while the old judge was on the bench. After she retired, it only took a single request from the new one.

The rapist violated the protection order five times the first day. The cops kept refusing to arrest him no matter how cocky he got until I finally broke down on them and accused them of protecting a known drug dealer for a reason.

I finally faced him in court on the protection order violation. I sat in a room full of people that I had known my whole life and told the story while he glared me down. He accused me of being crazy, and asked me if I was on any psychotropic medications. He questioned every word I said and forced me to repeat myself. He never denied the events, but he never admitted to them either. He just pushed me and pushed me.

Then, he pushed too far.

I realized that day that intimidation was his weapon. It had been all along. He wasn't just trying to scare us, he wanted to watch us live in fear. As long as I was afraid of him, he was in control.

But he pushed me past fear and straight to pissed.

He was sentenced to 90 days, and did 45 on work release. They never even notified me when he was released. The cops spent more time protecting him than they did us. We couldn't set up interviews. They dragged their feet on the investigation, lost important evidence, and refused to respond to reports. Eventually we went away, but none of us went quietly.

It isn't fair, it isn't right, and no, it really shouldn't be that way, but it is.

Some victims get so desperate that they turn to vigilante justice, but at what cost? To add physical bars to the emotional prison they already live in? Walking in the courtroom with a felony charge isn't going to win any friends on the other side of the bench, and prison certainly isn't going to help your situation any.

There is no shame in admitting that you want to see the person who harmed you pay for their crimes. Yes, you can win in court. They can receive jail time.

If it is only to see them pay for the pain they have caused you then you need to slow down and wait until you are thinking rationally. Know when to act and when it's the right time to withdraw. Sometimes, you have to choose peace .

Standing up against the person who raped you is noble. To remove them from society and place them in a safe place is worthy. Getting even with the ex-boyfriend who spent all of your money, slapped you around, and cheated however many times? Probably not. He's a jerk for sure, but you won't be doing yourself or society any good in giving up your own freedoms to get there.

> A lot of people have ideas about what causes abuse and what you as the victim should do about it.
>
> ⬤
>
> If little experience with abuse is present in someone's past, the person functions with different programming that we do.

Put your energy into you, not them.

You can easily put out tens of thousands of dollars just to get to court. Even if you have that kind of cash just lying around waiting to be burned, you still have to convince a judge and sometimes a jury. Then, if you are lucky, the judge will decide in your favor. Then, if they don't find a way of getting out of restitution you might come out with something.

It is rarely ever worth it.

Long after their conscience had been wiped clean, you were the one suffering. You had the nightmares. You had the flashbacks. You were the one who had to learn how to trust people again.

You have already given your abuser so much.

It doesn't matter what you are waiting for; if it is coming from outside of yourself, you will be waiting a very long time. Take it back. Take all of it back. Don't wait for the approval of others. Don't wait for your abusers to ask for forgiveness. Don't wait for someone to say, "I believe you."

Don't wait.

We all want acceptance, acceptance of our pain, and acceptance of our experiences. That doesn't mean that we will get it.

Instead we get the mother who refused to hear our stories and maybe even protected the abuser. We get the legal system that still asks us if we were wearing a short skirt the night we were raped. We get the cops who refuse to enforce protection orders, "cuz' man, women can be a real drag and they've been there."

When someone outside of a situation can believe that a victim is somehow responsible for their own predicament, they don't feel the burden of responsibility. Admitting that your own judgment is flawed can be scary. Years of denial can build up some fairly impressive defense systems in the human brain.

If it isn't their own personal problem, it's really hard to get someone to do something about it. It can be hard to get them to even care.

When you seek support and comfort and you find judgment, guilt, and blame, it really does feel very personal. It's not personal. It is human nature.

People tend to live within their own realm of experience, and very rarely do they look outside of it. Many people will defend themselves or their beliefs, even at the cost of another. When that happens, the reaction is more about them than about you.

When someone else rejects your emotions or your experiences, it can feel like the most personal of rejections. It isn't. When abuse isn't on someone else's radar, you need to understand that they aren't rejecting you, they are rejecting what they are not ready for.

Sometimes in the past we've reached out for a helping hand only to have our hands slapped away. It feels like they are rejecting you, but they have their own ghosts to deal with and you have yours. If they are not capable of offering you acceptance, then find someone who can.

You might not be able to remove the negative people from your life totally, but you can create an insulated barrier between yourself and the rest of the world by developing a network of safe people that can offer support.

Those who truly love you and value your presence in their life will accept the changes in you. The ones who can't will fall by the wayside. Just keep your focus on where you are going and you can send them a postcard when you get there.

You can't afford to let them hold you back anymore. Happiness will always be just out of your reach as long as it hinges on another person.

Survivors tend to seek approval from those around them, but they so often fail to filter out the healthy influences from the unhealthy. You absolutely cannot please everybody, and trying to is guaranteed to fail. Some people can never be pleased no matter how hard you try. Placing the bulk of your relationship energies into people who only take is a sure way to be drained to the point of exhaustion.

Instead of healing your wounds the system often aggravates them. This process takes years upon years.

The legal system takes a toll on your financial and emotional resources. It can strain your other relationships and goes on far longer than one could imagine.

I only know this because I can't seem to stop trying.

You owe it to yourself to differentiate between those who see you as a priority and those who see you as an option in their lives. We tend to give all of our attention to those who demand it the most but when our own storms hit, they are nowhere to be found.

You need semi-healthy people in your life, people you can trust and rely on, whom you can feel safe with. You can be friendly with many people, but your inner circle–the ones you lean on, and who lean on you in return–is different. Not everyone needs to be allowed into that inner circle, nor should you try to fit everyone in. It should be a place only for the closest of friends and safe loved ones. This is where your therapist fits in, and perhaps a victim's advocate or counselor.

Starting with a support group can open up the door to new and healthy relationships. If you call your local crisis line or advocacy hotline, they may be able to give you some idea of where to look either locally or online to find a group that fits your needs.

You are going to find that a lot of your toughest work comes from inside of yourself. You are going to have to tear down defenses that you have relied on for a very long time. You do not need people's permission to heal, but you do need your own permission to get on with your life or you aren't going anywhere.

You need someone who isn't going to put up with any of your old "victim" crap to guide you through for a while.

Even professionals will run out of options for helping you after a while if you keep running to them with crisis after crisis. You are going to have to change the way you view the world.

The change you crave has been within you all along.

The amount of time and energy you are putting into staying stuck is exhausting for you and for everybody else around you. Stop fixing the world and take some time to fix your relationship with yourself. You can put it off for as long as you would like. You can ignore it and hope it goes away. You can spend your whole life running from the truth, or you can just admit that the time has come to give yourself and the world a break.

You can be the Survivor that you were meant to be.

Ask any abuse victim who has gone to court and they will tell you that the abuser gets the dignity of being the innocent party.

The victim is the one that is often assumed guilty until proven otherwise.

Each moment may seem very much like the next, with so little potential for real change, but before you know it hours have become days and days have become years, and change has occurred.

If you find yourself resisting a suggestion from someone, there is usually a reason. The harder you fight it the more likely it is that there is something there that you need to pay attention to. Take the blinders off and look at what is really bothering you.

Once your perspective changes, as bit by bit your old flawed thoughts are replaced with new ones, you will start to understand what they are telling you. As the scenery changes, you begin to see life in new and different ways.

You don't just find happy relationships under a rock. When your life is ready, it will happen. Learn to base your relationships on healthy concepts like respect, dignity, and equality, and create new constructive patterns within your life.

I assure you, the strength is there–the strength to stand up for yourself, to assert your rights without aggression, to heal yourself, and even heal the world. Your Survivor Spirit may seem such a fragile thing after all of these years of neglect, but it grows as you feed it, just like anything else. You are a Survivor. You are a fighter.

The only difference between those who will remain victims throughout their lives and those who will go on to survive and thrive is simply a decision to keep going forward no matter what gets in the way. You have used your Survivor Spirit to come this far, and it will take you wherever you need to go from here if you learn to trust it.

You owe it to yourself to move on, to heal, and to overcome. Change will not happen until you are ready to MAKE it happen.

Being passive is fine if you want to remain a doormat. Take an active approach to your healing. Take an active role in your own life. Slowly but surely you will move towards your focal point, whatever it may be.

The first step forward breaks the paralysis, and sometimes that's all you need.

Roll Call

Gabriel Byrne
Actor
Child Physical & Sexual Abuse

Joyce Meyer
Televangelist, Author
Child Physical & Sexual Abuse

Kirk Hammett
Musician
Child Physical & Sexual Abuse

Queen Latifah
Musician/Actress/Model
Child Sexual Abuse Survivor

Sinead O'Conner
Singer
Child Physical & Sexual Abuse

"In fairy tales, the princesses kiss the frogs, and the frogs become princes. In real life, the princesses kiss princes, and the princes turn into frogs."

~Paulo Coelho

A Kingdom Of Entitlement

Every little girl knows that "once upon a time" is possible for any would-be princess if she just kisses the right frog. We set out upon our journeys knowing that we would have to kiss a lot of frogs to find our prince, but the idea that there is a *right* frog implies that there are bound to be at least a few *wrong* frogs to wade through along the way, so wade we have.

It isn't as if every handsome stranger promises to be charming, and kind, and not to mention financially stable, but you can't win the jackpot if you don't play the game, right? And so what if frogs are a bit icky? "Happily ever after" is worth a bit of ickiness, isn't it?

To stop this cycle, someone has to make the conscious decision to do something different.

Step 1. Stop hanging out in swamps.

Someday love will overcome all of your hardships... eventually... any minute now... tick... tock... tick...

Still waiting? There were so many things that the fairy tales forgot to tell us.

Almost every chick-flick ever made has attempted to prove that love really does conquer all. Even the dirtiest of dawgs can be kept contentedly at home when the right woman comes along. As though a woman's love is a super power, and she can heal the ills of all simply by loving just a little bit harder and a little bit longer.

If a frog can turn into a prince, then is it all that unthinkable that Prince Charming could someday turn into a Toad?

Toads tend to come with a strong "since" of entitlement.

Since they are there... Since you are there... Since you have something that they desire...

The Toad has filled the bare spot that personal responsibility should occupy with an overdeveloped sense of entitlement. The king in his castle, the man on his throne. If his happiness comes at other people's expense, it can't be helped.

Toads don't just have wants like other people, they have *neeeeds*. *Neeeeds* are wants with some whine on them, and it is a rather convincing whine.

Lie? Steal? Cheat? Kill? Maybe, but emotional manipulation is so much easier. Toads are capable of finding some pretty creative ways of getting their *neeeeds* met. They can throw a tantrum to rival any preschooler, or they can freeze you out for days. They are waiting for the magic words, the ones that mean they win. It just depends on what they want out of it. "NO" means nothing to a Toad.

Just like the spoiled little princes Toads think they are, some Toads are charming, some Toads are needy, and some Toads are just plain greedy. The Toad relies on emotional manipulation and guilt because...they work.

Where we need things like food, water, and shelter, the Toad *neeeeds* things like your car keys, your wallet, all of your free time, unrestricted access to your personal belongings.

The fulfillment of these types of needs are somehow inevitably linked to your future happiness. Once they are free to move on, our long-promised reward tends to move on with it.

In a castle. On a cloud. Once upon a time and happily ever after.

There are some telltale traits to your average Toad if you look very closely, but that is usually the problem. We get so wrapped up in finding the right frog that even when the signs are there we brush them away. It can be difficult to tell the difference between a frog and a Toad at first glance. They don't look all that different after all.

Toads can pop up just about anywhere in your life. They will be friends, they will be neighbors, they will be bosses. Caught somewhere in the cycle of perpetual victim, they can't seem to escape the notion that it is everybody's responsibility but their own.

Toads are the friends that always seem to show up when they want something, yet become scarce when you are the one in need. They are the husbands who convince you work to put them through law school then trade you in on a new model as soon as their needs have been met. They are the sibling that always seems to have a drama in their life that only you can fix. They are the parents who are always talking about what you owe them.

Let's say you were to catch a Toad breaking into your house. Their defense could easily be that they only got caught stealing because they had no food, or maybe they only cased your neighborhood because they felt the residents had more than enough to spare. It could be that they only broke into your home because the window was open and inviting, and in case you doubt their true inner goodness, they meant to give the leftovers to starving children anyhow.

Does any of this sound familiar? Yep, you've probably got yourself a Toad.

You hang on because even in the darkest of circumstance, hope remains.

🌐

But there is a big difference between hope, and fantasy.

Toads can't catch a fair break and someone else is always to blame. They always have a really good story. This person or that is always responsible for their misery. Never them, though. Never them.

Starting to sound familiar?

Their constant feats of heroism place the weight of the world on their shoulders, and the world owes it to them to help them shoulder that impossible burden.

Wait. That sounds a lot like a victim. Glad you caught that.

Yes, victims can be bullies and bullies can be genuine victims. There really isn't much of a difference actually. It's all in how they deal with it, and how much they expect other people to deal with it for them.

There can be more than one villain in a story.

A wounded animal can seriously injure those who try to help them. This does not lessen either party's pain. A person in pain is only reacting to their own internal scripts, just guessing at what normal behavior is, and so are we. You can even be a bully and a victim at the same time.

If you do your part, they'll do theirs. That's the deal, right? If you just behave and mind your manners, if you can just be a good little girl and follow the rules, if you can just wait long enough, Prince charming will return, and this time he will stay! He will promise. He will even mean it when he says it.

Things could be a lot worse after all...

So, we stay.

You can count on the seasons changing. You can count on birth and on death. You can count on both laughter and tears. And you can always count on abuse coming back around again.

With each turning of the cycle, the threat of irreparable injury becomes more and more likely. Little things can become big things, and then bigger still.

The cycle of abuse does repeat itself, and what seems unthinkable from your partner at first can become routine at an alarming pace. By the time you realize that you are in over your head, you have lost your voice. You don't know what to say, and you wouldn't dare say it if you did. Eventually you find you no longer have the power to speak up at all.

If you were sexually abused as a child, your chance of being a victim of rape or domestic violence in your adult years increases. If your father was an alcoholic, there is a good chance your future husband will be one. If you were abused, your children are more likely to be victims themselves. The deeper you go, the more cycles unfold, in families, in cultures, in human nature.

Their presence in our lives, even for a few moments, is not likely to be forgotten. With a smile to rival any crocodile, some Toads can charm the skin right off of a snake. It is only upon close inspection that the cracks in the facade show through.

The Toad may start throwing tantrums, insulting you, or breaking things. It may start with bizarre accusations. It may just be a blowup over something trivial. Try as you might, there is nothing you can do to avoid it. Playing offense, playing defense, dodging left, dodging right, then, with the flip of a switch, the rules change...again.

When this happens they say they lost control, but they weren't losing it so much as unleashing it. They don't destroy their own things, they only damage yours. They can still maintain control of a vehicle, but not of themselves.

Once the disguise begins to slip, once you have seen them for what they really are, there is little reason for them to keep up the illusion anymore. What goes around once comes back around again and again like a bad virus, growing and mutating with each incarnation. From sweet to savage and back again, and you never quite know which is which.

As time passes, the cycle continues to spin out of control. Prince Charming seems to visit less and less. Sometimes all that you have left is the memory of what was, and fond wishes for what could be. You still catch glimpses of that side sometimes, just long enough to keep you hoping for a revival.

If you happen to have a fairy godmother handy, tell her she had better start waving her wand if not, you are on your own. Don't waste your time waiting for Prince Charming to fix himself. Nothing short of magical intervention is going to change another human being against their will. There is no magic frog, or golden ball, or wishing well. There is no knight in shining armor coming to save you.

> Somehow the Toad learned that the proper use of power was to control other people. Somehow we learned to accept it.
>
> ⊜
>
> Bullies are hiding behind their own walls, and we are hiding behind ours.

When Prince Charming has come to the rescue again, all of the problems magically go away for a time. The illusion is restored just long enough. They clean up the messes they made, promise to try harder, and become caring and attentive for a little while. They apologize for their actions. They offer to get help for their problems. They promise to catch you a falling star.

And they really do mean it this time.

The "kiss and make up" part is one of the best parts of the relationship. Heaven is the only thing that can make up for the trips through hell. Just like a drug, the lower the lows, the higher the highs.

That promise is in there somewhere.

If that fairy tale was there once upon a time, you hold on through the rotten parts in hopes that the person from your fantasy returns. Everybody goes back to pretending that life is just peachy. You are lulled into lowering your defenses again.

Place a tissue paper bandage over the gaping wound and forgive and forget.

Toads are so damned good at making you believe that you can find your "happily ever after" if you only believe in fairy tales just a little bit longer. Oh yes, they are charming as hell, but be careful, that smile hides razor-sharp fangs. Once Prince Charming, aka The Toad, is no longer on his best behavior, you will find that their famous charm is just the bait.

The ability of a relationship to be both pleasurable and painful doesn't fit into the fairy tale mold. Few things about abuse do. If bullies were always unpleasant and controlling then they wouldn't get very far in life; instead, Toads can be the sweetest and most caring people you know, often charming and attentive in public they are someone quite different in private.

People are supposed to be one or the other. It is so difficult to swallow the idea that someone can be sweet and caring, AND still be abusive and controlling. They can be a genuinely nice person in one circumstance and still be highly dangerous in another. They can be both black AND white.

Instead of focusing their anger inward like victims tend to do, they have externalized it, pushed it outward. Once the world is righted, and their control over the world is restored, they can go back to their pacified state. Until then, watch out.

When it's bad, it can be really bad, but oh does the "honeymoon phase" earn its name. When it's good, it is also *very* good.

On rare occasions, Toads do get help. It isn't the rule but a very rare exception to it. They find healthy ways of dealing with their problems and learn to treat others in what could even be considered a fair and respectful manner. Before they can do that however, they have to take full responsibility for the damage they have caused.

And that is where it usually stops. They can promise all they want, but money talks and bullshit walks as they say. A promise is not action.

The problem is they rarely have to take responsibility for anything.

Bullies can gather sympathy and support for themselves in the strangest of places. They can ruin our lives ten times over, but their mothers will still bail them out of jail, friends will take their side, and people who see them on the news will send them money anyway.

Toads have little trouble attracting people into their lives who will make excuses for their behavior. People can't resist a child in need, and many people can't resist a bully either, especially when they are playing the victim. They just seem so helpless sometimes. They always seem to have family members and friends waiting in the wings to protect them from the consequences of their own actions.

Chances are you made your fair share of excuses for them.

If you are going to invite someone else to narrate your fairy tale, be careful. Don't waste your time playing nice because you are hoping to make it out of this looking like the good guy. Everybody has a healthy dose of self-interest as part of their survival skills, but the Toad has an overabundance of it. Of course they blame you; it is a hell of a lot easier than taking responsibility for themselves.

Where their true nature leads, you will eventually follow. So if the game is rigged, at least do yourself a favor and admit it.

As more and more cracks become visible in their armor, you find out what every little princess finds out: castles in the sky are only illusions. Without a realistic support they eventually come crashing to the ground.

Toads always seem to have a past filled with crazy people who did horrible things to them for no reason at all. They are always having a run of bad luck. They are always innocent of the charges.

Prince Charming has left the building and he ain't coming back.

Those who help them get what they want are their friends. Anybody who gets in their way is the enemy. Look around them and you will find nothing but psycho ex-girlfriends, crazy former roommates, insane neighbors, dishonest coworkers, and so on.

That is your first clue.

When a Toad is telling a story, someone else will always be at fault. It doesn't matter how well the tale is told, the role of the hero depends on who is narrating and in most cases the role of villain is usually going to go to the person NOT telling the story.

Did you really think that you could be the hero in both tales?

It seems that everyone who has ever been a part of their life has screwed the

Toad over, so maybe those people now know something that you don't. Perhaps it is best if you find out what that is before you get hurt. Toads are no fun, and eventually they are going to pick up their toys and go home because we don't want to play their games anymore either. Someone who always sees themselves as the victim with others will eventually see themselves as a victim with you.

If you want to change your life, stop hanging out in swamps. If you must insist upon searching for Prince Charming in the deep and dark places of life, stop expecting other people to feel sorry for you. The red flags are there, pay attention to them.

Red means danger.

You can't polish up a Toad. Clean him up all you want, a Toad will remain a Toad. The more you have to discard, ignore, and make excuses for, the more cautious you should be. If they lie to get what they want from others, they will lie to us when they want something. If they steal from others, they will steal from us.

> Stop waiting for your knight in shining armor to come riding up on his shining steed.
>
> Damsels in distress are quite capable of saving themselves ...

You can ignore red flags all you want, but they will remain just as red.

Cheaters cheat. Liars lie. Abusers abuse.

Toads aren't really that concerned about your happiness, especially if it means giving up a piece of their own. Yes, it can be overcome, and many people do, but be honest with yourself. They aren't going to change until it is in their best interests to do so.

Someone who is getting what they want isn't likely to change on their own. Yes, there will be promises, but promises of change are short-lived. Even if they really did mean it this time, they meant it the time before that, and the time before that too.

Maybe your abuser will change, but it will take a lot more than a few promises to do it. There will come a day when you realize that you are filled to the brim with promises and apologies, but all you really want to see is action.

Trust me. It will come.

As a child I was told that touching a Toad could give you warts. Imagine my relief when I found that warts were really spread by a virus.

Misery is a virus of a different sort. If you are miserable in your relationship then you are doing nobody any favors. You are spreading your misery just as the Toad spreads theirs.

No abusive relationship is ever worth it. In the end, both people die, emotionally, spiritually, and sometimes even physically.

It is a slow death. It is a painful death. It's so not worth it.

Multiple Trauma Survivors

Cady Groves
Musician
Child Physical, Emotional & Sexual Abuse Survivor

Missy Elliot
Rapper/Producer
Child Sexual Abuse & Childhood Domestic Violence Survivor

Lynn C. Tolson
Author
Incest/Domestic Violence/Sexual Assault Survivor

Eva Mendes
Actress
Sexual Abuse & Bullying Survivor

Mary Murphy
Reality TV Star
Rape & Domestic Violence Survivor

"Superman is in-destructible, and you can't be brave if you're indestructible. It's people like you and your mother. People who are different, and can be crushed, and know it. Yet they keep on going out there every time."

~"Angus," 1995, Angus Bethune

Superheroes Aren't Brave

I was six years old when I got my first pair of Wonder Woman Underoos. With a towel safety-pinned around my neck, I made the stealth leap from the sofa to the loveseat hundreds of times while my mother's back was safely turned. It only took a few years of bumps and bruises to figure out that I was lacking something very important: I'm not invincible.

I waited and I waited, but my superpowers never did show up.

Mythology is full of people who have found a secret that somehow transformed them from helpless victim to a hero of the common masses. Ordinary people who through some sort of bizarre circumstances inherited supernatural powers (and an undeniable need to save those in peril. Sounds familiar, doesn't it?), and through those powers their helplessness is overcome and they make the world a better place.

Today we call those people superheroes.

Human beings can be hurt. We can be maimed. We can be killed. It isn't hard to face life with a brave face when nothing can harm you. Superheroes have little to fear.

That's why Batman has always been my favorite modern hero. Bruce Wayne had a whole life full of secrets tucked away beneath his public persona. As the story goes, one of Bruce Wayne's earliest memories was that of his mother and father being murdered.

On some level, I think every Survivor understands his secret world.

What about you? Childhood abuse? Incest? Domestic violence? Rape? Emotional abuse? Verbal abuse? The average abuse Survivor could fill their very own Batcave with the nightmares that haunt their lives.

As a child, it was at night that my imagination ran away. Visions would visit in the darkness, images of people I loved being taken away, and I would dream of fractured memories of abuse I had suffered. In my dreams there was always loss. Always.

I became terrified of going to bed, and I delayed every second I could. The adults in my life never understood what was going on with me. They assumed my fits were tantrums, so they yelled at me, spanked me, punished me and made me go to bed even earlier the next night. I came to be afraid of more than the dark.

How can someone fight crime if they are still afraid of the dark?

Without superpowers, we have no hope of leading a fear-free life. Fear is a normal human response that involves chemical and biological reactions as old as time. It is an indicator that something needs your attention, a response to threats in your environment. Fear means you are still human and everything is still in working order.

> Survivors tend to have excellent imaginations. We should; we certainly exercise them often enough.
>
> A life lived in fear is no life at all.

Batman's superpowers never showed up either. He had no supernatural aid, no toxic waste infusion, no magic wand. While most of the other superheroes were granted powers by some outside source, the Dark Knight drew his from within. The superpowers he didn't have, he created.

Little Bruce Wayne was certainly afraid of many things, but as Batman he used his own resources to build a life dedicated to bringing bad guys to justice. Those who overcome their fears are the people who truly live life. The rest just get by.

If you ever plan on leaving the Batcave you are going to have to accept that fear is a part of life. An imagination allowed to run wild can amplify your anxieties beyond your control. If you've ever had a panic attack you know exactly what I mean.

When we don't expect the unexpected, bad things sometimes happen so it's almost as if we try to expect it all. We imagine that a bus will hit us on our way to cash in our lottery ticket, so we don't buy one. We imagine that our partner is cheating because they are exactly 17 minutes late getting home. We imagine that our uncle's footsteps are coming down the hallway when he has been dead for many years.

Batman had to face his fears without help just like the rest of us. He was determined only to make things right. He refused to play the victim in or out of character. He didn't always deal with his trauma in the healthiest of manners, but I imagine the same can be said of many Survivors. Unfortunately, he is a fictional character, and we have real lives to lead, so we are going to have to do a little bit better than that.

F.E.A.R.

False

Evidence

Appearing

Real.

Fears centering around words like "could," "should," and "didn't" infect your mind with F.E.A.R.

Your mind is your most powerful asset. If you can find a way to block out significant moments of your life, if you have convinced yourself that you somehow deserved to be abused, then you have a gift. Whether you use that gift for ill or for good is entirely up to you.

That power that allowed you to keep believing that nasty Toad would change into Prince Charming someday is the same power that pushes you towards your "happily ever after."

There have been times when I thought that going for even one more day was impossible. My memories of the darkness in my life always seemed to be with me in vivid clarity, and it muted everything else. As my mind continually turned to the negative, that became all I could see.

That shadow settles in and makes itself at home. They told me that this feeling was called depression. Depression and writing have a lot in common. It's all about the creative powers of the human brain.

We build up fears based on half-truths and outright falsehoods that were placed there so long ago. The abuse you suffered is a fact, but so many of the thoughts that were left behind are pure fiction. You have to learn to see them for the lies they really are. Negative thoughts lead to negative feelings, so a professional will help you weed through your automatic thoughts and find ways to weigh them against reality.

Some of your fears are very, very real, but most aren't.

Some people will never move beyond these fears. They believe they are a victim of other people, a victim of circumstances, a victim of the universe even, but they are really victims of "false evidence appearing real."

F.E.A.R.

Fear is a survival response. It's there to keep you safe in dangerous situations. It lets you know when something isn't right. It lets you know when you need to fight and when you need to run. Sometimes your best response is to freeze, to choose to do nothing.

Some people are afraid of spiders while others can handle them as if they were the most domestic of pets. In both cases the person, not the spider, has chosen their response. We spend a lot of time wondering where individual fears come from, but in the end it doesn't matter; it doesn't make it any less real in our minds.

You may remember the root of your fear of spiders very clearly, while the origins of your fear of water remain a mystery. A single event you no longer remember? Several smaller events that built up? A terrifying scene from a movie? Or maybe you really did have a past life as a third-class male passenger on the Titanic.

Either way they are not real here and now. They can't hurt you.

A lot of people are afraid of heights, or public places, or water, but they can and do overcome it. It is the Survivor's nature to push through, no matter how hard it is. That is how superheroes become super in the first place.

Emotions fueled by imagination are no less real than those powered by reality, at least not to the human brain. It isn't the dangers that we face in life that makes our path so difficult, but the strong emotions that come with them.

The human mind doesn't always know the difference between a threat that is real or imagined. If you think there is a bear outside your window, your mind prepares your body to react as if there is one. Your body still responds with the same stress reactions either way.

So what if you start to think that every noise outside of your window is a bear?

Sometimes our fears came from a real event, and others were formed through complex associations that are long forgotten. If you are camping in the woods, a fear of bears is perfectly logical. If you are at home safe in your bed in the middle of New York City, perhaps not.

If you have spent a great deal of time living with anxiety then you have built up some very powerful conditioned responses. "Triggers" are common for victims of abuse, whether they call them by name or not. A trigger is something that sets off an unexpected emotional response in a person. Everybody has them, but they can be incapacitating to victims of abuse. Our fears have a way of taking over if we let them, manifesting themselves in any number of obsessive and compulsive behaviors.

You can't see what is going on right here and now while you are stuck in the past or building up anxiety over the future.

When fears are fed they grow, sometimes to the point that we feel completely out of control.

Something as simple as the wrong phrase or image can incite a chain reaction in the victim's mind. What those triggers are and the reaction they elicit depends on the person and the situation. Some triggers are obvious, like graphic descriptions of sex acts or violence, while others are unique to the individual.

One of mine is the powdered candy that comes in the brightly colored straws. Yeah. I know.

But to this day when I see a candy straw clutched in one of my children's hands I remember having my innocence stripped away, and being handed candy as a reward for my silence. It wasn't even the worst of my memories, but the emotions tied to it are still strong nearly 40 years later.

The power of the emotions linked to our triggers can range from mild discomfort to unexplained rage.

If in the past your partner became violent when they drank, your mind and body may go into high-alert when they come home with a case of beer. Your survival instincts are telling you that this could be an unsafe situation.

Based on prior experience, this is probably a rational fear.

What was true before is not necessarily still true today, but if your mind can't tell the difference then there essentially isn't one. Sometimes just seeing a can of beer sitting on the table in a public place can cause that same state of alert in a victim's brain. If the mere thought of alcohol makes you feel unsafe then you have a trigger. You will still react as if there were danger even if there isn't.

Your mind is always attempting to make decisions based on the evidence it has already collected. Being reminded of past unsafe situations can also remind you of your vulnerability, even if the risk is no longer there. Very much like war veterans who hear loud noises and dive for cover, if an event was impressionable enough it will leave a mark.

We will all have to face our fears eventually, and no, it isn't easy. All superheroes have obstacles to overcome. Something that hasn't happened yet can feel very real, but a lot of things could happen.

It's okay to be aware of your true weaknesses and learn how to work with them instead of against them.

Superman didn't have to be strong, he was as close to invincible as someone could get. Bullets didn't hurt him, and neither did speeding trains. There wasn't much that gave him cause for alarm.

Every superhero has a weakness, something that no superpower can save them from. While we think of them as fearless, everyone is afraid of the things that can actually hurt them.

That isn't cowardice, it is intelligence.

He knew how to find the rational part of the brain, the part that actually kept him safe. Even though his weakness was kryptonite but he didn't avoid all green rocks because of it.

Heroes don't act in an absence of fear. They act - despite it.

Every hero has a process to go through. It doesn't matter if they have superhuman abilities or subhuman. At first, most heroes are a danger to themselves and others. You may have to face a fear until you are sick and tired of it, but that is exactly what you want. The more you look it in the eye, the less control it will have over you. Even fictional characters can't avoid extensive training montages and a whole lot of mistakes on the way.

The difference between a novice and a master in any field is always the same: practice. Peter Parker fell on his face and made a mess of things while learning to sling his spider webs, and a long time ago in a galaxy far, far away, Luke Skywalker's overconfidence in his new Jedi abilities led to a disastrous victory for the evil Empire, at least at first. He eventually got it right, and so did Spidey.

You will too.

They didn't just wake up one day with a nifty new identity, they had to work at it. The polished exterior presented in the tales of their bravery is only the end product.

All superheroes had to start somewhere. They had to take risks and so will you. You aren't a comic book superhero and you aren't fictional. Maybe we can't all be Wonder Woman, but a hero just the same. A real life hero. No superpowers included, some assembly required...but you are the honest to goodness real deal.

Every Survivor has a little bit of superhero inside of them.

Victims Turned Activist

Andrea Dworkin
Activist/ Author
Rape Survivor

Angela Rose
Activist
Rape Survivor

Chris Gavagan
Filmmaker/Activist
Child Sexual Abuse Survivor

Florence Holway
Activist/Artist
Rape Survivor

Mukhtar Mai
Activist
Rape Survivor

Quanitta Underwood
Professional Boxer
Incest Survivor

" Telling someone who's depressed to 'Just get over it.' is like telling a blind person to 'Just look harder.'

~Unknown

Don't Leave Your Behind In Your Past

Yes, we've all heard it. "It's in the past. You should just move on. Put it behind you."

It never fails. When you are struggling most, some well-meaning helping-type person comes along and tells you to "just snap out of it," that "it's all in your head."

Thanks, that really helps. No. Really.

You've likely had a lot of advice over the years, haven't you? From parents. From siblings. From friends. If other people's ways worked for you, you would already be fixed by now. Several times over. The "I've been through tough things in my lifetime , and I'm just fine" method of therapy has never been particularly effective in the past, has it?

The fact that Uncle Joe got over his war experiences with no outside help is great. We don't discuss the drink that is always in his hand, or the way he makes everyone miserable with his frequent outbursts.

Repression works for him. Sort of.

Or maybe it is dear Aunt Edna who drives you crazy. The one that converted to some new faith and now sells vitamins on the side. Sure, she's happy but you aren't into aliens or houses full of cats.

You were meant for very different paths than those around you. Others can call it "getting over it," but you can call it something else.

You weren't born to be Uncle Joe, and thank goodness for that. If we did things the exact same way as him our lives would very likely be just like his.

Let Uncle Joe live his life of biscuits and gravy and the NRA, if that is what makes him happy. He found his way to survive, and it works for him.

But you aren't Uncle Joe, and you aren't Aunt Edna either.

You have your own way of dealing with things. There is never any harm in looking at theirs, of course, but it doesn't mean that you have to use them. You have your own life to live.

If we were all given the same education and experiences we would still handle things differently, because that is just how humans are. It is the chaos theory in full effect.

Even when a source is questionable, the information can still change your life. Even Uncle Joe can be right sometimes.

If help is offered, take it, as long as it will make your life better. Don't let the word victim become just another limitation.

Don't become your diagnosis, overcome it. Make it just another part of your Survivor story.

Despite his "beer before five and whiskey after dinner" policy, his advice about getting a gun is worth considering if you do feel your life is in danger. In some cases a firearm may be your best choice, but only if you are comfortable with the idea of having one.

Then maybe it isn't the weapon itself but the spirit of the advice. Maybe Uncle Joe is really saying that it is time to look into adding some sort of protective measures to your life, such as pepper spray or a stun gun. Maybe it is time to take a self-defense class. Maybe you just need a really big dog.

Maybes are okay sometimes.

If you need to take extra measures to feel safe, then do it. Don't get hung up on the how.

Don't let Aunt Edna's strange ways keep you from finding a satisfying spiritual life a bit closer to home either. Maybe a religion that believes aliens are the master race isn't your style, but that doesn't mean that all of them are wrong. Leave Aunt Edna's aliens behind and her collection of cats too.

But don't set the idea of having faith in something aside. When you are dealing with things that are bigger than yourself, you need a faith big enough to handle it. Your spiritual safety is important to your healing as well.

People who have something to believe in have extra strength to see them through the hard times. They aren't dealing with their problems alone.

Are you beginning to detect a theme here?

Aunt Edna may be a little crazy, but she can still be right about something. Find what works for you and throw away the rest.

Healing takes time, and it takes support. There is no way around it. Your friends, family, or loved ones may be pressuring you to heal, but they are bound to be ready long before you are.

If someone else bought you this book as a polite nudge to fix your issues, I do apologize. If you give it back to them, I will not be offended.

They may be not so politely telling you to just put it behind you, but you will when you are ready. Forcing yourself to do something you aren't ready to do is exactly what got you into this situation in the first place. Destroying your confidence will not force you to rebuild it.

You might have to call in the professionals, but that's okay. If you need a diagnosis, get it, but only if it is going to help you understand your world and make it better. In the end a diagnosis is just another word, a label for other people, not for you. It may help them understand a small piece of you, but it is not who you are.

A lot of the situations in our lives have been crazy, but don't expect anybody else to understand that. Even the so-called professional only has limited knowledge of your world. They label you, diagnose you, medicate you, and treat you, but they still don't really understand you. Surely you have heard hundreds of "All you need to do's..." by now, if not thousands.

Your whole life has been a paradox, trying to convince the outside world that everything was "fine and dandy, thank you very much," when inside it was anything but.

People have been telling you all along that it was all in your head and, well, they were right.

It is in your head, body, brain chemistry, and chemical makeup. Some of us will always be on edge around balloons, or jump when a car backfires outside, or be uncomfortable with our backs exposed, or feel panicked in large crowds. It doesn't make you crazy, it just makes you normal in your world.

Wondering if you are crazy is normal. Really.

We don't need any more victims in this world, but we sure could use a whole lot more Survivors.

Roll Call

Alexander Pushkin
Poet
Abuse

Rosario Dawson
Actress
Bullying

Sally Field
Actress
Child Abuse

Scott Brown
U.S. Senator
Child Sexual Abuse

Tony Rogers
Teacher
Child Sexual Abuse

Virginia Woolf
Author
Incest

"... and then I decided I was a lemon for a couple of weeks."

~Douglas Adams

Call Me Crazy

As it turns out, I'm a bit different. Yes, other people have noticed the cracks, even if they don't want to know the cause.

I've been called crazy a time or two. Weird, strange, and of course odd as well. It has happened so many times that my ex-husband bought me a shirt that says "You call me a freak like it's a bad thing" just before our divorce.

I wore it until it rotted.

Personally, I prefer to think of myself as eccentric. At least it sounds classy. Like a wealthy recluse who wears velvet and lace, and collects teacups and hats. I like being different, and I like being me, as odd as that may sound.

In my youth there was a lot of pressure to be normal and I was ashamed for being unable to conform. I was supposed to hide it, and I couldn't.

I'm still not very good at fitting in, and never have been. I get some strange looks, but people can be very uncomfortable around those that can't be fit into neat little packages with nice, tidy labels.

Sometimes that rejection hurts, but it's better than pretending to be someone I'm not to impress people who never cared in the first place. The more other people tried to force me into their definition of normal, the more chaotic my life got.

So far my strange colors of hair and odd clothes have harmed neither people nor animals. And I am happy just being me. Something got a little twisted along the way. And yeah, it probably is all in my head, but I wouldn't be me without it and those who truly love me know that.

In turn, my loved ones have learned to allow me to be a little bit chaotic, (just a little.)

I'm not easy to live with, and I know that. I try to make up for it whenever I can.

Are you responsible for your issues? Probably not. But you are responsible for any damage done to others.

Survivors Often Struggle With

> *Behavioral issues*
>
> *Criminal activity*
>
> *Depression & suicidal thoughts*
>
> *Difficulty sleeping*
>
> *Drug or alcohol abuse*
>
> *Emotional problems*
>
> *Excessive absences*
>
> *Fear of authority figures*
>
> *Feelings of guilt and shame*
>
> *Frequent headaches*
>
> *Obesity*
>
> *Over-achieving*
>
> *Poor body image & low self esteem*
>
> *Poor decisions*
>
> *Stomach aches & digestive issues*
>
> *Trouble with intimacy*
>
> *Withdrawal & isolation*

You do a lot of things to try to make the abuse in your life right. You strike out. You strike in. You cling. You push away. You love them, and you hate them. Yes, sometimes we all wonder if we are crazy - at least the sane ones do. Actually being crazy, for the most part though, is rare.

If you are hurting other people, you are continuing the cycle of abuse.

STOP.

Nothing gives you the excuse to hurt others. Even if you aren't striking them physically you are just as responsible for your own words as your abusers are for theirs.

There is a reason they call it losing control.

I am a control freak, at least when it comes to some areas of my life - my body, my belongings. I can't do anything about my need to have a safe environment. I can learn to live with it though.

And I can control myself. When things get bad, they can get really bad fast. Reacting in anger is only continuing the cycle.

I've learned to remove myself from the situation until I've calmed myself down. I've learned to consider all angles, and look at things from other people's positions before reacting. When people are angry my world feels off-balance, so thinking things through has to be a priority.

Be honest with yourself; abuse Survivors aren't always the easiest people to live with. Our families have to put up with some strange quirks.

My kids grew up with the weird mom, so they've adjusted pretty well. Living with me is just their normal. They know that mom has a panic disorder so the only acceptable time for anyone to scream is during emergencies, and there had better be blood or smoke to back you up. They make sure to let me know they've entered a room if my back is turned, and they are careful not to pop balloons in the house.

We all know the drill for Mommy Meltdowns. If I get backed into a corner, stop, get me safe, get me calm, and then tell it like it is. And they know I will listen. It isn't their fault I've been through the things I have, and I can't change who I am either, but I love my family. I owe it to them to do what I can to stay on the sane side of the eccentricity line.

That's the deal.

I am still wired towards excess. I am still wired towards extremes. To this day I find myself being defensive about something and realize that it is old pro-gramming doing the talking. Our first reactions are usually the emotional ones, and while they may be a part of the truth, there are a lot of things to think about before I can trust myself to make a rational decision.

I like chaos; in fact, I am attracted to it. I don't mean to be, but it is the closest thing to home I have ever known. I still owe it to my loved ones to try to control that chaos.

There have been times that all my husband could do was hold me while I cried. Where people in my past pushed me to get over it, get past it, move beyond it, he doesn't push at all. He waits patiently while I get it together again, and we move on side by side.

When I had children, I brought them into my choatic world. They didn't ask me for any of this. They know their mom is a bit off sometimes, but they accept it because they don't have much of a choice. It has taken us awhile, but we have learned to face it together.

"What's remarkable is that women with an average age in their late 40s still suffer consequences from abuse that occurred decades ago…We are able to say pretty confidently that it was the abuse itself that is driving higher healthcare use and costs in these women."

⊜

~Amy Bonomi

Associate Professor of Human Development and Family Science

Ohio State University

If I use my past as an excuse, we all suffer.

It isn't normal for a child to be able to tell their parent that they are being irrational, but not all moms have PTSD either. You adjust. My husband, my children, and I are all a part of the same team. If one of us is broken, then all of us will be.

I count on them to tell me when I'm crossing a line and they have my promise that I will try not to make them responsible for my problems. I expect them to own theirs in return.

You can't expect other people to live with you if you can't figure out how to live with yourself. Hell, we all have skeletons in our closets. I just figure if I have to live with them I might as well make mine dance.

When my depression was at its worst, it seemed that everyone was offering me their version of a fix, and I tried many of them. What worked for other people seldom worked for me though. I can't just make what happened in my life go away.

According to a study conducted by Ohio State University, women who suffered sexual abuse spend about $380 more per year on healthcare than the average woman, while those who were abused physically spent around $500 more. For those who come from a history of both physical and sexual abuse, their expenses climb to almost $800 more every year than those who have not been abused.

There is no nice way to say it, being a victim of abuse sucks. Abuse doesn't just go away; it hangs around for years. It's pretty inconvenient all the way around. When you hold all of that old garbage in, every area of your life is eventually infected, and it spreads from there.

Changing your life isn't easy, even when you are moving from the darkness into the light. It really does help to have a navigator to help you find your way.

That's what the professionals are for.

The most successful therapeutic approach found for abuse Survivors by far has been cognitive behavioral therapy which is a close examination of the relationship between your thoughts, your feelings, and your behaviors. Problem solving skills and coping skills are focused on and strengthened. You challenge your beliefs about yourself and your life by experimenting with those beliefs and by testing them.

Don't waste your time in counseling until you are ready to commit to change. The only way therapy is going to help anybody is if they go in prepared to let go of their defenses. If you really are afraid that you are crazy then stop trying to hide it; make an appointment to discuss it.

Yes, you can do it alone. Some people have, but the help of a therapist will ease the pain of that transition. A professional not only knows how to approach this but when, and they can help you learn to handle the stresses that come with facing your fears as well.

It is difficult to label abuse Survivors because symptoms coexist, overlap, and mimic other conditions. There are no tests and no concrete definitions for many of these conditions. Even though most victims of abuse are diagnosed somewhere under the broad category of personality disorders, the range of conditions that fall under that umbrella is astounding.

Labels That Survivors Wear...

Antisocial Personality: Disregard for the rights of others

Avoidant Personality: Inadequacy and extreme sensitivity

Borderline Personality: Instability in relationships, self-image, and emotions, poor impulse control

Dependent Personality: Dependent and submissive behaviors designed to elicit sympathy and care-giving

Depressive Personality: Pattern of depressive attitudes and behaviors

Histrionic Personality: Pattern of attention-seeking behavior and extreme emotionality

Multiple Personality: Two or more distinct identities or personality states

Narcissistic Personality: Grandiosity, need for admiration, and lack of empathy

Obsessive-Compulsive Personality: Perfectionism, orderliness, and control over environment

Paranoid Personality: Distrust and suspicion of others and their motives

Passive-Aggressive Personality: Appears to comply with others while passively resisting

Schizoid Personality: Detachment from social relationships, loner

Schizotypal Personality: Difficulty in establishing and maintaining close relationships, eccentricities interfere with normal social functioning.

Self-defeating Personality: Masochistic, avoiding pleasurable experiences, drawn to painful situations, and refusing outside help

Despite all of these labels for our personalities, most of us are just people who survived some strange stuff and adapted accordingly. A diagnosis doesn't mean a damn thing if it isn't back up with solid treatment options.

You need to have someone on the outside that can help you see through the walls you have constructed for yourself. There are many, many different approaches to therapy, and it sometimes takes a few tries to find the one that clicks for you.

In my experience, doctors gave me a lot of medications that actually worsened my condition. Stimulants, dual anti-depressants, and new experimental drugs that made my life hell. Antidepressants can actual worsen depression and anxiety in some people, and I was one of them.

Your experience may vary, and if you or your doctor think that it is best for you to take medications, do what you feel is best for you. Research may help you to decide what that is.

If you go that route, I recommend that you don't automatically reject or discount everything that comes from someone else. I learned to research it online thoroughly before I took anything. If I can find a natural option I use it, and I stay away from anything that isn't tried and tested completely.

Being brave enough to ask for help is an important strength.

You are responsible for managing your own mental health, for seeking appropriate treatment and for following it. If there is medication that actually helps you then take it, but don't let them shove you into a box that you don't fit into. Fight for what is best for you.

Maintaining balance in your life can be very difficult, and sometimes you need daily reminders to keep yourself from leaning towards one extreme or another.

There are so many things in life that are acceptable or even healthy in moderation but dangerous in excess. Eating is required for a healthy body, but eating more than you need to can cause a myriad of health problems.

A glass of wine a few nights a week is encouraged by many in the medical profession, but a few glasses of wine a night could lead to dependency.

Some girls who are molested go on to become sexually promiscuous, as they grow older, while others move to the opposite extreme and shun sex altogether. Neither is healthy, but both were learned. Sex is supposed to be a good thing. We are supposed to enjoy it as consenting adults, but someone came in and messed with the wiring.

When love came to you through food, food became linked with pleasure. When it came to you through fear, you learned to seek out high-risk situations. If it came to you through sexual attention, you may have learned to associate feeling loved with feeling sexual. If sex was bad, and wrong and nasty, then we thought we must be those things too.

Nobody told us that it was simply human.

If your interests easily translate into obsessions, then you must always be cautious of your tendency to overdo it. Working when you need to work is fine, but you will sometimes deny yourself the ability to rest when you need to. Binging and purging is never healthy, whether it is in food, in work, in exercise, or even in love.

Emotions elicit actual chemical responses within your body. Not just love, but anger, sadness, fear, and pain. If you learned love through unhealthy means, you probably got those love chemicals a little mixed up in the process.

Survivors have a chemical dependency and they aren't even aware of it.

Your brain made these connections the first time, and every time you repeated the pattern those connections got stronger. You have repeated those cycles over and over in your life, in part because you have become addicted to the chemical highs and lows that come with them.

> There is nothing wrong with allowing yourself the pleasure of good food, good wine, and even good company as long as it isn't causing problems in your life or the lives of others.
>
> ⬣
>
> Survivors are already wired for dependency so be warned, those who dance with addiction are bound to lose.

Sometimes chemical addictions mutate, and you need more of your emotional drug to sustain the high. Sexual addictions and fetishes are very much chemical in nature, As the demand increases the tolerance levels continue to rise. As the addict's need grows, they go from leather to rubber, from rubber to steel.

When the object of an addiction stops working, an addict needs to adapt and find another outlet. It could be a new relationship, a new obsession, or even a whole new persona.

The former dominatrix begins going to church. The drunk gives up booze and switches to gambling. The housewife picks up jogging and a year later she is obsessed with roller derby. They will do anything to keep the chemical rush from their emotional addictions flowing.

Locate a competent counselor if you have not done so already; ask around and find someone you can trust. Be honest about everything, especially your concerns about your mental health. If you go in trying to protect your secrets, you will get nowhere. They can only help you if you give them a clear picture of what is really going on.

There is no single step to healing, no way for the Survivor to make it go away.

⚜

Roll Call

Eve Ensler
Playwright/Actress
Incest Survivor

Madonna
Singer, Actress
Domestic Violence Survivor

Ellen DeGeneres
Comedian/Actress/Talk Show Host
Underage Rape

Lady Gaga
Singer/Advocate
Bullying Survivor

Tom Arnold
Actor
Child Physical & Sexual Abuse

"I will punish you because you don't fit in, and I will continue to punish you until you do."

~ Seth Godin on Bullying

Redefining Normal For Yourself

Sometimes things happen in our lives that are well outside of the realm of normal.

Imagine getting up and going to school one day, just an average American teenager, and walking straight into a war zone. That is exactly what happened at Columbine High School on April 20, 1999. More than a dozen people were killed when two students opened fire on fellow classmates.

It was the first of its kind. A military style assault on American schools was unthinkable before that moment. Columbine was not just a shooting, but a full on massacre. Had things gone as planned, had the propane bombs in the cafeteria actually exploded during lunch, had the confused Survivors come staggering out into the daylight and found two very prepared gunmen... as bad as things were that day, what could have been was far, far worse.

Thirteen lives were cut short for no conceivable reason at all.

Books have been written, monuments erected, and foundations have been started in the victims names. Even a decade later the stories of Rachel Scott and Cassie Bernall are still being used to inspire others. They are remembered as the victims of Columbine, but there were so many more.

Two dozen people were wounded and survived. They were barricaded in classrooms and hiding in kitchens. They survived, but many of their friends and loved ones did not, and they must live with that knowledge every day. Some walked out without a scratch, but the nightmares and flashbacks still haunt them over a decade later. Some were never able to walk again. Others will suffer chronic pain for the rest of their lives.

And most of us will never know their names.

Dylan Klebold and Eric Harris became anti-heroes and inspired other marginalized boys who had been bullied the world over. People who felt that they had been victimized in the past identified with the images splashed all over the media.

Many of the school shooters' writings ranted about revenge and retribution, and even natural selection, but what the shooters seemed to crave above all else was attention. They wanted people to fear them. They wanted fame. They wanted notoriety. They wanted people to know their name.

Unfortunately, thanks to the media, they got all of that and more.

The media was only interested in those who were killed and those who did the killing, and not with the real heroes of that day. The real heroes of Columbine were the people who found the courage to go on with their lives. The real heroes are the people who learned to walk and talk again, those who learned to use wheelchairs and have had to learn to live with chronic pain. Those who had to learn how to live again.

The Columbine shooters were not Survivors. Nobody who goes on to perpetrate abuse on another human being can wear that badge. There was nothing brave about picking up a gun and shooting at unarmed civilians. They chose the coward's way out.

If the media focused coverage on the Survivors instead of the killers, perhaps violence wouldn't be one the easiest ways to get attention. Self-destructive behaviors and negative attention seeking are very common among abuse Survivors, but they don't have to be. You can learn how to trade the bad attention for the good, to be recognized for who you are, not what you do for others. Nobody has to choose a path of destruction in their lives.

Suffering abuse of your own is no excuse. The Survivor Spirit is all about stopping abuse, and making the world a better place.

Many school shooters claim that they were bullied. If bullying really was part of their motivation, if it was bad enough that they felt they needed to get revenge on the people who perpetuated the abuse it would still be difficult to understand. At Columbine, none of the students they killed or injured had been part of that bullying.

Many different organizations have tried to develop a profile of the typical school shooter, and have discovered none. It is hard to imagine what is going on in these shooters heads, let alone think far enough ahead to actually stop them.

If these shootings are a cry for attention, then it is time for us to listen.

People seek out attention throughout their lives. We all want to be accepted by somebody. What we usually fail to ask is: what sort of attention are we seeking, and why?

As the shooters wallowed in their misery and played out their revenge fantasies against those who had bullied them they grew a false sense of power. Through video games like Doom and movies like Natural Born Killers violence became their normal

"Let Columbine be a benchmark for change, not despair. It left me with a hole in my heart. The hole doesn't get any smaller. But Columbine also taught me the goal is to make my heart bigger."

~Dawn Townsend – Daughter Lauren Townsend was killed at Columbine.

No rational person could blame the video games for these acts, but the immersion in a fantasy world was fairly intense by all accounts. It took two years for them to plan their shooting spree, and in that time most of the students they had originally planned to target had graduated. But the boys went ahead with their plan anyhow.

That fantasy did not translate into reality though. Towards the end of the Columbine shooting spree witnesses noted that the boys began wandering around in what seemed to be an aimless manner. They had enough ammunition to continue their spree for some time, the police were not advancing, but they stopped and committed suicide. Their purpose lost.

It is strange that so many school shooters cite "survival of the fittest" as their motive. They clearly did not understand the concept at all.

They had spent a great deal of time fantasizing about the shootings, and I honestly think that the reality let them down. Fantasies so often do. They thought they would gain power over their lives by controlling others.

They declared war on the American definition of "normal," and lost.

Most of these boys were what would be considered "abnormal," and their targets were the so-called "normal" students. These kids did not just target the people who hurt them but the environment that they associated with that hurt. A place that could be considered the headquarters of the Normal Patrol: the average American High school.

Studies have shown that perpetrators of school shootings are more than twice as likely to have been bullied by peers than their victims were.

As our schools have faced budget cuts and overcrowding, conformity has become even more important. We are literally raising our children like cattle. There is no room for those who stand out, or do things differently.

For the kids that are able to conform, it's a great system, and it works for the schools, but many kids have no hope of ever measuring up. Kids who stand out risk being singled out by bullies.

Many, many children are bullied every year in the United States, more than half of all American students report being bullied at their schools and 10% of children report repeated episodes according to BullyingStatistics.org.

> "The time I spent living in the mountains was one of my darkest hours. I say this to give others hope that it's possible to rebound from such a dark place, but I contemplated suicide in the mountains. I was no longer able to attend school, and I was not working. I sat around watching TV all day, and it was awful, but I realize now that I had to go down before I could go back up."
>
> ●
>
> ~Anne Marie Hochhalter - Columbine Survivor

Were the shooters at Columbine bullied? All indicators say yes. I found several incidents in their histories where the boys were bullied by more popular students. They were singled out, had drinks thrown at them, and were called faggots.

Sexuality is not an uncommon target for bullies. Dating is a competitive sport in the super-straight, jock-oriented cult of America's high schools, and all that really matters is the score. A close look at the types of bullying boys reacted most violently to were those that attacked their sexuality.

But there are also stories where the shooters were the bullies. They had a lot of anger built up inside, and while they hid it fairly well from the adult world the signs were always there. They were victims who allowed themselves to become the bullies.

They chose to continue the cycle of abuse.

Suffering somehow became normal for them. Sadly, a person, a family, and even a country can adjust to just about anything.

I have seen a lot of people who sympathized with the shooters, but I have also seen a lot of people who sympathized with the bullies. Uncle Joe and his comments like, "I was bullied and I didn't go out and shoot up the school," and "It'll make a man out of 'em," is just as much a part of the cycle as the kids who worship Columbine are.

What could make a boy fear life more than death? I have spent the years since Columbine researching that question from every angle I could to find seeking the answer. As every new shooting emerged, I watched for the story beneath the story to come out. I've studied more than two dozen school shooters in depth, and still have no answer.

> "Because I had been there before, I knew that people needed to hear that it would be OK. Thirteen years ago, I didn't have that confidence, but I want those in Aurora to know that it will be OK. An incredibly difficult journey lies ahead, one that you didn't choose, but don't you give up."
>
> ~Liz Carlston – Columbine Survivor (To Aurora Theater shooting victims)

Wayne Lo was one of the first school shooters of the 1990s. He will spend his entire adult life in prison, and he knows this. Many years have passed and whatever his motives really were for his shooting spree they are no longer in existence.

He and I have corresponded for several years now and have shared an interesting friendship. While I do consider him a friend, he knows what he did was wrong, and he never tried to convince me that he wasn't a killer. I wrote to him to tell him that I was interested in interviewing him for a book about a school shooting and those left behind to pick up the pieces.

I never really did interview him though. When I asked him why he had done it, all that he could say was that he didn't know.

In the dozens of cases that I have studied, the assumed motive was different, the background was different, and the locations varied dramatically. They have a few things in common, but very few: school shootings tend to happen in rural areas, are more likely around long vacations, and nearly all of the shooters had been on anti-depressants but for the most part they are totally random. There is still no way to tell who will snap and who will not.

For now, there is no way to stop school shootings from happening, and as long as they continue, the number of Survivors left behind to pick up the pieces will continue to grow.

Many Survivors say they simply want to get back to normal, but how do you do that after something so fundamentally life-changing? You can't stop living just because something horrible happened.

For many of the Columbine Survivors, the world really did stop spinning for a while. There was so much to mourn: the loss of friends and loved ones, the loss of their healthy and functional bodies, the psychological toll.

How many of the staff and students witnessed the mass murder of their friends and loved ones? How many families rushed to the school and waited only to find that their children were among those who would not be coming home? In less than one hour, thousands of lives were changed. Columbine

> "From the day of the shooting I was determined not to be a victim.
>
> Columbine was simply an event. Now it should be a word for hope and courage."
>
> ~Patrick Ireland,
> Columbine Survivor –

has since spun copycat acts all around the globe, and the number of affected has continued to climb.

Columbine Principal Frank DeAngelis has been there for many of the Survivors of subsequent shootings. He bravely led 20 students to safety that day while his good friend, teacher Dave Sanders, lay dying. In the end twelve of his students were murdered, and two more of his students were responsible. Some people considered him responsible for the shootings, saying he should blame himself.

Things sometimes happen in our lives that are out of our control. The wrong person, the wrong place, the wrong time, and a victim is born.

But the final choice always rests with us.

Principal DeAngelis joined the ranks of the Survivors that day. Many people in his situation would have taken early retirement, and nobody could expect someone to go back to the hallways of Columbine after what had happened.

Like many Survivors, he struggled to find his place in the world again. His marriage crumbled. He suffered anxiety attacks and Survivor's guilt and struggled to come to terms with the events of that tragic day. On the outside he was a hero, but his emotional scars ran deep.

His life was spared, and he does not take that for granted. He no longer mourns the lives lost that day, saying that he prefers to celebrate the lives they lived. Through counseling and faith he made a new path for himself and along the way became engaged to his high school sweetheart.

He has survived the halls of Columbine every day since the shooting. At first he promised that he would stick it out as principal until those who were freshmen in 1999 had graduated, but he kept extending his stay. He finally announced his retirement as principal in 2013, 15 years after the shootings.

> "We will never get back to normal, we just had to redefine what normal is."
>
> ●
>
> ~Frank DeAngelis – Columbine High School Principal

Frank DeAngelis spoke for every Survivor when he said, "We will never get back to normal, we just had to redefine what normal is."

When normal isn't working for you anymore then it really is time to redefine it.

Finding healing isn't about fitting into someone else's view of what is normal. It is about finding your own definitions. A lot of people had to redefine normal after Columbine, and in dozens of mass shootings since.

Five students that were at Columbine that day went on to become teachers at their old school. They have become angels watching over students today. It wasn't easy for any of them, but they did what they had to do. They did what they felt was right.

I've had to learn to live with a lot of the things I can't change about my past. We all do. My life has not been normal. My experiences have not been normal, but my reactions to them were as normal as could be expected given the circumstances.

Being a victim is only normal if you accept it to be so.

I'm almost forty years old now, and I still have no idea what normal is. I've come to the conclusion that I'm probably not going to get there in this lifetime. Holding on to the hope that something will happen that magically makes your past traumas go away only holds you in place. Nothing can change what has already happened. It will still be there tomorrow morning and every day after.

People who are different spend a lot of time wishing that they were normal, but whatever normal is, you can't trust anybody else to define it for you.

We will always be too fat, too thin, too short, or too tall. Some of us will need glasses, or braces, or even prosthetic devices. We will be too old for some, and too young for others. Those who have curly hair wish they had straight hair, and those who have straight hair envy those with curls.

They say, "To be normal, you should just be yourself," but then they always seem to point to what everybody else is doing. Normal is the people on TV. Normal is the clothes your friends and neighbors wear. Normal is a skin type.

Normal is a kind of shampoo. Normal is a test result.

Normal is a myth.

School Massacres Remembered

1927 The Bath School Disaster
58 Wounded
44 Killed

2007 The Virginia Tech Massacre
17 Wounded
32 Killed

2012 Sandy Hook Elementary Massacre
2 Wounded
26 Killed

1966 University of Texas Massacre
32 Wounded
14 Killed

1999 Columbine High Massacre
28 Wounded
15 Killed

To all of those who will never forget...

*"Stress does not
cause pain, but it
can exacerbate it
and make it worse.
Much of chronic
pain is 're-
membered' pain.
It's the constant
firing of brain cells
leading to a
memory of pain
that lasts, even
though the bodily
symptoms causing
the pain are no
longer there. The
pain is residing be-
cause of the neuro-
logical connections
in the brain itself."*

~Dr. Herbert Benson

Real Life With Imaginary Illnesses

When we hear the word terrorism, images of bombings and mass casualties arise, but what is terrorism really but bullying on a large scale?

A life lived in fear.

On September 11, 2001, the world watched as the great towers fell. Through the media we re-experienced the event over and over for the next few months. There have been numerous attempts to define the word terrorism since then. Most have centered around the use of violence or threats to create fear in another person, and the danger posed to innocent parties. In terrorism, goals are often ideological, but then again...so is bullying. The difference is simply scope. A bully, if given enough power, can take down schools, buildings and even countries.

In the days following 9/11, acute stress symptoms such as anxiety, avoidance, hyper-arousal, and re-experiencing of the event were reported by at least 1/3 of respondents to a questionnaire by the Journal of the American Medical Association. Another 12 percent of respondents reported difficulty sleeping, exaggerated startle responses, feeling on edge, helplessness, nightmares, trouble concentrating, and unexplained terror gripping them for no reason.

So-called normal people were dissociating and triggering. For the first time in my life, I was almost normal.

Other people finally knew what it was like to have a body and brain on high-alert in a world full of things for us to worry about. That flow of adrenaline coursing through your body again at the slightest provocation, constantly preparing it to fight or flee.

That's my life.

More than 13 million people have post traumatic stress disorder at any given time, and 8% of Americans will experience PTSD at some point in their lives. In nearly any case of trauma, 5% of those exposed to trauma will suffer with long-term symptoms. Chronic PTSD.

Within six months of the attacks, all but 5% of participants in the original JAMA questionnaire reported that their symptoms had diminished. As the events of September 11 faded from our nightmares, individual stress began to return to normal again nationwide. For a time, a lot of people understood what it felt like to be one of US. They knew.

It was in the 1960s that therapists began noticing a similar group of symptoms reported by Survivors of the Holocaust: nightmares, depression, social withdrawal, sleep disturbances, and a persistent feeling of guilt for their own survival. They called this "Survivor's syndrome," or "Survivor's guilt," a condition that is now listed as a subset of post-traumatic stress disorder.

It's a learned response, a mind doing exactly what it is supposed to do: keep you alive. PTSD is fear that has become habit.

Sufferers are told that there is something wrong in their heads when it is really their bodies doing exactly what they've been trained to do. Survive.

Survivor's syndrome may very well exist, and not just in Survivors of the Holocaust but in Survivors of many different kinds of abuse. Long-term threats in your environment can train you to stay in a heightened state of alert a majority of the time. It's what your body is supposed to do when it senses danger, and it's perfectly normal and natural.

PTSD sufferers sometimes feel like life is unpredictable so it pays to be ready for anything. You brace yourself for the worst and dare not hope for the best. The resulting adrenaline rush causes fear, and the fear pumps more adrenaline into your body, creating a pattern that cycles, builds, and continues to increase. You end up in an almost permanent state of alert.

What is unnatural about PTSD is the self-perpetuating cycle it causes when your natural fear responses begin to take control of your life.

PTSD is my normal. It's just something I have learned to live with. Avoid large crowds. Stay away from drunk people or those with temper problems. Always sit with your back protected. Talk yourself through the panic attacks.

Get it together and get back to life.

So you do what you can to avoid anything that might remind you of what you have been through. You don't want to leave the house. You don't want to remember it or talk about it. You don't want to deal with people or situations that might trigger an unexpected reaction.

I've had it since I was very young so nobody ever knew anything was wrong to begin with. Sure, they told my that I was broken, that something about me wasn't right but they all assumed it was something that I was doing consciously. I wasn't. I've always been high strung, talked way too much, made impulsive decisions and jumped at loud noises.

It quickly became my normal.

Survivors often complain of a mysterious cluster of symptoms that baffle the best of doctors. Labeled as psychosomatic, psychiatric disorders, or hypochondria, patients may even begin to think they are imagining their own symptoms.

PTSD should be the first thing that doctors ask about when they discover a history of abuse, but they often don't. We don't talk about our abuse, and our healthcare providers don't ask. Long term effects of living with abuse are rarely properly diagnosed and dealt with.

A lot of those things that make you feel crazy are just side-effects of recovering from trauma. Our fear response came in handy in man's most primitive days. It was crucial to the survival of the species in those moments when the saber-toothed tiger roared out its warning, and it is needed now when someone runs the red light as you are crossing the intersection. It was supposed to keep you alive long enough to flee if possible, and if not, to turn and fight.

When you have PTSD, you are already prepared for danger, so anything in your environment can be viewed as a potential threat to your survival. You make irrational connections in your brain. You get defensive. You mistrust others. You strike out at the slightest provocation. You hurt people who don't deserve it.

Sometimes you might have been left wondering if you were still in possession of your rational mind at all. You were. It was just on vacation for a while.

I've had many "diagnoses" over the years. As a child, they said I had a learning disability, or perhaps attachment difficulties due to frequent moves and changes of caretaker. As a teen, it was clinical depression or chronic depression. Even a mention or two of manic-depressive disorder found their way into my file. And that was just the beginning. By the time I was an adult, they had a comprehensive list of labels placed in my files, but they still had no idea what was making me so different.

I've struggled with panic attacks most of my life. People kept telling me that it was just my imagination playing tricks on me. But it didn't matter what it was, I had no control over it.

As a young mother, I would be standing in line at the grocery store when I felt it coming on. Suddenly there were too many people. The walls were closing in. I was aware of every breath. My eyes darted from one exit to another, trying to find the fastest way out.

Everyday events can bring old memories to the surface, and with them feelings so intense that it's just like reliving them all over again.

I was doing all I could to avoid freaking my children out, but I was barely able to keep myself calm. Inside my whole body had suddenly gone tense.

Living in your imagination is a nightmare few can understand.

Most of the time there was no real cause. It wasn't as if I was in danger, or my children were being threatened. I was safe, but I was inexplicably terrified.

I have scooped up my children and left carts full of groceries sitting at checkouts many times much to the confusion of those around me.

Then there were the not so obvious side-effects of PTSD.

My first two pregnancies did not reach term, ending in miscarriages. I lost my first child 5 ½ months into the pregnancy, and the second at 9 weeks. My body was actively trying to abort them every time I had a panic attack.

With my oldest, Brooke, I was on bed rest for a good portion of my pregnancy. I was allowed to take a shower and watch TV for an hour each day. They placed me on medications that amped me up and told me to lay down. I had to take them every six hours to keep my contractions under control. She was born full-term, but she only weighed 5 pounds, 4 ounces.

My only son, Justin, was born six weeks early. After we took our very first ambulance rides together, he spent the next four weeks in the hospital. He barely made it home for his first Christmas, and for the next few months our lives were filled with tubes and wires and sleep apnea alarms.

My body just couldn't carry kids after stress, but none of the doctors ever tried to figure out why. Every time my husband and I fought, every time I was startled, every time the stress built up, my body tried to abort my children.

Even those that survived came with a surprise...

My first labor lasted a total of 45 minutes. The doctor barely made it in time. My son took around three and a half hours. We really don't know, as he was born in the ambulance 25 miles away from the hospital. I almost had Mystery, my youngest, at home, but my husband and grandmother objected. The security guard that told my husband he couldn't park in the ER entrance was in for a hell of a surprise. It took me 18 minutes from first contraction to delivery.

> Nobody knows for sure what the effects of the events in our lives are on the human brain, because no two human brains are the same. When dealing with a life-altering event, some people will bounce back and some won't bounce at all.
>
> ⬤
>
> While a group of people can witness the same thing, each of them reacts in a very different manner and heals in entirely different ways.

My children should not be here. My super-fast labor with Mystery left me with a cracked tailbone, and she still has a lump on her jaw from the fracture she received and her entire face was bruised. My children were my most precious gifts, and I treasure each of them. Knowing that I was lucky to have them at all, makes them even more of a blessing in my life.

After I left my first husband my stress levels decreased significantly. I am sure that his did as well.

I remarried, and tried to go on with my life. For long periods of time, I would do very well but then my whole system would just crash. Some insisted that I was just lazy, but it was more than that. I was exhausted. I slept a lot, couldn't keep up with my daily tasks and struggled to keep working in some capacity.

I had two speeds: go and stop. There was no in between. The minute I stopped, I was totally drained. People kept telling me to push harder and my body would eventually get used to it. They promised the energy would come to me if I kept ignoring the fatigue. It never happened.

Then it began to build up. I tried to make up for all of the time I was sick by pushing myself even harder, and I would be back in bed again within weeks, and then days. I was stuck in bed for longer periods of time.

My illness was trying to tell me something, and it had to put me flat on my back before I was willing to listen.

In my mid-thirties it all began to decline rapidly. I lost strength in my muscles and found it hard to keep food down. The pain that had been a constant companion from the onset was increasing. My ribcage felt bruised, and the pressure came from all sides, as if I were wearing a corset. My legs felt swollen and overworked, as if I were running marathons in my free time. They grew too weak to fully support me, I was confined to bed for weeks at a time.

That's when I first started hearing the rumors that I was on drugs. That's the problem with living in a small town, it's like high school but it never ends. I hadn't done drugs in twenty years, but I couldn't blame people for their guesses about my condition. I couldn't even explain it, whatever it was affecting me was unaided by external causes, and there was nothing I could do to control it.

I was too miserable to be doing it to myself on purpose.

By then the doctors began to suspect that I had multiple sclerosis, but an MRI revealed no lesions on my brain or spine. They did all of the standard blood tests, but they came back normal. Four different doctors had weighed in on my diagnosis before I finally managed to get past the "it's all in your head" phase and made to the "guess we'll call it Fibromyalgia" phase.

There wasn't a blood test or tissue sample that could clarify my condition, just an educated guess. In many doctors' minds, if symptoms cannot be seen in charts or graphs then they can't possibly be real.

After years of tests and specialists I finally had a tentative diagnosis, everything fit, and all we needed was the confirmation.

The nearest rheumatologist, Dr. Cocky, was booked for nearly a year in advance, so I had to wait it out. Some of the strength had returned to my muscles by then but I still required the use of a cane for balance.

I walked into Dr. Cocky's office filled with hope, but it didn't take long for him to crush it entirely.

He blustered through our time like a Banty rooster. Rushing through the interview without pause. Make no mistake about it, it was an interview, not an appointment. He hastily gathered my family history and took a few notes. The exam itself lasted just a few minutes.

New links were being explored at that time, ideas that abuse and Fibro are much more closely related than previously realized. I had seen a few of these articles, and the symptoms were strikingly similar. I mentioned the rape, my history of abuse, and pointed to the new studies. He was more worried about the fact that I did not know my father well and was not married to the father of my children than my actual symptoms.

A recent study found fibromyalgia in 49% of male soldiers with long-diagnosed PTSD . While there was no fibromyalgia at all in the control group.

Not all fibromyalgia sufferers have had significant trauma in their lives, but for those who have, the pieces are finally starting to fall together. Trauma sticks around.

~Hadassah Hebrew University School of Medicine

Beneath his judgmental gaze I felt like nothing more than another white-trash, stay-at-home mom looking to "get on the welfare." The instant I mentioned Fibromyalgia and PTSD the interview was over.

"I am the doctor. You don't come in here and tell me anything. I tell you."

He simply poked me a few times and announced that all I needed was to lose weight and get a better bra, and then excused me from his presence without a single test. At least with a Fibromyalgia diagnosis I had something to go on, but he had even taken that much away. I left his office in tears. Defeated.

Not that a diagnosis of Fibromyalgia held much hope. There was no known cause, no known cure. Many in the medical profession see it as the latest fad diagnosis, and more than a few still don't believe that it exists at all.

If I had not met Shirley Olsen, I don't know if I would still be here today. It would be three years before I would be brave enough to repeat my suspicions to another health professional. At that time, Shirley and her husband were commuting from Ouray to our small clinic a few times each week. I loved them for that 70 miles drive every day.

I spent many years living from my bed, trying to work and raise children, managing a marriage. The doctors told me that there was no known cause, and no known cure. They could medicate the symptoms, but they couldn't give me my life back. Living life half awake, half medicated. Living half a life.

My health had declined to the point that I was bedridden about half of the time. I had a lot of female troubles, and they eventually led to a diagnosis of endometriosis and a hysterectomy.

I fell a lot, and for no good reason. I would just get lightheaded and down I went. I was vomiting a lot, and it continued to get worse. I had trouble keeping a full meal down, and I lost 60 pounds. Whenever I ate, I had to consciously swallow because my throat sometimes seemed to get stuck.

My blood pressure had always been low, but by then it was in the 90/20 range. The doctors and nurses all saw it as a good sign, but it bothered me. Every indicator was that my blood pressure should have been through the roof, but it was barely there at all. I was a smoker, I ate salt like candy, and my life was constant stress. Sometimes it was so low they couldn't find it without elevating my arm.

> In May of 2011 researchers found that women who were physically abused as children had double the rate of chronic fatigue syndrome and chemical sensitivities and an astounding 65 percent higher risk of having fibromyalgia than those without past trauma.
>
> ~UT's Factor-Inwentash Faculty of Social Work and Department of Family and Community Medicine
>
> "These findings persisted even after controlling for potentially confounding factors, such as other adverse childhood experiences, age, race, mental health, and adult socioeconomic status."
>
> ~ Professor Esme Fuller-Thomson

Shirley Olsen was the first person to agree that it made no sense. It turned out that my wonky blood pressure was the key all along.

After she commented on my blood pressure I took a deep breath and told her everything. That I had been doing some research on my own, and all of my random diagnoses had overlapping symptoms. ADHD, fibromyalgia, chronic fatigue, post-traumatic stress disorder. What if they were all the same thing in my case?

Shirley not only knew exactly what she was looking at when she saw it, she knew how to treat it. My whole body was literally exhausted. I had been sick far longer than anyone suspected. Shirley, and her husband, have many years of experience in treating people like me. Low blood pressure was a classic symptom of adrenal exhaustion.

Years of going too hard for too long had finally caught up with me in a big way. I was so tired that I could barely function, but too wound up to sleep. Even in high school my fatigue was so great that I slept through many of my morning classes and I missed at least one day each week to stay home and sleep but I never felt rested.

Shirley ordered a series of tests for hormone levels and we confirmed that my system was shot. My body was not producing testosterone or progesterone properly anymore, and my cortisol levels were nonexistent. She also found a gluten sensitivity that was interfering with my whole system. She put me on massive doses of vitamins and minerals, and stripped my diet down to the essentials.

Most of the time our adrenals recover with time, but I had chronic PTSD, so mine stayed in a heightened state for long periods.

> After the death of a loved one, financial ruin, public scandal, a rape, or any other traumatic event, your body does the best it can to keep up, but it is a short-term solution.
>
> 🔵
>
> Adrenal fatigue can happen to anyone; in fact, it is fairly common. If the pressures continue to build, the stress response doesn't get a chance to fully reset and your adrenals can't keep up.

Shirley and I went through my history, both physical and psychological. On average, I had a trauma or major change occur in my life around every six months for almost 20 years. I was molested from four to eight. I attended twenty-two different schools before graduating. My mother was married and divorced three times in my childhood, and she had several long-term relationships, some live-in, some not. Most of her relationships were troubled, and none of the men stayed in my life after the divorce. Many of my adult relationships had been emotionally and verbally, and sometimes physically, abusive.

When those stress responses make themselves at home, the functions that were designed to keep you alive turn against you. Your body becomes its own enemy.

When faced with danger, your nervous system floods your bloodstream with "stress" hormones; adrenaline, noradrenaline, and cortisol. Your heart rate and blood pressure rise. Your respiratory rate increases, your pupils dilate, and your awareness heightens. Your body is ready to face the enemy, whatever it may be, and you are in fight-or-flight mode. Your reaction times quicken, you feel less pain, and your impulses are primed and ready for action.

Cortisol is always present in your body, but in times of danger your nervous system dumps higher amounts of hormones into your bloodstream. When faced with long-term stressors your body is unable to keep up production and it drops.

It isn't just your mental faculties that are affected though. Your essential bodily functions become the main priority. The ones needed for your immediate survival get bumped to the front of the line. Blood is redirected from your digestive tract to feed your muscles and limbs, resulting in nausea and vomiting. Your reproductive organs are non-essential to your survival, so your body does what it has to to keep you alive. Miscarriages and premature births can occur in times of high stress.

Insufficient levels of cortisol can lead to fuzzy thinking, fatigue, muscle pain, weakness, sleep disturbances, and mood swings–all classic Fibromyalgia symptoms.

Participants in one study reported that their depression symptoms fell to 57% among participants, without the use of pharmaceuticals. How? By games with positive outcomes such the ones many people play on Facebook and like minded sites daily.

◉

Participants reported decreases in:

Fatigue (58%)

Anger (55%)

Confusion (50%)

Depression (50%)

Tension (49.6%)

Increase in vigor (33%).

~ East Carolina University's Psycho–physiology Lab and Biofeedback Clinic

Shirley and I began the road to my healing. She started me on a program designed to strengthen my adrenals. Slowly my health returned and even went beyond anything I had ever experienced before. I even found out what it was like to wake up feeling rested for the first time in my life.

After five years of pain and pills and living life in a haze, my health began to improve. Handfuls of prescriptions for pain and sleep and nausea were replaced with vitamins. We cut out gluten and most junk food. When my adrenals are in need of an extra push I add in licorice root and ashwaganda root tinctures. Sometimes I need B12 shots when I'm really stressed. It took almost two years of treatment, but for the first time in my life my body was functioning properly. Slowly but surely we discovered that I was ALIVE!

I spent a lot of time taking care of other people, but had I ignored my own needs for too long. Shirley made me find time to take care of me. She prescribed frequent periods of rest throughout the day, as well as a low-energy, no-impact exercise program.Just learning to take care of myself is finally becoming a part of my routine. I still have relapses, especially under high stress, but we've learned to head most of the symptoms off before they get serious. I often have very limited energy, so I have to take great care in deciding what and even whom that energy should go to. .

The way the entire medical field looks at Fibromyalgia and PTSD is changing. Fibromyalgia and trauma are linked. More and more studies are finding these links every day.

We now know that both conditions can be marked by low cortisol. This deficiency does not appear in standard blood tests, but a 24-hour cortisol saliva test (available online without a prescription) will show your doctor how low your levels really are and help them formulate a treatment plan.

I can only hope this means that more doctors will begin to recognize the symptoms and offer treatment. All along they have been looking at Fibromyalgia and PTSD as two separate conditions, but it very well may be that they are the same condition manifested in different ways.

Fibromyalgia is not curable as of this writing, but for trauma Survivors there is now hope. It was the last piece in the puzzle.

Dr. Cocky had all of the information that he needed, but already knew too much listen to me. It was there all along. Post Traumatic Stress Disorder was frying my adrenals.

As a PTSD sufferer, you might be easily startled when people sneak up behind you. You might be frightened when you are in large groups, or avoid sitting near an open door, leaving your back exposed. You might feel unsafe no matter where you are. You might be afraid that someone is following you. Maybe you stay awake all night listening for strange noises. If you had a reason to react a certain way in a type of situation once, your body doesn't easily forget, and is still on guard.

When it is allowed to roam free, our imaginations can make us prisoners in our lives, our homes, and even our own bodies. I've had to learn to be observant of my thoughts to a much greater extent than I was in my past.

Keeping your adrenals healthy means keeping them calm. Prayer, visualization, and meditation have all been successful in treating PTSD symptoms with great success.

When harnessed and redirected, the same mind that brought so many PTSD Survivors a life of hell can be what finally brings them peace. Strange isn't it?

Some of the most successful treatments so far have come from areas you never would have expected. Anti-depressants and anti-anxiety pills can help some people but they can also keep your from dealing with the real roots of the problem. If we don't fix our minds, we will never fix our bodies.

Medical marijuana is proving to be more effective with PTSD patients than any other treatment they have tried, including antidepressants. Researchers now believe that it may have something to do with an inability to process memories properly, and thus recover from them. Cannabinoid receptors in the human brain are strongly linked to this ability.

Brain imaging has shown a connection between cannabinoid receptors in the brain and PTSD.

New research is coming out that shows exposure to severe trauma can significantly alter the function of the natural endocannabinoid receptors.

The bodies endocannabinoid system affects how we move, react, and feel. In those who have experienced trauma, that system is not functioning properly.

Marijuana, or cannabis, can activate the natural cannabinoid receptors in the human brain. Allowing them it to better process and let go of traumatic memories and reduce overall anxiety.

~New York University Langone Medical Center

Even certain video games are showing promise for treating depression and anxiety, which are common with abuse Survivors. We may have to look at things in whole new ways, but the help is out there.

Those with PTSD have to control their minds or their minds will control them. Our imagination is just another survival skill that came from a life spent living on eggshells. It is part of Survivor's syndrome as much as anything else is, and it is sharpened to a fine edge.

All along there was hope, but I had to find it in some pretty unlikely places. I wasn't broken either, or lazy, or crazy. I was just different.

My husband always wants to drive here or there, and I can't seem to get him to understand I really would rather walk. I got a second chance at life, and I don't want to waste it. I don't want the closest parking spot to the door, and I don't want to drive a block and a half to the store. I can walk again without help, and there was a time I wasn't sure that would be possible.

The door to my imaginary cage has been opened, and now all I want to do is fly.

Famous Survivors

Connie Francis
Singer
Rape Survivor

Corey Feldman
Actor
Child Sexual Abuse

Emilie Autumn
Singer/Writer/Poet/Musician
Multiple Abuse

Marilyn Monroe
Actress/SingerChild
Sexual Abuse

Roseanne
Actress
Child Sexual Abuse

Winona Ryder
Actress
Bullying

"Sticks and stones may break your bones but words can hurt like hell."

~Chuck Palahniuk

Sticks And Stones And Broken Homes

All of our lives the Big People have told us that "Sticks and stones may break your bones, but words can never hurt you." It was supposed to make us feel better, but it never really did. Did it?

In 2010 alone, it is believed that 33 bullied children took their lives rather than face continued bullying at the hands of their peers. These deaths have brought a new term to the school bullying forefront: "bullycide." Words can induce fear, lower self-esteem, and increase anxiety.

George Carlin once said that there are no bad words, only bad intentions. How many words does it take to wear a person down to the point of suicide? Nobody knows. But what is certain is that suicides don't usually happen after a single encounter. It is only after a child's fear of death is surpassed by his fear of life.

Sticks and stones indeed.

Children are literally being bullied to the point that suicide appears to be a viable option. If a near-stranger's words can cut someone so deeply that they begin to believe that suicide is their only escape, what of the bullies that they may be living with?

Words can hurt; even more, what is behind those words can hurt. They can cause you to rise up, and they can help others keep you down. Some can put you into a certain place, and others can pull you out. Some words were created with the express intent of doing harm.

Words have a power that few people respect. There is a reason words like "white trash" and "nig-er" bring an emotional rise out of people. The target of such words is meant to feel shame, or inferiority, or even pain.

For the person using the insult, it gives them a feeling of power over another human being, a sense of superiority. It is meant to weaken the other person, to wear them away while they build themselves up. All insults are.

All abuse is. An old Chinese proverb says, "The beginning of wisdom is to call things by their right names," but it isn't easy to call abuse what it is. Sometimes you call it "concern," others you may call it "passion," and when things get really bad you just call it "a bad temper."

Sometimes you just call it "normal."

I never did call any of the things I endured abuse either, it was just my secret. As an adult with my back against the wall and a hand around my throat, I still excused it. I understood it as just the way things sometimes were. When you broke the rules, you got punished, and someone else was making the rules at that moment.

> You have to show other people how you want to be spoken to, and do it consistently.
>
> ⬤
>
> Think about your words before you use them, it's really that simple. Simple, but never easy.

I accepted that right up to the age of 29.

Then the rape happened and everything changed.

I knew that my no meant no. I whispered it at first, and then I screamed it. I began to understand the true power of words that night. Almost a dozen people found me there. We all had the word written all on our faces, but nobody said it. It took three years before any of us could say it out loud. Even me.

Rape.

The word still gets stuck sometimes.

Even after telling the story over and over to stone faces and deaf ears, the word did not fall easily from my lips. It was the bad thing, a rough night, the thing I didn't talk about. It was something that happened to other people, not to me.

How I was in high school was no secret, but it was no source of pride either.

Trading my body for love only deepened my shame in the end, but it was the only way that I knew how to feel loved.

I had heard people talking that night, "You know Angel, you know how she has always been." As if the things I had done in my past excused the rape all of those years later.

Sexuality is a struggle for many Survivors. Girls are taught that being a "slut" or a "whore" is bad, but the alternatives are words like "frigid," "tease," and "prude." Words demean boys as well and, like the girls, their sexuality makes the easiest target.

Where women are expected to remain within a tidy little square of not too little, not too much, not too good, and not too bad, men are expected to "sow their wild oats," "spread their seed," and "get their needs met." In fact, a very big part of the definition of "being a man" involves his sexual relationships with women.

If you want to compliment a male, you praise his sexual prowess. If you want to demean them, just pull out the insults like "sissy" and "faggot." For a straight boy, being teased about being gay is a deep insult, and can ruin his self-image. If that boy already has emotional problems, then it can only add to an already volatile mix. And for those teens that are coping with the reality of homosexuality the pain teasing of can become unbearable.

Some say that these children were simply weaker that their peers. More vulnerable? Perhaps. Weaker? Rarely.

These children were not born weak; they were slowly weakened by long-term verbal abuse that sometimes crossed over into the physical kind. Harassment. Humiliation. Taunts. Challenges.

As long as it is effective, bullies will continue to bully. Many victims reported long-term harassment and even stalking behaviors. These are behaviors illegal in the adult world, but are excused in the schoolyard as children just being children.

Society has taught us that abuse always leaves signs on the outside–black eyes, broken bones, wounds that need stitching. Tangible injuries. Injuries that anybody could identify. While you were waiting for blood, waiting for bruises, waiting for some outward indicator, you may never have realized the toll abuse had already taken on your life.

We so often speak without considering the long-term consequences. Not all abuse is physical, but physical abuse almost never occurs without its verbal counterpart.

When something has been misused, it has been used in an incorrect or improper manner. When something has been abused, it has been misused to the point of being damaged. In its most simple definition, to abuse someone is to damage them.

Abuse is not a broken nose or a black eye. It is something that is done to you over a long period of time. Survivors are people that you know and interact with every single day. You live next door to them. You work with them. Your children go to school with them.

I am a Survivor, and if you are reading this book then you are probably a Survivor, too. If you are not a Survivor yourself, one out of every five people that you know is.

If the words of a stranger can make a child fear life more than death, what of the words used by a bully that lives within their own home? What about the words of a bully that lives within their own heart?

How many children are verbally and emotionally abused at the hands of school bullies each year? How many are abused by adults in positions of power? Partners? Parents? Children?

Too many.

Calling abuse by its proper name isn't easy.

When my stepfather teased my mother about her weight, he always said it was just her sensitive nature that made her so unreceptive to his humor.

He called her duck, and it was the cutest nickname ever. When he began coming home with duck figurines, a collection grew. The rest of the family added to my mother's duck collection in support and she packed them around with her for fifteen years.

I protested the day my mother added her duck collection to our yard sale goods. All of us had added to that collection, all of us had given her those gifts. That's when she finally told me the truth. He called my mother duck because he said she waddled like one.

It was only then that I remembered laughing with him as he called her "thunder-thighs." Sometimes he mooed at her as she walked across the room, referring to her as his "old milk cow."

I remember thinking this was perfectly normal.

I never saw him hit her, bu the true damage came from the daily trickle of words that went almost unnoticed. Violent and angry words, insults, infidelity, and accusations, but I still had no way to recognize it as abuse.

Many women have told me if they had been beaten a single time, they would have left. They understood that physical violence was wrong and would never have stood for it. Yet over time, they grew so used to the slow trickle of insults and demands that they didn't even notice the effect it had on them.

They knew that violence was abuse, but they didn't know that words and even silence cold also be abuse.

You don't have to convince anybody else of what happened. It is doubtful that the courts will ever consider name calling and insults as serious as physical injury, and it wouldn't be a good thing if they did. It would do no good if anyone who ever got their feelings hurt was running around crying about being a victim.

We already have a judicial system full of "victims." People become millionaires overnight at the expense of others. Being a victim has become a lifestyle in the United States, and we don't need to encourage it any further.

How easily we become perpetual victims, choosing to be passive participants in our own lives. As long as things keep happening *to* us, the cycle of abuse will continue. So call abuse what it is, but remember that you are far more than just another victim.

My mother finally found a man that values her as a person, and it took more than a few Toads to get there. She's pretty damn cool. It's about time someone else figured that out. She says having such a smart daughter might have something to do with it, but I disagree. Everything I am today came from having her as a mother.

Our darkest secrets have a way of being passed down, and with our secrets comes a certain acceptance of the abuse. Your children are always watching, always learning. Knowing without knowing. Saying without saying.

There are no bad words, only bad intentions.

Roll Call

Casper Van Dien
Actor
Childhood Sexual Abuse

Derek Luke
Actor
Child Sexual Abuse

James Dean
Actor
Child Sexual Abuse

Jill Saward
Activist
Rape

R.A. Dickey
Professional Baseball Player
Child Sexual Abuse

"The more a daughter knows the details of her mother's life [...] the stronger the daughter."

~Anita Diamant, The Red Tent

Like A Set Of Fine Silver

My mother has always said that we put the fun back in dysfunction, and that we did... but there were a lot of parts that were no fun for anybody involved. She is a little wacky, but I love her dearly. We are a matched set it seems.

She still has a bit of Peter Pan in her today and we still have a hell of a lot of fun in a toy aisle together and we have three accomplices to join in the fun now.

Free spirits were never meant to be kept down, and in reality, they can't be. The harder you try, the more they will fight to break free. My mother really struggled when I was a child, but it is only now that I can see that much of that was her Survivor Spirit trying to break free.

My children are pretty much doomed in that regard.

We all inherit traits from those who came before us, like the Wilson green eyes I inherited from my grandfather's side of the family, and the small frame that came from my grandmother's side. My oldest daughter Brooke is 19, and stands only 4 feet 11 inches tall. The other two children favor their father, tall and slender but if Brooke has been small her entire life.

I am a small person who had a baby with a small person and I wouldn't trade my beautiful baby girl for the world. Petite though she may be.

There is no doubt that she got it from me. I am also a fourth-generation divorcee. My mother pointed out how rare this was just after my first marriage crumbled. It isn't something we are proud of in any way, each of us considered marriage as the most serious of covenants but sometimes life has other plans.

Women in my family have been willing to put up with an awful lot of shit in the name of love, that's all. My mother, my grandmother, my great-grand-mother...who knows how far back these cycles go? Handed down from one generation to the next like a set of fine silver.

Children have lived with abuse in my family for as long as anybody can remember, sometimes as witnesses, sometimes as victims. From mother to daughter, from grandmother to granddaughter, from one generation to the next.

Dysfunctional Family Heirlooms: A One-sided Conversation With A Brick Wall

⊜

Just like that great big elephant in the living room, anything that is not seen as acceptable just isn't seen at all.

Talk all you want, bring evidence to prove your point, call in the experts and...still, nothing.

It's the old magician's slight of hand trick on a psychic level. If we only see the things we want to see, the other stuff just magically goes away.

As long as you keep your eye on the fantasy, you don't see the reality.

Four generations of women who swore to themselves that their children would not be brought up in a divorced home, but they life had other plans. Our promises to the next generation were broken. Again.

But with good reason.

A dysfunctional home is not working for anybody. What does the word dysfunctional really mean? A home that doesn't function properly? A family that doesn't function properly? Individual parts that don't function properly? Something that is dysfunctional can still function, but not to its optimal level.

The goal of the dysfunctional relationship is the exact opposite of the functional one. Relationships are supposed to be about getting closer, in unhealthy relationships it is all about keeping your distance. That doesn't mean that we are broken beyond repair, but parts of our world have been.

We've learned to see the world in a broken way, and to react in kind. It's not necessarily genetic, but almost as deeply ingrained within some of us as if it were.

One of the men who molested me had victimized dozens of other children. His crimes have spanned many decades, and he may very well have begun with my own mother.

My mother was obsessively protective of me, and truly believed that would always be enough. Her abuser had disappeared for a long time, but then while I was staying with another family member, he showed up unexpectedly. No one had ever told anyone about the abuse, so nobody knew the threat he posed to me or the other children he victimized.

The cycle of abuse had begun in a new generation. Like my mother before me, I became one in five. For one in five children under the age of 18, sexual abuse is normal.

Abuse does have its effects, everything that happens to us does. We can't change it, and we can't deny it. It only takes one event to start a lifelong cycle. From bully to victim, from victim to bully, and around again, the pattern continues.

If we are used to being treated poorly, we will have no difficulty in this life locating people who will continue to do so. In abuse circles this is known as "going home," but what it really means is we seek out what we're used to.

A domineering parent makes way for verbally abusive friendships, which lead to a physically abusive spouse. Manipulators, users, liars, cheaters, thieves. They just seem to find us. It is as if we are drawing them to us like a magnet.

If you have lived with abuse long enough, it becomes your normal. Where some may see blame, judgment, or weakness, the observant Survivor sees a strong family resemblance.

Before someone can begin to see that something in their world is wrong, they have to have something to compare it to. So what are we supposed to compare our lives to when it has been estimated that 85% of people in the United States

---

Dysfunctional Family Heirlooms: But We Don't Talk About It

In the unhealthy homes, people are usually avoiding more conversations than they are participating in, not talking about far more than they are actually saying.

This results in long periods of saying nothing broken by great explosions where everyone says everything all at once. And everybody complains that nobody is listening.

Confused yet?

Exactly.

The more side roads the conversation takes, the less likely anybody will have to actually do something.

---

come from dysfunctional homes?

Let's face it, normal has been nothing more than a fairy tale in some of our pasts. Abuse, alcoholism, lengthy work hours, chronic illness, depression, frequent relocation, and recurring changes of primary caretaker all make it difficult for a family to form proper attachments with one another. The way adults interact within their relationships teaches children how to interact with their own friends and loved ones later in life.

A lot of the things that my children will have to contend with in life will come from those who came before them. They will inherit genes for alcoholism from both sides. I got the addictive behaviors that came to me from generations back on both sides.

Dysfunctional Family Heirlooms: My House, My Rules

⬣

Because the world is black and white, it stands to reason that authority is the be all and end all in the dysfunctional home. We do as we are told. We don't delay. And we do not, under any circumstances, question that authority. Unless of course we need a reminder of where we really belong. Nobody really needs to hear what anybody else is saying, so long as nothing productive comes from it.

I've raised my children to be aware of this, and to know that messing around with alcohol beyond the occasional celebration is bound to end in disaster. It isn't necessary to avoid it totally, but if they don't moderate it carefully they will be just as prone to addiction as their parents are.

It really is amazing what human beings can get used to. Habits are formed so easily, sometimes without us even realizing they exist at all until someone else points them out to us. You can even get so used to abuse in different forms that when somebody else isn't around to abuse you, you abuse yourself.

In unhealthy families, children learn that problems are best handled through the most indirect means possible. Outside appearances mean everything in the dysfunctional family but inside you find only chaos. More time is spent trying to avoid intimacy and honesty than seeking it. You ignore other people's boundaries.

You can complain to everybody BUT the person you are angry with. Start trouble, choose sides, backstab, but by all means, don't repair. Rather than going to the people that hurt us and confronting the problem head-on, you can act up, you can storm out, you can pout, you can rage, or you can throw temper tantrums. But simply saying "That hurt my feelings" and moving on is too easy.

We will pass a lot of these things on to our children simply because nobody has ever taught us anything different.

Dysfunctional family 101: Life is serious, so no fun allowed. Don't bring up problems; it rocks the boat. Just be a good little girl, do as you are told, and follow the family rules, no matter how often they may change.

Sometimes family traditions have been going on for so long that nobody stops to question them anymore.

Once many years ago I heard a story about a newly married couple that was preparing for their first dinner party. The wife busied herself in the kitchen making the main course. Laying the roast on the cutting board, she sliced a thick slab of meat from each end before placing it into the pan. Her husband watched this strange behavior, frowning.

He'd thought perhaps she had a purpose for the cuts of meat but then was puzzled when she dis-

---

Dysfunctional Family Heirlooms: You Make-A Me Crazy

You will hear the term "crazy-making" from time to time in support fields, and if there was ever a self-defining term, crazy-making is it.

If you have ever dreamed of traveling back in time to record an event just to prove to yourself that it really happened, you know exactly what I am talking about.

Crazy-making is supposed to make you feel crazy, that is the whole point.

---

posed of the excess and busied herself with other tasks. "Honey, why did you cut off the ends of that roast?" he asked.

The bride shrugged her shoulders. "That's what my mother always did."

"But...why?" Honestly, the new bride had no idea. Now she was curious too. Picking up the phone, she dialed her mother's number.

She asked her mother the same question, "Why do you always cut the ends off of the roast?"

"I don't really know, that's just how my mother always did it."

They hung up and still nobody knew. So, the bride dialed her grandmother's phone number and asked her. "Why do you always cut the ends off when you are making a roast?"

Her grandmother laughed, "When your grandfather and I first got married, all I had was the one small roasting pan. I had to make do, so I cut the ends off of the roast to make it fit."

We do the same things over and over without ever really asking why we are doing it.

I had no idea how abnormal my world really was until I walked into my fathers family. My parents divorced when I was two, and did not see my father again for fourteen years. I first visited him at sixteen, knowing very little about the man who had given me his last name. While my mother and I had struggled, my father went on to build a happy life of his own with a new family.

> **Dysfunctional Family Heirlooms: The Portrait That Never Changes**
>
> ⊜
>
> When you buy a new picture frame, it usually comes with a sample portrait that you are supposed to remove and replace with your own personal photograph.
>
> In some families, that perfect family image is still in the frame. There is no room for anybody in the family who doesn't live up to that image.
>
> They are either forced into conformity or pushed out of the frame altogether.

They had problems just like everybody else, but they handled them in ways I had never seen before. When one person was disappointed with another, they talked about it. They even set out to repair it. They were actually healthy.

It was weird.

I saw respect between my father and his new bride, and between them and their children. Being together was more important than being right. I had never really seen that before. It was just too good to be true. It doesn't make much sense at all, unless of course you are me.

I learned to get my needs met in totally different ways than my brothers and sisters had. I still felt like I had to act out, pull in, and push away to be in a relationship. They had learned the direct route.

I witnessed their strange and loving interactions from an emotional distance they didn't always understand. I always knew that I would be going back to my world. The methods I had used to survive my life before then wouldn't have worked in their home.

Dysfunction is a habit.

I never, ever thought my father or anybody else in my second family would hurt me; in that respect, I knew I was safe. It was more like being a stray puppy that accidentally wandered into a dog show. A happy family just didn't fit with my definition of normal.

> *"We spent our childhood maintaining a shroud of 'silence and secrecy' around our perverse experiences of child abuse. We coped by 'suppressing memories,' 'learning to forget,' 'disengaging,' 'disassociating,' 'isolating ourselves emotionally and relationally,' 'trying to please everyone,' 'trying to adapt and accommodate our weird situation,' because there was 'no escape anyway.' This allowed us to survive our childhood. But as we became teenagers we came 'unstuck.' We knew we 'didn't fit in.' So we 'numbed our rotten feelings' by using alcohol, drugs and/or gambling."*
>
> *~Van Loon and Kralik Study, 2005*

I had always existed in a world of what I felt were unspoken expectations. Surely they would expect more of me than ever before in return. I ran like hell. If I couldn't live up to the expectations of a broken few in my life then there was no way I could ever live up to whatever it was that a healthy family would want from me.

Once my other family got close enough to see how broken I really was it would all be over. Someday they would see me as I really was. A lot of people left me in my life, eventually I just started leaving first.

My second family had a power to hurt me in ways they would never understand. Their world was the fairy tale, mine was the reality. No matter how kind they were to me, I knew I had to go back to my real life, my own normal.

My father spent the years before his death wondering how it was he let me down, thinking he had given me too little in my eyes. He never realized it was just too much.

Years later, after my father had passed away, my stepmother told me that marriage is all about meeting each other's needs. I have carried that with me ever since.

Some families in my life were very normal; they were happy, and ultimately healthy. They were like a television show to me, something to be watched and enjoyed, but eventually the real world returns. You learn not to trust anything too bright and shiny after a while.

Those members of my own family that had escaped the family curse seemed to have formed an exclusive club. I saw what looked like happiness from a cautious distance but I couldn't get close enough to tell for certain. Living a life outside of the drama you have come to know seems plastic. Forced. Faked.

I've never really felt that I belonged anywhere .

Dysfunctional Family Heirlooms: What Happens In The Family...

We might have our own versions of those secrets, but the one rule that remains the same no matter who we may be is that we all have them.

We deny them, we hide them, we avoid them, and we refuse to discuss them, but still the secrets remain. What happens in the family stays in the family. Going outside is traitorous. We don't talk about them outside of the family. We don't talk about them inside of the family either. In fact it is best if we don't talk at all. Bringing those moldy secrets out of the darkness could have untold consequences, so few dare try.

I spent a childhood wanting more than anything for life to be like a musical, with people smiling and bursting into song in the streets. I still sometimes secretly wish I could live there. At least I knew that it was a fantasy.

That standard American *Leave it to Beaver* cardboard cutout of a family where the soccer mom's hair is always done and father's shoes are always polished has always scared the hell out of me. Even as a small child I was convinced happy families had to be hiding something.

Rosanne was probably the first show I ever saw on television that made me feel like my family was okay. We sure weren't the Cosby family, and *Growing Pains* was beyond comprehension. At least I understood what was going on with the Conner family.

If you are still struggling in relationships years later, it's no wonder. You were raised to destroy them, not build them up. Some traditions have been a part of your life for so long that they don't even make sense anymore.

Take a good hard look at those family traditions that you have brought with you through the years. Those defense mechanisms learned in the dysfunction-al home are still there, and chances are they are hurting, far more than helping you now.

Instead of asking if our stubborn old ways work, we just go right on trying to get our needs met in non-functional ways, even if those methods hurt us. Along the way we develop an awful lot of unhealthy ways of getting other people to meet those needs for us.

You have both the right and the responsibility to choose which patterns will remain in your life, which you will pass on to those you influence. Some can be repaired, and others will need to be left behind.

I've never hidden the fact that I am an abuse Survivor from my children. I have just taught them to see that word in a very different way than the rest of the world, to see it as just another asset in life.

I would not be the mother I am today without the abuse I went through. I've been criticized by grandparents for not forcing them to give hugs to strangers, and glared at by teachers for insisting that my child's personal boundaries were concrete. If their behavior extended to harming others I would be there to back the school up and I would follow up at home, but when my child said no, they meant no.

Dysfunctional Family Heirlooms: Know Your Role

Every member of the dysfunctional family has a role, and once that role has been assigned there are no negotiations. Anyone who tries to step outside of their role will be reminded ever so non-gently to get the hell back to their proper place.

A woman's place is in the kitchen, a child is seen and not heard, and the family screw-up might as well just accept what they are, because nobody is ever going to let them forget it. If one person changes then everyone must change, and we can't have that.

If I had not been sexually abused, I would never have been so intent upon teaching them to keep their own body safe. It was the neglect of my own innocence that made me treasure theirs so deeply, to help them learn to protect it from the many people in this world who would steal it.

I wanted to give my children a better world. I wanted children who would make the world a better place. And they have. Survivors have a way of doing that.

It doesn't matter who we are or where we come from, we are all trying to accomplish the exact same thing in our lives: to find ways of meeting our needs. In unhealthy relationships we are so busy scrambling to get our own needs met that nobody is getting anywhere.

A child prone to violent outbursts in class could very well be holding in some very big secrets. The woman who skitters back into her house like a frightened deer when neighbors wave has her own secrets. Some hide it better than others, but abuse is all about secrets. And many of these victims keep their abuse a secret simply because they don't know any better.

If we had nobody to teach us, then we had no way of knowing right from wrong. We might not even know there is anything wrong in our lives at all. Generation after generation may have lived with the abuse in your family. You may be the first to break free. You may be the only one who ever does.

Overcoming that sacred Survivor commandment burned into your brain of "Thou shalt not talk about it" is one of the more difficult tasks faced by Survivors. You might have to risk being called selfish. You might have to confront not just your bullies but also their supporters. You might have to set boundaries for yourself that limit your contact with certain people, even if they are blood.

> Dysfunctional Family Heirlooms: And Nothing In Between
>
> 🌀
>
> In the black-and-white world of dysfunction there are only ever two options. If you are not thin then you must be fat. If you are not sane then you must be crazy. If you are not good, you must therefore be bad.
>
> There is good, and there is evil, and nothing at all in between.
>
> Dysfunction has no room for variation.

In the end, what's done is done and there's no changing it. Our parents taught us what they were capable of teaching us, and to that end, they have nothing more to offer. We're adults now, and we are the only people who can fix our adult lives. You can afford to wait for your family's permission to stop the cycle no longer.

You have to work through a lot of tears and a lot of fears, but it's in your blood.

I knew what heirlooms I was passing down to my children all along. I can't really change it, but the least I can do is teach them to turn it into positives. While I'm at it, I figure I might as well teach them how to be the best Survivors they can be.

I learned that from my momma.

My mother was trying to contain what was never meant to be contained. She was the silly lady that hated white walls, and conventions, and normal clothing. My mom dressed in a really weird way when I was a kid, and so do I, and so do all of my kids.

Someone left the cage door open, and we flew. We will always stand out in a crowd. We will always talk way too much. We will always turn talking books into rap songs. And we will always get excited about Halloween.

They are all family traditions.

Generation after generation may have lived with the abuse in your family. You may be the first to break free. You may be the only one who ever does.

I inherited a lot of things from the women that came before me. The Hilleary women–my predecessors–were strong women, and dedicated mothers who walked away from abuse in order to give their children a fighting chance. They were small but mighty, each with a set to her jaw and a spring in her step. We are tiny, but we are stubborn when it comes to fighting for those we love.

Just knowing that their blood flows through my veins gives me strength. They had the strength to change their lives, and so do I.

So do you.

Famous Domestic Violence Survivors

Angie Dickenson
Actress

Beth Chapman
Reality TV Star

Bill Clinton
Former President of U.S.

Brett Butler
Actress

Christina Crawford
Author

Patsy Cline
Singer

*"Still she haunts
me, phantom-wise,
Alice moving under
skies. Never seen
by waking eyes."*

~Lewis Carroll

Behind The Looking Glass, Beyond It

When Alice stepped through her looking glass, she found a world where nothing was as it seemed. That's the problem with mirrors: what we find is often just a reflection of what we already expect to see. They offer illusion, not reality.

When you look in the mirror, do you see someone who deserves to love and be loved? Someone who genuinely cares about themselves and others? Someone who has wants, needs, and desires, and isn't afraid to make them known? Someone who is allowed to make mistakes because they are capable of learning from them?

I didn't think so.

Perhaps you are viewing yourself through a cracked pane of glass. Abuse kind of does that to you. It distorts your life, magnifies your flaws, and accents the negative parts.

You shouldn't have to be perfect to win your own approval, but a lot of people seem to think so.

As a child, I would spend hours looking into the mirror, wishing I could go to the world where normal beings were the strange ones and time ran backwards. As things changed in my outside world my reflection began to make me more and more uncomfortable. I eventually began avoiding mirrors entirely.

People thought it must have been because I didn't care how I looked.

Close, but not quite.

I didn't care to look at all. What I saw before me was a total stranger, and I didn't like her much. Every criticism I had ever heard was there, waiting in my reflection.

I couldn't stand the sight of the girl in the mirror, but I couldn't avoid looking inward.

Sometimes in your reflection you see only flaws. Discount merchandise. Damaged goods. No matter how hard you try to reach perfection you will always come up short. It will never be hard enough. It will never be good enough. It will never be perfect enough.

It will never be YOU.

You can't define yourself from the outside, in. The real gift that was meant for you is on the inside.

Get lost in your own thoughts and see where they lead you. Find out what you do, and do not, believe about the world around you. Then find out why. Question everything.

Discover what you like and what you don't like. Avoid the latter and seek out the former.

The life of a victim so easily becomes fractured into parts, bits here, pieces there. Looking at the parts you choose to see and discarding the rest. All Survivors have learned to see the dark side of our reflections, but where there are shadows there must also be light.

When someone gives you a gift, you might take time to admire the wrapping paper. You might linger on the pretty bow. But then what do you do? You rip open the gift and ruin the whole thing. Who you are on the inside is the real person, and the rest is just paper and trimmings.

For many victims, the thought of loving yourself brings on all sorts of confusing feelings. There may be past hurts and regrets. There may have been breaches of trust in the relationship, but they can be forgiven. Abuse forces you into a false Self, and who you really are as a person gets lost along the way. It's up to you to find that person.

Your relationship with yourself takes work. Every relationship does. You can rebuild that trust in yourself. You can strengthen the relationship. Nobody has known you longer and more deeply than you.

You know all of the things about yourself that you have never told anybody else. Only you really know who you are.

You are your oldest and bestest friend.

The wonderful thing about an old friend is that sense of knowing you have. You have shared successes and tears. You know each others' secrets and desires. They have seen you at your very best and at your very worst. Years and years of history are built up behind that friendship.

You should see the same in yourself.

It has been twenty years since the counselor asked me to make a list of my most positive qualities for our next session. When I returned to his office the next week, I handed him a sheet with only two items on it.

"I have pretty eyes," and "I'm good in bed." He was, shall we say, less than impressed.

If he had asked me for a list of my flaws, that list would have been miles long. Sex was all I had ever had to offer, even as a child, and that was all I was convinced that I had to offer for a large portion of my life. I never considered myself pretty, or thin, or smart, or even slightly talented. I never considered myself as much of anything, and that was the real problem.

I was always so busy looking at the things I thought I was missing that I was completely blind to the real me. I did not want to think about my past. I only wanted to escape my present, and try as I might, I could see no real future. Even when it seemed I had something to offer that someone else might want, as soon as that person left, I was back at square one.

No matter how my counselor pressed me to find one more good thing, I just shrugged my shoulders. I had nothing else. I suppose I looked to my counselor to answer that question for me, and I have looked to many people since, but the answers never came.

For years, I saw everything that was wrong with me and could find so little that was right. I did not know who I was or what I wanted. I wasn't even certain why I was getting out of bed in the morning most days. I had to keep going; I had three beautiful children to live for. There were times that they were the only thing that got me out of bed. They needed me whether I wanted to function, or not.

But it wasn't really living either.

Rarely, if ever, did I see myself as a whole person. My kids were totally worth living for but in the rest of my life, I felt so disconnected from myself that I didn't feel like a real person at all. I was an accessory. I was a robot. '

I was trying to find purpose in what other people had told me that I could do for them. I needed to find it inside of me.

Then, from time to time the thought would come, what if something happened to my children? What purpose would I have in life then? It was a very bleak place to be.

I had to find a reason to be excited about getting up every morning.

I can't promise you that a reason for your pain will ever become clear. I really do wish I could, but that's just not how life works. Some people don't wait for a purpose to find them, they go out and find it for themselves. That's what families who start scholarships in the name of their loved ones do. That's what volunteers do. That's what the founders of non-profits do.

Figure out what you do want and what you don't want out of life, and find ways to make the things you do want happen.

When something truly makes you happy, give yourself permission to go for it.

We spend a lot of time seeking perfection in our reflections, but perhaps what you were really looking for was purpose. Purpose is that inner voice that keeps you going long after the rest of you has given up. When you truly believe in your goals, you will push through anything to keep moving towards it.

The Nazis were professionals at breaking the human spirit, it's what they did. Yet after spending two and a half years in various internment camps, Dr. Viktor Frankl had bent but would not be broken. What little he had left had been taken from him upon entering. When he asked a fellow inmate where his young bride and parents had been taken, the man pointed to the smokestacks. He truly had lost everything. Men who were friends and bunk mates at noon were reduced to an extra pair of shoes and bowl of broth by supper. Human beings were tossed out like garbage.

Viktor Frankl continued to find meaning in the world around him, never letting go of his sense of purpose. Everything Dr. Frankl needed to survive came from within. Sometimes when the pressures of his internment became too great he would go outside and lecture imaginary groups on the *"Psycho-therapeutic Experiences in a Concentration Camp,"* just to keep himself going.

Everything was still alive inside of his head. All of it was, his wife, his parents, his book...

He kept the manuscript he had been working on, the one that had been taken at the gates and presumably destroyed with the rest of his previous life, stored in his mind. It might seem like Dr. Frankl had some special hero quality that helped him along, but he didn't. He held on to what he did have left: his spirit.

After he was liberated, Dr. Frankl went on to write about his experiences in *Man's Search For Meaning*, where he spoke of his unshakable belief that man could find meaning in all forms of existence, even in suffering. How he found such idealistic lessons about humanity in Nazi Germany is incomprehensible.

But he did.

While you may marvel at the strength it took for Holocaust Survivors to keep going, there is no superpower to it. Everything, even simple comfort, had been taken from them. Upon their release, many had no lives left to return to. Some held on to a book, others held on to a loved one's memory, and some held on to the hope of another sunrise... but they did hold on. Whatever it may have been, they refused to let go of their sense of purpose.

Nearly every successful Holocaust Survivor said the same thing: they just didn't give up.

Despite all he saw, Dr. Frankl's experiences led him to believe that love was the ultimate and highest goal to which a man could aspire. For the rest of his life he taught that the salvation of man was both *through* love and *in* love. Dr. Frankl's motivation was more than just his book, it was love.

He chose to be better, not bitter, and that made all the difference.

Don't waste your time looking for the outside world—in the mirror, in the bottom of a bottle, in a lover's bed, through a wall of awards at work, or through your child's performance at school. You won't find purpose in any of those places, just distractions.

The distractions and external parts of life are all beyond your control. They can leave. They can change. They can be taken away. The more purpose that you can find in living, the better position you are in to weather the bumpy roads in life.

We all have at least "one thing,"that we are good at. That one thing that truly makes life worth living. You don't know what your purpose is yet? Join the club.

The meaning of life has never made itself easy to find, but the important part is that it *can* be found.

In the 1991 movie *City Slickers*, the grizzled, old trail boss Curly is one of those rare people that does not doubt his purpose. In the movie, Curly asks the main character Mitch if he knows what the meaning of life is.

Mitch does not.

So Curly holds up a finger and says "This."

"Your finger?" Mitch asks.

Curly smiles, "One thing. Just one thing. You stick to that and the rest don't mean shit."

> Become aware of your wants, and decide if they are indeed needs or merely desires.
>
> Believe that you truly deserve happiness, and desire it to be so. Know that you deserve better. Do what is best for you.

As Mitch gazes at Curly's uplifted finger, he asks, "But, what is the one thing?"

And Curly answers, "That's what *you* have to find out."

Purpose doesn't come from "out there," it comes from somewhere deep inside. For each of us there is at least one thing that we truly enjoy doing even if we aren't particularly confident in our skill. We've convinced ourselves that talent is something that just happens, but it isn't.

We are all amateurs at first, every single one of us. The only difference between a beginner and a master is the amount of hours they have spent practicing their skill.

Besides, nobody ever said you had to be good at something to enjoy it.

It doesn't matter if all you know how to do is create pictures from belly button lint. If that's the case, then by God what is stopping you from being the best belly button lint artist there is? You don't have to make money doing it. We're talking about passion here, not profession.

Chances are you are living your passion already, even if it's deep within your mind. Take a look at where your interests lie. What do you do in your free time? What types of movies do you watch? What books do you read?

Figure out what you truly enjoy doing. Then do it some more.

Everybody, I repeat, *everybody*, has a talent. Sometimes they are suppressed, sometimes they are unrealized, and sometimes they are just undeveloped, but they are always there. Even when we hide them from others, they are there.

Even if we hide them from ourselves, they are there.

When I was young, my grandmother would find my notebooks lying around, and comment on a poem or short story. A few class assignments were published in the school paper, and my teachers tried to encourage me to explore it further, but I brushed them away. Writing was fun, and I liked it, but it certainly wasn't something worth pursuing seriously.

Pay attention to your own physical and emotional needs.

Actively protect yourself from the people and situations that will harm you.

Besides...who'd want to read it?

By the end of my first marriage, I had a trunk full of notebooks I still refused to show anybody. Writing my thoughts and words down was nothing more than a guilty pleasure. I wrote in the darkness, late at night. Most of what I did was promptly tucked away where I wouldn't see it again for years.

What can I say? Secrets are my specialty.

Whatever thoughts rambled through my head during my teen years and first marriage went into those notebooks. All of those spinning thoughts became hundreds of thousands of words hidden away on shelves and eventually on hard drives. At first it was mostly disconnected ideas, odd streams of consciousness that didn't make a lot of sense to anybody but me. My ADHD was always at play, and sometimes I wasn't even sure what it all meant.

After I remarried, Ed saw the guilty look on my face when he caught me writing and thought I must be hiding something, that I was writing something bad about him. That first time he took my notebook from me so he could see what I was scribbling, I wanted to cry. I tried to yank it back but he wouldn't let me. I was afraid that he would laugh at me, afraid he would discourage me, afraid it wouldn't be good enough. *More than anything, I was afraid that he would take it away from me somehow.*

But he didn't criticize me, or make fun of me, he just looked at me and asked me why I never showed it to anybody. I just knew that I wasn't good enough. Good enough for whom? I had no idea, just the stone cold certainty that it could never be good enough. It was all I had, and it would crush me to have it taken away.

I tried to explain this to my husband, and he smiled. "Screw 'em."

My husband does not love words nearly as much as I do, but what he really said to me was: "While you are busy worrying about what you can't do, what you can do is passing you by." He is a wise man, that one. With his encouragement I came out of my writer's closet and finally began showing others.

Boshemia took over from there, with her Squidoo accounts and multiple websites. At first, I wrote about the many lessons I'd learned in life, and eventually moved on to talking about my experiences with abuse. Hundreds of people have contacted me since then to thank me for my courage.

> Ask the questions that you have always wanted to be asked, and answer them for yourself.
>
> Then ask those questions that you have always been afraid to ask, and try to answer them as well.

You tend to find a way to follow at least part of the path you were destined to, even when you don't realize it.

Now, imagine if someone had told me then that that those scribblings would someday lead to a book, which would lead to a role in a movie, and eventually to a whole new life. I would have laughed in their faces just a few years ago but, instead, here I am.

Our lists of things that we can't do are nothing but a cage.

What would happen if you explored those passions further and tried to work them into your life in other ways, perhaps by joining volunteer groups, taking a college course, or pursuing a new career path? Open up your arms and embrace your passions. Allow them to bloom.

My shame kept my talents hidden for a very long time, but it couldn't squash it entirely. Dreams have a way of feeding themselves after awhile. A small dream began to grow, and a little was all it took. You just have to nurture them through the early days and watch them grow from there. Take a class, learn more about it through research, or ask someone else to teach you something new.

I truly believe that one of the greatest sins in this world is to let a God-given talent go to waste, no matter what that talent may be. I know, I know, I am the biggest hypocrite there is, and I admit it fully.

Hopefully you can learn these lessons far faster than I did.

Everyone has something to offer, but hiding it away in a trunk isn't going to do anybody any good. Somewhere inside of you is the person you were meant to be, the real you as it were. Open your eyes and your mind to yourself. Spend some time getting to know you, and find the parts you like and expand on them. Free yourself from the need for perfection and just enjoy being you for a while.

We all have strengths and weaknesses. There will always be some things that we are good at and other things that we would be best to avoid. Don't magnify your weaknesses, save that energy for your strengths. For a change, instead of counting all of the things that are wrong, try counting the things that are right.

People are supposed to be made up of many, many parts. Once you know your strengths you can build on them, and once you know your weaknesses you can minimize them, but do yourself a favor and be honest about them.

When you look in the mirror, you deserve to see someone that you honestly and genuinely love.

Take yourself apart and take a really good look at all of those pieces. Your skills, your talents, your strengths, and your know-how are unique to you. Nobody else has ever been put together from the exact same combination of parts as you. Nobody else has ever been able to live the life you have led. Nobody else has ever been able to *be* you.

This is your story. From beginning to end, it belongs to you. Will you be the hero? Will you be the villain? Will you be the victim? Or will you be the victor? You, and you alone, can give your story the meaning it deserves.

You will be a stranger to many people in life, but you should never be a stranger to yourself. Your attitudes, beliefs, motivations, dreams, hopes, fears, and character are all important in defining who you really are. Your definition of yourself should not be based on one or two, but many factors.

Abuse may have taught you to focus on the things that you can't do, but healing requires you to focus on the things you CAN do. Somewhere in there, that free spirit that you were born with does still exist. The more you acknowledge it, nourish it, and above all treasure it, the stronger it will grow.

Find out who is behind the looking glass, beyond it.

The mirror is only a reflection of what you already expect to find. Next time you look in the mirror, try doing it in a new way. Don't just look at the same old image that you have always seen. Expect new and different things, and like Alice and her looking glass, you will find a whole new you waiting to be discovered.

Roll Call

Chris Witty
Olympic Speed Skater
Child Sexual Abuse

Desi Arnaz Jr.
Actor
Domestic Violence

Humphrey Bogart
Actor
Domestic Violence

Robert Downey Jr.
Actor
Rape Survivor

Tim Roth
Actor
Incest

Sometimes I lie awake at night and I ask, "Why me?" Then a voice answers, "Nothing personal, your name just happened to come up."

~Charles Schulz

The Victim Tattoo

If you have ever looked for the invisible victim tattoo stamped across your forehead, then you aren't alone. We all have. Feeling as if you have some sort of mark that everyone but you can see is pretty normal for Survivors.

It may feel like bullies have some sort of radar to locate us, that we are somehow to blame, but people tend to find whatever it is they are looking for in life. Every abuser knows how to spot a power advantage and use it to their benefit. Most of the time that power balance is just an illusion, but that doesn't matter as long as it works.

A victim is no more to blame for their abuse than a deer is at fault for becoming the hunter's prey. It's just that people who think they are powerless are less likely to fight back or defend.

Abusers are often true hunters.

Abusers find us because they are looking for us. Doesn't the predator always seek out the weakest in the pack, those that are easily isolated and manipulated? You just had the unfortunate luck of walking into the wrong cross-hairs.

Hunters don't go into the wilderness on equal footing as their targets. They take weapons. They take protective gear. They take a higher-functioning brain. A good hunter knows where to look, what bait to use, and when to strike.

Adults are in natural positions of power over children, and a pedophile knows how to use that. They know how to play the role of the concerned adult, to keep themselves above suspicion, to charm their way out of getting caught. One study found that the average pedophile committed 281 acts with nearly 150 different victims before getting caught. No amateur could accomplish a record like that. These are clearly professionals.

People do not become predators by accident.

It only takes one person to listen to a child and stop the abuse, but the average child tells seven adults before one believes them. Even when they are talking, nobody is listening.

One in four girls, and one in seven boys under the age of 18 will be victims of abuse in their lifetime, and it is believed that the number of reports is increasing. Five of the girls and three of the boys in your average grade school classroom will not make it out of their school years without at least one sexual assault.

No child deserves to be abused, but abusers really aren't concerned with such things. Pedophiles are looking for targets who will allow their bodies, their lives, and even their minds to be controlled with as little resistance as possible.

You aren't a hunter, so you might not even notice the type of people the serial abuser does, and certainly not in the same ways. The hunters watch for kids who exist under the radar. Kids who are just a bit too friendly with strangers. Kids who try their best to be invisible, those who have a sense of isolation or sadness.

To add to the victim's pain and confusion, the abuse often continues with new offenders. It can last a whole childhood, and even a lifetime. Studies have shown that childhood victims of sexual abuse are more than twice as likely to be re-victimized later in life. On some level they know it isn't their fault but, like me, in all of the abuse they will suffer the only common denominator will be the person in the mirror.

It can be difficult NOT to blame yourself.

What qualities the hunter is looking for depends on the individual, but it so often seems that injured prey is preferred to those who can put up a healthy fight. They seek out kids who have troubled relationships at home, and with their peers, and children without support or protection or perhaps they are just the type to do as they are told.

It's hard to say what it is they seek when predators look for the victim tattoo...

Children who come from abusive or neglectful homes are easier to control than most. Abuse strips them of their self worth, of their personal boundaries.

Children are vulnerable, and that's about it. That is all it takes to become a victim. Being targeted by a single abuser doesn't make one a serial victim, it just gets a lot easier to be used with practice. The work has been done for them, the ground softened. People who see themselves as victims tend to function as victims.

Anybody can find themselves in a relationship with an abuser. Having abuse in your past just softens up the ground ahead of time and makes it easier. Those who have suffered abuse in the past have been taught to disregard their own safety and personal needs. They have learned to disregard their instincts as to what constitutes a safe person or situation and what does not. They have learned to ignore red flags.

Those traits that are so often sought after in codependent homes serve later abusers well. Learning to obey authority blindly. Becoming afraid of fighting back. Trying so hard to please others. Such a good little girl. Such a compliant little boy. We train our children to behave, but we sometimes fail to teach them to be safe. As Dr. Haim Ginnott noted, we should raise polite children, but for their sake we must raise empowered children.

> It's like bullies are drawn to you... and they kind of are.
>
> How else do you explain the way certain types of people seem to find you no matter where you go?

A solid sense of self-esteem will not prevent abuse, but it is an added safety net. Abusers don't like complications, and the more difficult you can make their task, the better. Children who are close to their parents and have a supportive circle of friends have an added layer of protection. As children, we need someone nearby to protect us, to pick up the signals that something is wrong.

If we do not have support in our home lives, we begin looking outside of the home to get our needs fulfilled. As we grow older, that circle expands to peers and various authority figures. Some may find themselves playing out the same abusive relationships over and over despite the change of partners. Each time believing that...

"This time things will be better."

Even when you start with a relatively healthy partner, some version of that old dysfunction can follow. You can bring it with you and reintegrate them in your new relationships without even realizing it. Violent arguments, failed peer relationships, abusive marriages...

You can even become abusive yourself.

The very concept of victimization is a passive one, an inherent acceptance that life is controlled by something or someone outside of the self. Someone else is defining the victim's reality. The chronic victim may find themselves attracted to the same types of people over and over. Perhaps in a misguided attempt to fix the mistakes of the past or maybe they think it is what they deserved. Sometimes they just accept abuse as a normal part of life.

People who are willing to accept abuse as a part of their life are a requirement for the cycle of abuse to continue. Nothing is going to change until YOU do.

Someone who doesn't value themselves displays it in ways the hunter is trained to watch for: an avoidance of eye contact, a passive speaking voice, not taking care of hygiene or appearance, the slouch of their shoulders.

When you believe yourself to be helpless you give up on the hope of change entirely. Why else do you think that abusers crush our hopes so readily? They sense the true power they hold.

Many of these children will spend their lives thinking the abuse is their fault, when they simply wandered into the wrong hunters cross hairs.

Being compassionate with a genuine desire to help others is not a bad thing. Don't give up the best parts of you to the abuse. Don't allow anybody to take those things away. They are your strengths. Many of the traits bullies seek out are, for the most part, positive qualities.

There are people out there who will take advantage of those qualities, but healthy people will love you because of them.

As long as you continue to see yourself as powerless, you will be. As long as you see your situation as unchangeable, it will be. As long as you see love as something as rare and precious as diamonds, it will continue to be.

You weren't born to be a victim, but many of us were granted that label just the same. Like an invisible tattoo across our foreheads, it marks us for those that care to see it. Maybe you can't remove that label entirely, but labels can be changed.

They can even be cast out entirely.

◈⊶⊷◈

Roll Call

Charlize Theron
Actress
Childhood Domestic Violence

Elizabeth Smart
Kidnapped as a Child
Sexual Abuse, Imprisonment, Unknown...

Margaret Hoelzer
Swimmer, Olympic Medalist
Child Sexual Abuse

Mike Patton
Musician
Neglect/Child Sexual Abuse

Stephen Hawking
Scientist
Domestic Violence

"Don't rely too much on labels, for too often they are fables."

Charles H. Spurgeon

The Labels We Wear

If I ask you to tell me who you are, you might begin with mother, wife, sister, daughter, or perhaps housewife, manager, store clerk, and so on. It takes hundreds of labels to even begin to describe a single person. You might find that you couldn't describe yourself using a thousand labels once you really get going. Where you allow yourself to see "white trash," "slob," or "unemployed," you might totally miss "good mother" and "excellent cook."

Your self is what differentiates you from the billions of other people on this planet. It is what sets you apart, and makes you, YOU. Self is the one label you should wear proudly. Not the self you have built up in order to please others, but the real self that existed somewhere beneath the defenses, the lies, and the shame.

Whatever you have been told you were in the past is still somewhere inside of you, for better and for worse. The fat kid, the drama queen, the social outcast, the good girl, the wild child, the princess, the slut...

The problem with labels is they are always limited. Always. It's like describing an entire mountain range by the small portion you can see through the lenses of your binoculars.

When you have allowed others to define you through power and control tactics, it can be hard to find yourself under the years of junk.

One of the very first things that children are taught is that the world can be divided into two distinct categories: things that are the same, and things that are different. As soon as you are taught the concept of same and different you naturally begin applying those lessons to the people that make up your world.

I still remember watching the whole "which one of these is not like the other" segments on TV as a kid and gleefully pointing out the one that was different. Now I find entire groups, faiths, hobbies, occupations, and political parties dedicated to keeping those labels together, arranged neatly by likes and dislikes, loves and hates, things that they have in common and things they don't.

What we don't teach kids, but really should, is that someone can have differences but still be the same. Humanity comes in many shapes, colors, sizes, and personalities. Even when the most glaring differences are present, we are all still basically similar in that we are all human. We all have the same basic components, the same basic emotional range, and the same basic feelings.

You play a lot of roles in life: roles in your family, roles at work, and roles in your social circles. Who you are in life, what you have done, what you wish to do...these things may all make up a part of who you are, but many of the things that you consider yourself to be are simply roles that you played for a time.

> The thing is, that label isn't real. It never existed in the first place.
>
> Someone who knows who and what they really are will not allow themselves to be defined otherwise.
>
> ⬤
>
> Take control of your labels before they take control of you.

From birth you are labeled–the good one, the smart one, the moody one, the quiet one, the whiny one, and so on. People will try to get you to conform to labels they have chosen for you your whole life. Sometimes those same people who gave us the labels keep them going long after they have stopped sticking.

People like labels. Once you can fit something in a neat and tidy box, it gives us a false sense of security. If we can label something then we can pretend to understand it.

Comparisons are made, shortcomings are magnified.

By school age you may become the fat kid, the kid with braces, the geek kid, or the school bully. As you grow you gather more labels, some more personal than others. And along the way those labels begin to define you–the prude and the whore, the ladies' man and the sissy, the overachiever and the screw-up, the victim...

And the more focus we put on those labels, the truer they become. Even when they are long gone from your life, you still see them as a part of that reflection in the mirror. Underneath all of those labels and restrictions lies the real person you were meant to be.

Labels have a way of sticking, and they have a way of keeping you stuck. It takes a whole lifetime to define who you are, and there are no shortcuts. Chances are "the fat kid" isn't going to make it into your obituary unless, of course, you are the one who puts it there.

Still, we reason that someone who isn't the skinny kid must be the fat kid. We look at ourselves the same way. If we aren't a prude, then we are a whore. If we aren't a whore, we are a tease. Men don't get off any easier in the labeling department. If he isn't a ladies' man then he must be a sissy.

Labels don't even begin to describe who you are, or what you can and can't do. They only set up psychological barriers that can be nearly impossible to overcome. .

The labels you accept, both those given to you by others and those you choose for yourself, play a very important role in your self-image. When you become fixated on a label, you subconsciously become that label. You don't see the parts of life that contradict that belief anymore. They are there, but you have blocked them from your vision entirely.

> Codependents often have trouble with black-and-white thinking.
>
> Never forget that you live in a Technicolor panoramic world. There are not just the two options but a whole spectrum of color in between that you are choosing not to see.

The "fat kid" can also be the "super-intelligent, but really shy, child that will someday grow up to create the computer program that cures cancer." That kid might also end up being quite average for his or her weight and height and be nothing like the kid he once was.

A lot of . It came from living in a world where there was no room for error, a world in which you weren't allowed to question things. You weren't allowed to figure things out for yourself, and someone else defined your reality.

The label of victim is no different. The word brings up images of abuse, neglect, powerlessness, and hopelessness. It brings to mind pictures of what happened to you. That label keeps you stuck in victim-mode long after the abuse has ended. It reminds you that a victim you are and a victim you will always be.

You live as a victim. You act as a victim. You love as a victim.

If our labels really were written in stone then they would apply to us in every situation. Labels must be fluid. They must allow for differences, because those differences will always exist.

Human beings are far too complex to fit into a single label of any sort. We can become so attached to labels that we clutch them to our chests like favored toys.

If you slapped a label on a girl who has sworn to keep her virginity, that said "Hello. My Name Is: Slut" it isn't as if it would magically transform into something she was never meant to be. She could choose to accept it, but she could just as easily replace it with her own choice of labels.

Where you have been and where you are going are just more parts of the whole. Your past labels are such small parts of who we really are.

When you are part of one bad relationship after another you tell yourself that all relationships are bad. When you have been hurt over and over you begin to think that all men are bad, or all women, or all friends.

You label.

You erected most of those barriers for good reasons. They served to keep you safe when you needed them; to keep your mind from dealing with things that you weren't ready to deal with; or to make you feel like you had some control. Those walls will come crashing down someday, and you will have to face it.

Until then, your brain will perform some amazing tricks to keep you from seeing what is right in front of your face.

If you don't want to know your spouse is cheating on you, no amount of blonde hairs in the bed or lipstick stains on their t-shirts will convince you otherwise. If you want to believe that your political views are the only possibility, then you will see nothing bad that your side does and nothing good on the other. If you see every person that is different as a threat, then you will find them slipping right into that role.

Labels were meant to be ever changing, but some of us have made them a permanent part of our lives. Someone handed us that label, and we are still wearing it even today.

Pamela C. Hancock LPC of Art Alchemy in Telluride, Colorado, taught me that art therapy works particularly well with abused children. Where her office becomes a safe place for them to illustrate their feelings.

Counseling children who were abused can be very difficult because they don't have the verbal or emotional skills to articulate thoughts, feelings, and ideas into something concrete for the therapist to work with. These kids know the guilt, the shame, the anger, and the confusion, even if they aren't yet able to name them.

Understanding that something happened in their lives which made them different can be hard for anybody to deal with. Even at a young age, an abused child is aware of their status as a victim. That awareness may only come in the form of "same and different," but it is there. They already wear the label, even if they have never heard the word.

> You were not born to be the broken one, the drug addict, the alcoholic, the battered, the abused, or the victim. You were not made to be the whore, the screw-up, or the pitiful.
>
> Cast those labels off. And choose your own.

Pam has a beautiful way of getting around that barrier. She meets the child on their own level. Through their art, her patients learn to identify and label their feelings. Children may color, sculpt, paint, or create any other unique means of expressing themselves.

As they create and talk with Pam, the feelings caused by the abuse have a way of leaking out. They express themselves with a candor, that unashamed honesty that only a child possesses, that many adults have long since forgotten. Pam's children create representations of not just what has happened in their life, but of how it made them feel. This, in turn, helps them to cope with experiences far too large for them to deal with alone.

I was deeply touched when Pam described the children who walked into her office bearing the label of "victim" and walking out of therapy with a new self-chosen identity: "The Artist."

They chose new labels for themselves.

Nothing on the outside of these children was different. The events still happened. They were still molested, still witnessed domestic violence, still lived with abuse and neglect. They might have learned new words to describe what happened to them, but what they really learned were new words to describe themselves.

If worn long enough, labels will confine you and constrict any growth you might accomplish otherwise. Each time you insist that you are too stupid to understand something, that you are too weak to handle a person or situation, or that you are incapable of having healthy relationships, you are labeling.

If you have to draw, paint, or sculpt your way to a new reality, then do so. Cut pictures from magazines. Print them from the Internet. Start shaping your own life today and choose your own labels for the mystery that is you.

In the beginning of my recovery I spent a lot of time at online message boards. One of the girls I knew there told us that she had been discussing this strange feeling that she had with her counselor, it was as if she had been branded with some sort of invisible tattoo.

Her therapist had asked what the tattoo said, and the girl had said "Victim." So, her counselor asked her what she would like to change that label to, and she wasn't sure... so she had come to the forum to ask. Many ideas were offered ranging from "strong," to "fighter", to "tough bitch," to "nobody's fool."

Finally one girl spoke up, saying that she just wanted her tattoo changed to the word "Survivor." Nobody could argue with her. That one word stopped the conversation for a time.

Survivor

A picture of strength, power, hope, and healing.
Survivors are those who refuse to let the circumstances in life keep them down.
Survivors do what they know best: they survive.

Then another woman joined the conversation. She said she was done with the label of victim, but she didn't want to be a Survivor either. She promised us that from then on her invisible tattoo would read "Thriver."

Thriver

(Insert your bio here.)

Roll Call

Christina Aguilera
Singer
Abuse

Stephen Fry
Actor/Comedian
Bullying

Patty Duke
Actress
Child Sexual Abuse

Christina Applegate
Actress
Childhood Sexual Abuse Survivor

Farrah Faucett
Actress
Domestic Violence Survivor

"When we are children we seldom think of the future. This innocence leaves us free to enjoy ourselves as few adults can. The day we fret about the future is the day we leave our childhood behind."

~Patrick Rothfuss, The Name of the Wind

Finding Innocence Lost

Innocence. Of all of the things you lose due to childhood abuse, your innocence is perhaps the most symbolic. Sometimes lost before you even knew it existed, taken by those who had no right to it.

We live in a world that will take your innocence the first chance it gets. The irresponsibility of adults–through abuse, alcoholism, or simply being absent when they are needed–forces children to be overly responsible. A child can't reasonably be expected to handle adult obligations, but many of them had no other choice. They raised siblings, ran households, woke themselves up in empty homes, and tucked themselves into bed alone at night.

Adults are supposed to handle the grownup worries, but not all adults can or will act the part. When grown-ups aren't present physically, emotionally, or mentally, children end up raising themselves.

From the moment I found out that I was going to be a mother, I knew I had to do better. I was going to bring another life into this world and the thought terrified the hell out of me. My innocence was gone long before I understood what it meant. I was forced into an adult world way too young.

I promised myself that my children would have their innocence as long as they wanted it.

My own childhood memories are filled with dark smudges that tend to taint even the happiest of times, so it wasn't a place I ventured often. Even in the happy times there was a risk of triggering the wrong memories again. I had to learn to disconnect from large periods of my life.

Then, many years later I had to learn to reconnect to those memories again. I had to see them in totally different ways.

It came to me one day while reading about young girls in other countries who have sexual experiences at young ages without the long-term trauma.

In cultures where sex is considered a passage into adulthood, children are sometimes introduced to sexuality by an older family member. Only these children don't suffer the trauma that many children do. If their culture sees it as a positive step towards adulthood then the kids do as well.

If I had been able to consent to the sex, it would not have affected me so deeply. If I had been more emotionally and physically mature. Being molested isn't what hurt me. Having something taken without my permission did.

I was trying to fit my experiences into a very different frame, one where sex was bad and wrong, and nasty. So, I was bad and wrong and nasty. *I was none of those things. I was simply a child.*

I had to see myself as just a child again.

People always wondered what that darkness was within my eyes. I have always wondered if Eve had the same darkness in her eyes after the snake and the apple. I had the body of a child, the knowledge of an adult, and the coping skills of a toddler.

I mourned the loss of the child I should have been. I mourned the childhood I should have had. I mourned the loss of my innocence.

I remember the big people asking me why I couldn't act more like a grownup, and wanting to respond that I never, ever wanted to be one. I had seen first hand what adult worries did to children and I wanted no part of their world. I was a kid, and I was supposed to be doing kid things like climbing trees and deciding which outfit my dolly would wear. My childhood had already seen too many adult worries. I wanted nothing to do with the rest.

After I became a mother, I saw the innocence in my own children and finally realized what a gift innocence really was. Brooke was a vibrant and intelligent little girl from day one. She would throw out her arms and dance around in circles as the rain fell on her face. Justin was my only boy, he wanted to know how everything worked. He was always taking things apart and putting them back together again. Mystery was just in love with life; from the ladybugs to the leaves, she wanted to experience it all.

As we played together side by side, my kids took off in new directions and, before long, they were teaching me new things. My kids have taught me so much about life, and I adore them for that.

Eventually Jaid joined our home as well, and something sort of odd happened. She didn't know a lot of the things that my children did, so we all pitched in to teach her. We were cooking together, and cleaning together. We played board games, without batteries or controllers. As I launched my writing career, they helped me tell stories. I helped them learn how to draw. To this day, just about everything we do, we do together.

Because we didn't have money, we were stuck with each other a lot of the time.

> We all play games with our own heads, the real trick is controlling it.
>
> ◉
>
> As long as you are imagining possible outcomes, why not imagine the best?

Have a conversation with a young child and you will find that anything and everything is possible. Children have the capability to see the magic that is left in our world, a magic that still exists everywhere you look. They can still loop-the-loop on the swing, because gravity doesn't exist yet. Santa has the power to make your dreams come true no matter how broke your parents say they are and if she really, really wanted, a little girl could grow up to be both a princess AND a ninja.

It didn't go away, you have simply forgotten. Before someone came in and told you all of the things you couldn't do in life, all you could see were the things that were possible. When you became an adult you forgot that magic existed at all.

As I followed my babies around, intent on protecting them, they pulled me into their innocent fantasies, bringing me into the world of a child for just a few moments. They asked me why mommies couldn't make mud pies.

I had no reasons to offer. I had just lost the ability to see mud as anything but mud.

The adult voice that says "Grownups don't..." always took over, and why I couldn't stop worrying about the laundry?

My children have made my world a better place. Being a mom with a panic disorder is hell sometimes. If I don't keep it under control, my anxiety will consume me. In the end I had to get it together for them.

They know they have a crazy momma, but they love me anyway. They also know that I have worked hard to overcome my issues so they would have a better life than I've had.

Brooke struggles with anxiety too sometimes, and the first time I saw her have a panic attack, I felt like a failure. Instead of telling her to knock it off or calling her a drama queen like people had with me, I asked her how long she had been having them and what triggered them. We learned to see them coming and head them off.

She would come to me, and I would hold her and talk her down, tell her that it would be okay, and that she was safe.

There are so many things that grown-ups aren't allowed to do once they wear the grown-up label.

No more catching snowflakes on their tongues, no more coloring books, no more making mud pies, and no more dancing in the rain. They stop putting their hair in piggy tails, and big people don't play dress-up anymore.

Who said so?

We have emotional triggers that we don't always understand, but we've learned to read ourselves pretty well and respond accordingly. We have a lot of the same triggers as it turns out: strangers touching us, people invading our personal space, being backed into a corner.

I couldn't always be there for her when she had an attack though, so we worked on ways that she could get herself through them. By helping Brooke learn to control her panic attacks, I learned to deal with my own in better ways.

I no longer deny it when I have a panic attack. It took becoming a mother to learn to talk to myself just as I would a frightened child. It doesn't matter where I am. If I feel the panic rising in the grocery store, I do exactly what I would do if one of my children were struggling. I find the nearest safe place and go into mommy mode.

I can even stop them before they start in the first place if I pay attention to the signs. It doesn't come easily to the abuse Survivor to stop and give yourself whatever it is you need at the moment to feel calm again, but it is crucial.

I had to learn to give myself the same things that a mother would. If you could see me, my arms would be wrapped around my body and I would most likely be rocking back and forth, quieting myself, centering myself. More than one person has no doubt heard me shushing a child in a bathroom stall only to exit alone but, hey, it's a crazy world.

We all need the nurturing love of a caring parent, even as adults.

On one hand, I was a natural mother. When they cried, I held them and comforted them. When they were hungry, I fed them. When they were sleepy, I tucked them in. That I was able to nurture them while being completely unable to do it for myself was lost on me for a very long time.

A child has a right to be a child, to worry about the cares of children. We were supposed to lose our childhood innocence in small pieces, but so many times we lost it in large chunks.

> Allow your self to take root and nobody can take YOU away from you.
>
> ◉
>
> A solid self anchored by strong roots is not blown about by the winds; it is safe and secure in just being.

My kids encourage me to explore the world through their eyes and to re-experience my childhood in different ways. I had no desire to control their spirit, I wanted to see what would happen if I taught them to use the power of their Survivor Spirit from the start. That, my friends, is an experiment still in progress. But, so far, it has been a pleasure.

I knew the world would take my children's innocence eventually, but I wanted to do what I could to slow the process down. That doesn't mean that they are weak by any means. There is very little that they will not attempt once they have set their minds to it. They will stand up for what is right over what is normal. They encourage me to look at life through the eyes of a child once again.

My kids still remember the mom who held herself back. They remember a woman who constantly tried to be perfect, and consistently failed. They remember the mom who only sang and danced with them when daddy wasn't around. The look, that their father still gives me today that says "Stop, you are embarrassing me..."

My ex husband couldn't hold my Survivor Spirit in when we were married, but he did contain it. He tried to take the child out of me and turn me into a serious adult, just like him. I eventually became an adult with or without his intervention but my way was a lot more fun.

My children also saw what happened when I was set free. Yes, I sing in public. Yes, I dance like a dork. Yes, I sometimes embarrass myself and everybody around me, but my darling Ed only laughs at me. "You're so silly."

My kids totally got that from me.

I wanted to give my children a perfect world free of abuse, but there is no way to prevent it. They all still had their traumas in life. People still violated their boundaries. I couldn't prevent bad things from happening to them at all. They were picked on for being poor. They still struggled with self-care. The teasing hurt, but it never once took away who they were. They have never been afraid of being themselves.

There were a lot of things that I didn't know how to teach them, but I tried. The only way that I could raise strong and independent children was to figure out where I had lost so much of my own childhood along the way. I never ex-pected them to give it back to me though...

I found out how to play again. I have found a way to sing at the top of my lungs again. I have found a way to feel like a child again if only for a moment. Through my children I have found a way to have a whole new innocence: a much healthier innocence, a much safer innocence, and a much more real in-nocence.

That childlike wonder is perhaps my favorite part of my Survivor Spirit.

Boshemia is my Survivor Spirit, and I have learned to channel her over the years when I need her most: in my writing, standing in front of a crowd, singing in public. The old me still pulls in, hesitates, and tries to decide what normal people would do. Boshemia just does it. It's all been an act, but it doesn't matter: it works.

We can do some pretty incredible things with our imaginations.

In 1992, while in therapy Beth Rutherford "remembered" becoming pregnant by her father twice and being forced to perform abortions on herself with a coat hanger. After her church counselor had helped her "remember" these things in therapy sessions, Beth went on to accuse her father of molesting her repeatedly between the ages of seven and fourteen, and she accused her mother of helping him.

She truly believed that these memories were accurate, until a physical examination revealed she was in fact still a virgin at the age of 22.

You can reprogram your memory in whatever ways you wish, taking control and redirecting it to more successful outcomes. Failure programs you for more failure. Success programs you for more success.

Think success and it really does follow.

In one study on visualization, Russian scientists compared four different groups of Olympic athletes. The first group stuck to old-fashioned physical training. The second spent three-quarters of their time training physically, while visualizing their practices the rest of the time. The third group split their training time evenly between the two, and the last devoted only one-quarter of their time to training physically and the remaining three-quarters to mental training alone.

Who says that Grown-ups don't?

Catch snowflakes on their tongues.

Make mud pies.

Put their hair up in piggy tails.

Dance in the rain.

Color with crayons.

Sing along with cartoons.

Play dress-up.

Amazingly, the group that had been instructed to imagine themselves performing successfully made the most improvements in their performance. Mental practice, it seemed, was more effective than actually doing it. Our minds really do create our realities good and bad.

After I had spent some time in counseling, he asked me to write a letter to the child I once was and tell her what she needed to hear. I ignored him for about six months. Like most of the things he taught me, it took a while to sink in. I'm a stubborn one. I am.

It took him awhile to get there.

My therapist knew that my children were my life, and he often used that to point out the difference in the pure love I felt for them and the sheer disgust I felt for my own childhood. I had to find a way to reconcile the two realities in my own life or I was never going to move forward.

When I got too hard on myself and started beating myself up, my therapist used to ask me how I would react to my children in the same situation. I wouldn't tell them that it was their fault, or to keep it to themselves, or allow them to beat themselves up. I'd most likely hold them, and comfort them, and then-I would do whatever I had to do to make it right.

Writing a letter to a long-gone child seems like a perfect waste of time, but what you imagine doing is even more powerful than actually doing it. Once I understood this, I sat down with a blank pad of paper and got a clear picture in my head of the little girl that everyone says reminded them of Wednesday Addams.

The one with the dark and somehow sad eyes even when she was happy. I was so surprised to actually find her in those forgotten memories that I had no idea what to say to her when I did. So much of my childhood had been blocked, but there she was just the same.

Your inner child is bound to act up now and then when she needs to feel safe and nurtured. She needs to feel loved. I know it feels silly, but just talk to her.

What happens in your imagination has powerful effects on your reality. That process, known as "re-parenting" among professionals, does seem pretty odd, but sometimes strange works.

I found her on the swing set at the old grade school. She knew that nobody else used the older swings, so that is where she usually spent recess. We sat there silently side by side for some time. I had always seen her from a distance, from where I was in my life. Now I looked at her as simply a child.

Her pudgy hands gripping the cold steel chains. Not swinging, merely swaying back and forth. She seemed so small and fragile. I thought of what I would say to my own children if I knew things about them that I knew about her. I understood things that she couldn't possibly comprehend. Things had happened to her that would drive me to madness if they happened to my babies. What was done to her was wrong. Very wrong. And I was an adult and knew it. I would have protected her, but I couldn't...not then.

She was convinced that she was invisible. Those she had counted on most had lost interest when she stopped being their little princess, but nobody had asked her what had happened to change things. She felt dirty and filthy and unclean, and she knew that everybody could see it when they looked at her.

For the first time ever I felt an anger rise up inside of me. It was exactly what I imagine when I hear someone speak of a "righteous anger." It wasn't foul and bitter like the anger I felt before, but pure and white and somehow right.

She was not an imaginary child, but a very real person, a little girl that was once me. She was a part of myself that I had fought long and hard to push away, but she was still there just as lost as ever. I had to reassure her, but I also had to reassure the adult she had become. I could finally take care of us and she needed to know that. I didn't have to ask her anything, I already knew. I was the ONLY one who would ever really know.

I also knew what she wanted to hear most, so I said it...

> *"I know things have been bad, but I'm here now, and everything is going to be okay. I am going to love you. I am going to protect you, and I am never going to leave you. You don't have to worry about anything anymore. I am going to take care of you. Now we're in this together. I am the adult now, and I have the strength to protect you from anything that can harm you."*

You can't make the things that have happened in your life be magically un-done, but it is never too late to tell yourself what you needed to hear. It doesn't matter if that child existed 10 years ago or 50 years ago, it is still there and still waiting for healing. That child belongs to you now. Visualize it being the way it should have been. Take your childhood back.

Smart grownups know that their inner child is always just a swing set away. You can bring that magic back into your life. Innocence lost can be found again. Letting that child out to play now and then is crucial to your healing.

I no longer fear that she is unable to protect herself. If she wants to dance in the rain, or get out the crayons and a coloring book, or even sing at the top of her lungs to an old musical...who am I to stop her? She's earned her childhood.

I don't hesitate to allow my inner child to guide me now. I can keep her safe.

Survivors of Childhood Sexual Abuse

Alison Arngrim
Actress

Anne Sexton
Poet

Antwone Fisher
Author

Ashley Judd
Actress

Billy Connoly
Comedian

Chuck Rosenthal
Professor/Author

"Never try to define love. Once defined love is confined. Once confined -- It dies."

~Unknown

The Very Definition Of Love

Ah, love. Thoughts of that certain someone fill your head and the blood instantly goes rushing to your brain. Without a doubt, they are unlike anybody else that you have ever met before. Just being in their general vicinity makes your knees go weak. You long to be with them, to touch them, hold them.

That's love, right?

Is love simply a deep longing, need, or desire? A craving? An appetite? A passion?

Maybe. And maybe not.

We all use the word love, but how we define it is as complex and ever changing as we are. We use it seriously, but we also use it casually. We say we love inanimate objects that can never love us in return. We love our cars, our homes, and our food. We can love someone wholly yet still not be *in* love with them.

> "Do you love me because I am beautiful, or am I beautiful because you love me?"
>
> ~ Rodgers & Hammerstein's
>
> Cinderella

No two people have the same definition, and each love is different. There is no unspoken rule in love that requires that it be returned; in fact, when it comes to love, there are no rules at all. Every age, every culture, every person has their very own definitions of love and it is constantly changing.

love /luv/

Noun: A deep feeling of fondness and affection.

Verb: Intense sexual or romantic desire.

Synonyms: noun. affection - fondness – passion

verb. like - be very fond of – adore

A noun and a verb. A feeling and a promise. You can have love. You can feel love. You can offer love. You can seek love. Love can find you. You can fall in love, but you can fall out of love, too. You can be in love. You can be in love with being in love.

> "Love: The irresistible desire to be irresistibly desired."
>
> ~Mark Twain

And as the immortal John, Paul, George, and Ringo once said, *"All you need is love."*

Your love for someone can change from day to day and sometimes from moment to moment. Your love for your parents is different than your love for your partner, which is different still than your love for your child. Beginning with your earliest experiences, you add to your definition, you subtract from it, you refine it, and throughout your life your definition of love defines you even as you seek to define it.

And to describe the indescribable, we have been given a single, lousy four-letter word.

The ancient Greeks had many words for the concept of love, and I think that they were on to something. First they considered the love of strangers, for which they used the word *xenia*. It is what we might call hospitality today.

Next they gave us *philios*, or "love of the mind," the kind of love we would call friendship, from this familiar word we get, *philadelphia,* which literally translates to "brotherly love."

What we might identify as family love, the Greeks called *storge*. This was a natural-born love like that between parent and child, or a sister and a brother. And still, we have not yet come to the kind of love associated with romantic passion.

Often translated as "love of the body," this is what the Greeks called *eros*. Ah, chocolate and roses, glasses of champagne, that's the stuff we're talking about.

All of that sensual desire and longing. You want to touch them, you want them to touch you, and you want to stay that way forever. It is new and exciting, but it does not last eternally, and it isn't the love for which we hunger.

Why are we stuck with one lousy word again?

What about those couples that last seemingly forever? You wouldn't call it passion, but it isn't exactly *philios* either. When we talk about love, aren't we really talking about friendship, devotion, and compassion? The other half to our whole?

Soul mates.

The soul part of the term implying some sort of deeper connection than just body parts and chemicals; otherwise they're just mates. Don't we all want to be half of that couple that still looks into each other's eyes like newlyweds after forty years?

In Plato's *Symposium*, Aristophanes spoke of a time before time where men and women were joined together as one being, twin souls in a single body. A time came when these beings angered the gods, so Zeus took a mighty thunderbolt and used it to cut them in two. Apollo then rearranged their features, *"taking out the wrinkles and tying the skin in a knot about the navel."*

> I wanna make you smile whenever you're sad.
>
> Carry you around when your arthritis is bad
>
> Oh, all I wanna do, is grow old with you
>
> ~Adam Sandler

From that time on according to Plato, we have all been split souls, driven to find and connect with our lost half, to seek our wholeness once again through love.

What a beautiful thought it is. Somewhere out there is the other half to your whole.

Your eyes will meet, your bodies will embrace, your souls will entwine, and in that moment your life will be finally be complete.

Every woman supposedly longs for that perfect relationship full of candlelight and roses. Many of those who do are disappointed.

In fantasy, falling in love happens as if by magic. If love were like the romance and fantasy novels, we would all have our own castles in the clouds complete with knights in shining armor and "happily ever after."

Passion is fine for about the first six months, and then the chemicals that led to all of that heaving and thrusting start to wear off. This isn't love; it's a chemical concoction, a bundle of hormones. It's lust.

Lust is all about what they do for you, how they make you feel, and what you get out of the relationship. It's fun sometimes, but you can't live in a world of lust forever. The moment the real world encroaches you find there is nothing of substance to hold it together If the relationship is built on passion alone, once the sparks fizzle so will everything else..

Instead of loving one another forever, the relationship disappears into the mists, leaving everyone wondering what the hell went wrong.

As long as two real people are required for a relationship, the perfect relationship will remain impossible, and just where do we find a perfect world for our two perfect people to live in anyhow?

"Someone once told me you trap yourself sometimes by thinking desire and need are love. He was right. Love is something far more precious, but something far more fragile. Hold on to it too tightly and it will crumble in your fingers. Hold it too loosely and the wind might blow it away and shatter it on the cold ground. Listen to the voice in your heart, but be absolutely sure the voice comes from your heart."

~ Unknown

A real-life relationship built on fantasy comes with a built-in requirement that the other person continue to fulfill their role and maintain the illusion. A crisis hits. The weather changes. Something more interesting comes along. People screw up. All people do. And there you go blaming it all on love again.

Lust can exist within the confines of love, but it can also exist completely separate from it, and completely devoid of it. Lust can just be lust.

Outside factors will forever remain beyond our control. If one partner changes, or grows, or faces a life-changing event, the other must either catch up or get left behind.

Nobody can guarantee you a "happily ever after." There ain't no fairy godmothers on the way either. There is no relationship out there that will fix your life. There will always be times that try even the strongest of relationships, but you can tilt the odds strongly in your favor by refusing to confuse fantasy with reality.

The love of love only leads to a need for more love. It never ends.

Try to fill a bucket with no bottom. The bigger the holes, the faster it runs out again. Pour all you want; there will never be enough liquid to stop the flow.

You will never be perfect. Eventually the rose-colored glasses are going to come off, and things never seem to be quite the way we thought they were. Maybe if you hadn't spent so much time defending what was wrong with the relationship, trying to fix it, trying to force it to work...

Abusive relationships are not love. Loving someone and hurting them are not one and the same, but popular culture would sometimes have you accept it as so. When violence is perpetrated in the name of jealousy, or parental concern, or even pure lovers' passion, people often call it love, but it isn't.

If someone loves you so much that they hurt you, it isn't proof of their love at all. It is proof of their lack of control over themselves. That's it.

You will not find love out there.

My beloved editor Matt (who plays triple-duty as BFF, personal assistant, and tireless editor) and I enjoy good food, so our business meetings are traditionally held in restaurants.

A few years ago we were having one of our "business meetings" to discuss the first draft of this book

> "The two halves went about looking for one another, and were ready to die of hunger in one another's arms...and when one of them meets with his other half, the actual half of himself, the pair are lost in an amazement of love and friendship and intimacy and one will not be out of the other's sight even for a moment."
>
> ~Collected Works of Plato

when a man sitting across from us mentioned that he was a writer, too. Far more than just a writer, Robert Subiaga Jr. introduced himself, and we found ourselves in the presence of a modern day renaissance man. It isn't often I can find someone who can keep up with my conversations, but Robert stayed ahead.

He joined our meeting, and through the many twists and turns our conversations took that day we finally drifted to the subject of love gone sour.

Robert shared one of the greatest truths about love that I have ever heard. It was so simple, yet profound that I asked him to repeat it for us, and I have repeated it for many people since.

"When you waste your love on someone who doesn't deserve

it, you are depriving someone who does."

Someone hurts you once and promises they won't do it again. They hurt you twice and their promises wear thin, but my, aren't you a little trooper? (Some circles prefer the term martyr.) Too many people have been brainwashed into thinking that love is rare, and precious and should be guarded at all costs. Worth fighting for. Worth dying for. Worth killing for.

> "You know, what do you know about love? What do you possibly think you know about love? You know, I am sick and tired of men using love like it's some kind of disease you just catch. LOVE should have brought your ass home last night!"
>
> ~Halle Berry - Boomerang

Once you get an idea like that in your head it's hard to get it out. A lot of ideas are. After a few different experiences in our lives you will find they aren't just linked but completely entwined in one another.

Because love feels good even when it is bad there will always be victims willing to put up with what hurts just to get a few moments of what doesn't. Your love is a gift. It cannot be taken against your will. Only you can decide who is worthy of it. So, why aren't you treating it like one?

Love is almost a life form of its own; a separate, distinct, and wholly uncontrollable being made up of many smaller parts: trust, intimacy, compassion, respect, concern, responsibility...

We keep trying to make love into one idea, but it is and always will be many. Love, lust, passion...so many different concepts all rolled into one!

Love is chaos. But love is order, too.

Love doesn't have to make sense.

> "Love itself is what is left over when being in love has burned away, and this is both an art and a fortunate accident. Your mother and I had it. We had roots that grew towards each other underground, and when all the pretty blossoms had fallen from our branches we found that we were one tree and not two."
>
> ~Captain Corelli's Mandolin

Out of the many definitions I have heard in my lifetime the description in 1 Corinthians is the one I have always returned to.

The Christian Bible offers what is perhaps the most beautiful and detailed definitions of love within its pages. At first I thought it was just a recipe of sorts, that it was only the love that we were supposed to give.

But Robert was right, love is supposed to given AND received.

Returning to those Greek definitions, *agape* has always been my favorite.

The Greek's version of unconditional love, *agape* is thought to be the purest of all forms, it translates to "love of the soul."

It is a love free of judgment, with no qualification of worthiness and no requirement for reciprocation. It is a wholly voluntary love that is offered with no strings attached.

Love is patient, Love is kind. It does not envy, It does not boast, It is not proud. It is not rude, It is not self-seeking,

It is not easily angered, It keeps no record of wrongs. Love does not delight in evil, But rejoices with the truth.

It always protects,

Always trusts,

Always hopes,

Always perseveres.

Love never fails.

~1 Corinthians 13:4 – 7

Of the many kinds of love this is the one most craved and least received. Agape is about as far from abuse as you can get.

"And now these three remain:

Faith, hope and love.
But the greatest of these is love. "

~1 Corinthians 13:13

Roll Call

Anne Heche
Actress
Incest Survivor

Marilyn Manson
Performance Artist
Childhood Sexual Abuse

Pamela Anderson
Actress
Rape Survivor, Domestic Violence

Rihanna
Singer
Domestic Violence Survivor, Childhood Abuse

Rosie O'Donnell
Actress/Talk Show Host/Comedian
Incest Survivor

Vanessa Williams
Singer & Actress
Childhood Sexual Abuse

"Romantic love is mental illness. But it's a pleasurable one. It's a drug. It distorts reality, and that's the point of it. It would be impossible to fall in love with someone that you really saw.."

~ Fran Lebowitz

The Next Big High

If you have lived with abuse, then love has been impatient. Love has been un-kind. It has been jealous. It has been boastful. It has been proud. It has been rude. It has been self-seeking. It has been easily angered. It has kept record of every wrong. It has delighted in evil. It has avoided the truth. It has harmed you. It has been untrustworthy. It has left you hopeless. It has left you help-less. Love has failed you.

That SO wasn't love.

How can one woman give her life for the sake of her children while another sacrifices her children to follow a lover? How can one man build a vast monu-ment while another destroys an entire city, both claiming that it was love that drove them to it?

Love is beautiful. Love is painful. Love is grand. Love is humbling. Love is clarity. Love is insanity.

Look at some of the decisions you have made in your past just to keep your supply of love going. Forgiving serial infidelity, turning a blind eye to the red flags, ignoring abuse, taking on their problems...

It's like an addiction.

Each person has mind labyrinths of their own to sort out, they've just taken different routes through the chaos. I've seen people do some pretty stupid things in pursuit of that almighty four-letter word. I've done some pretty dumb things myself.

Almost everyone has done something stupid in the name of love. We've alienated ourselves from friends and family, begged, borrowed, and even stolen, all just to keep that high going a little bit longer. Make no mistake about it, love is one of the most powerful drugs available. It is no less destructive than any other addiction though.

We all find different ways of making ourselves feel powerful, and for that reason anything can become an addiction. Sometimes we develop addictions to help us deal with our addictions. From obsessive thoughts, to OCD, to the bizarre world of fetish, you will find the same basic core: people in pursuit of that higher high.

If you have ever wondered why people do such unpredictable things in the name of love, you need look no further than chemicals.

You were getting high on your own chemical supply and didn't even know it. In the first stages of love, a chemical high is produced that activates the same areas of the brain that cocaine targets, and a similar feeling of euphoria takes over. Just like any other chemical addiction, you require more and more love to maintain the high you once felt.

> When you rely on something outside of yourself to get your needs met, dependency can so easily follow.
>
> 🌐
>
> A codependent relationship is a co-addiction.

Tolerance levels naturally increase with time, and you crave higher levels of your drug of choice. You are willing to take greater risks to get it. The supply must increase or renew in some way.

The chemicals that sustain the high we call love last about six months on average.

Addiction has a way of destroying its host if intervention does not come, and we are sort of okay with that. Addicts will do just about anything to avoid those horrible withdrawal pains. They will lie, steal, cheat, and even kill anything that gets in between them and their drug of choice. Their own mother can't trust them. They have no friends. As long as their supply holds out, life is good. When it is interrupted, things can get ugly.

As a teenager my friends and I began experimenting with drugs, but I stopped when things started getting serious and walked away. One of my friends in particular kept going deeper and deeper until finally heroin threatened to take his life. I remember talking to him, begging him to look at himself, but he brushed my concerns aside.

"But it's killing you!" I cried.

To which he very calmly replied, "Your first high is always the greatest. You can chase it all you want, but you will never find that first high again. Addiction is all about that higher high. The only high better than your first will be your last, and deep down that is what every junkie wants."

Many of our abusers have co-addictions, and we live with those, too. Drugs, alcohol, work, rage. Chemicals aren't the only addictions available to mask the pain, but they do tend to be the simplest. Even if you take all of the chemicals out of the equation, most people are just addicted to things that make them feel good, or at the very least leave them feeling less bad. Why is it that so many of us are attracted to drug users and alcoholics? It's almost as if we need them as much as they need their fix.

Your risk-taking behaviors increase as you scramble to maintain your supply. Just one more time. Just one more day. Just one more chance. When love stops feeling good, you keep chasing it. This person will fill all of those unmet needs. This relationship is the one you have been looking for. It will make you whole again. Just one more fix. This time it will be different.

No. It won't. Not really.

Damn junkies.

When you are in love with being in love there is little to distinguish your behaviors from that of the average junkie. You learn to depend on outside sources to fill your inside needs. As soon as that relationship sours, you seek a new one.

The pain will not go away until the real problem is addressed. You can't drink it away, you can't ignore it away, you can't deny it away, and you can't love it away. That big old elephant in the living room is going to stay in the living room stinking up the place for as long as you are willing to let it.

Codependents are so good at bad relationships that they even have unhealthy relationships with themselves. Lack of boundaries, obsessive behaviors, and low self-esteem become the norm. Anger and resentment build, along with depression, self-destructive behaviors, numbness...

An addict's survival is dependent upon the ability to ignore a lot of unpleasant things, and the same is true for the co-addict. Your reality is constantly being questioned. You become afraid of everything. Afraid of failure. Afraid of making mistakes. Afraid of rejection. Afraid of judgment. Afraid of abandonment. Sometimes simply afraid to move.

Instead of communicating in ways that will enrich the relationship we continue the dysfunction. We learn to distrust intimacy while longing for it at the same time. We become people-pleasers who care take.

You can find yourself dependent on another person, or even a certain set of circumstances, to meet your unmet needs so easily.

It doesn't take long for a want to become a *neeeed.*

My mother passed her addictions on to me, but it wasn't the family dependency on alcohol that took my mother from me for long periods of time. It was love. My mother was an addict for most of my life. She was a good mother when she was there, but her addiction sometimes separated me from my childhood, detached me from large parts of it.

There is no global shortage of love. Supplies are not running out. When you give love away there is no promise that it will be returned, but your capacity does not decrease. Love is one of the most important resources we have in this world and best of all it is 100% renewable.

My mother is one of the strongest women I know, but she somehow found herself needing to be needed just the same. She knew she couldn't fix the men in her life, but she was driven to keep trying. Through one unhealthy relationship after another she struggled to change things she couldn't change, to love people who only *neeeeded* her.

There always seemed to be another man who came along and promised to love her wholly, truly, and completely, and my mother would be reinvented overnight. She would do the best she could to become someone new for every relationship, but it always came down to the fact that she could never become the person they wanted her to be.

Even when she got away from one, another one very much like the last was there to take his place. All so very much like her daddy.

You can be addicted to people and their problems, just like you can be addicted to any other chemical. When your life becomes dedicated to satisfying a hunger within, the source makes little difference. Anyone can become a junkie. A food junkie. A drug junkie. A love junkie.

It is so easy to convince yourself that this person will fill all of those unmet needs when that is what you want to believe. This relationship is the one you have been looking for. It will make you whole again. Just one more fix. This time it will be different.

She was unable to be herself fully inside of or outside of a relationship, even unable to find a self at all sometimes. She traded in rock and roll collections for country music, and her hippie days for western bars. A shifting self can adapt to just about anything; that's how we survived abuse in the first place. So she adapted, she overcompensated, and she denied entire parts of herself.

In the end, the result was always the same. She could never be perfect enough.

Where your heart dwells, your attentions will follow.

You can be addicted to a substance. You can be addicted to a feeling, and you can most certainly be addicted to a person.

In her eyes, one person's rejection determined her likeability to the entire world. Her boyfriends cheated on her, conned her out of cars and money, left her destitute time and again. Then they blamed it all on her. I saw her go back to unhealthy partners time and time again, determined as ever to fix them, to fix her life through them. The bar was set impossibly high, but in all of those years she never realized that the game was rigged in the abusers' favor.

My mother learned to love through addiction. She needed a mess to clean up, or she didn't know what to do.

It took many years for her to find the real person underneath all of the disguises she had worn. Instead of being someone else, she is finally just free to be herself. It was never a man she needed to get there, it was a self. And a funny thing happened, she even found a man to love that person.

We fool ourselves into thinking that we learned from our parents' mistakes, but we sometimes go on to repeat them in surprising new ways. The daughter of the town drunk might never drink a drop of alcohol in her life, but years after he is gone she will find herself inexplicably drawn to people that need her in some way.

There are many generations of abuse in my family tree, but there are also many generations of alcoholism behind that abuse. The women in my family remained dry for the most part, but one after another they found alcoholics of their own.

I learned those oldest of family traditions well. I scrambled to find the love I longed for in my own life. I found myself dependent on one person after another. Love was always my drug of choice, and probably always will be.

My mother isn't the only hopeless romantic in the family.

Good, bad, or otherwise, relationships are a basic human need for survival. I struggled most of my life to find a way to be in a relationship without being consumed by it, but it wasn't easy.

Abuse Survivors often try to get their needs met in the same ways they were taught to deal with them as victims. When we turn our anger outward we risk damaging others. When we hold it in we damage ourselves. Addictions will cover the pain temporarily, but the problems will still be there.

When you do not possess a strong sense of self you can so easily become your relationships, changing who you are in the process.

There are many destructive ways to get your needs filled, and victims seem to be drawn to the worst of them.

You can even lose yourself totally.

Our self-destructive behaviors will take over not just our own lives, but everyone we come into contact with.

If the first thing you do when a relationship fails is replace it with a new one then you are bound to repeat the same dance over and over throughout your life. No matter how often you change partners, the steps will stay the same. Those lessons will keep repeating themselves until you finally learn them, and they have a way of getting more painful as they go.

When one relationship goes sour it isn't time to rush into the next. It's time to figure out what lessons you can learn from your past relationships to better your future. You can't keep believing that you can bring bad habits into your relationships and still somehow get good results. Nobody else is going to change it for you.

We find the strangest ways of restoring balance to our lives, some more constructive than others.

Many of the self-destructive behaviors that Survivors struggle with can be traced back to that paradox within them, that need to find some sort of balance, as precarious as it may be. Going to extremes in one direction can leave us totally lacking in others.

If you need help dealing with your addictions, whatever they may be, there are twelve-step programs available for nearly every dependency. Reach out for help, and someone will be there to answer the call. There is even a group out there formed specifically for sex and love addiction problems.

Any recovering addict will be glad to share the twelve steps of recovery with you, and they will tell you that the first step to recovery from any addiction is...

> *We admit that we are powerless over our addiction - that our lives have become unmanageable.*

Survivors Who Have Struggled With Addictions

Axl Rose
Musician
Childhood Sexual Abuse

Corey Haimm
Actor
Child Sexual Abuse

Dorothy Dandridge
Singer, Actress
Child Sexual Abuse

Mackenzie Phillips
Actress/Singer
Incest

Michael Jackson
King of Pop
Abuse

Ozzy Osbourne
Singer
Childhood Sexual Abuse, Domestic Violence

"You yourself, as much as anybody in the entire universe, deserve your love and affection."

~Buddha

Getting What You Deserved

There are people out there who would never dream of accepting knock-off clothing or cheap jewelry, but they will accept any old love that comes along.

As soon as one relationship ends they set out to find another just like it just to get everything back to normal. If you ask them why, they can't quite say, but they seem comforted just knowing someone is there.

It's the same reason that people keep their old gallon of milk on the shelf long after it has gone bad. It's turning green and is stinking up the fridge, but they are still holding on. Someday when they get around to it they will replace it, but for now sour milk is better than no milk at all.

Some of us need someone in close proximity so badly that we settle for "close enough" in many our relationships. They become painful, and we hold on. They become depressing, and we hold on. They become toxic, and we hold on. We act as if there is a shortage.

Everybody wants to be wanted. Everyone else can see that the relationship is toxic, but maybe in their mind it's better than being alone. When we need to be needed, being single is a fate worse than death. It is hard to wait for the love we truly deserve.

Or is it because someone wanting us means there must be something about us worth wanting?

Abuse is so often a perversion of your most intimate relationships, but that wasn't an accident. There is a twisting of the things you long for most in life: love, acceptance, security... Victims want love and abusers use that knowledge like a dog trainer uses treats.

Look into the eyes of the love deprived and you will see that same hunger you see in the eyes of starving children on the streets. Deprivation of the physical body and deprivation of the soul will both kill eventually, and it is a very long and painful process. People in positions of power over vulnerable individuals can abuse that power all too easily, and there are so few places to turn to for help. Parents, partners, youth group leaders, teachers, and daycare providers are all common abusers. They are people who are supposed to love and nurture those they care for, so they are the people that we least expect.

Every child deserves...

Loving and supportive adults who understood the healthy boundaries a child needs.

Adults who could act like responsible adults and allow you to just be a kid.

The knowledge that you were loved.

The knowledge that you were safe.

A sane world to grow up in.

We all deserve those things; support, healthy boundaries, responsible partners, love, safety, sanity.

If pain is a consistent part of your relationship then whatever you want to call it, it isn't love.

Your abusers may even believe that you should feel guilty about your abuse. Most bullies do, it sure beats the alternative. In a dysfunctional or abusive relationship you are often held responsible for far more than just yourself.

They can blame you for a lot of thing. Their thoughts, their feelings, their actions, and even their expectations. But that doesn't make it true.

Abuse focuses its attention on your weaknesses. Love in its most perfect form magnifies your strengths and minimizes those weaknesses. When someone truly loves you they don't suffocate you, they help you grow.

Love is a very effective weapon when wielded by the abuser. At its heart, abuse is all about power and control–controlling you, controlling the situation controlling others through you. There is a twisted logic there, and in many different types of abuse that perversion centers on love.

A child does not have the authority to insist upon these things, but thankfully as adults, we do.

What we deserve in relationships...

People who seek out opportunities to spend time together.

People who protect us from harm.

People who want us to be happy.

People who try to remain aware our needs, wants, and desires.

People who are aware of our physical needs.

People who do not need to fake being perfect for outsiders.

People who speak positively to and about us.

People who encouraging us to share thoughts and feelings openly.

Love that works in ways that you both can understand.

Honest and direct communication.

Abuse doesn't work for society, and it doesn't work for the victims, but someone is still getting his or her needs met through abuse. A relationship with an abusive person is always going to hurt because they are masters at playing the ME game. They want what they want, that can't be helped, but how far will they push you to get it? How deeply are they willing to drive that hurt?

Pain and love are not as intimately connected as the bullies of this world would have you think.

Bullies have a way of ensuring that they remain the focus of the relationship. After a while in an abusive relationship your life is lived from the outside-in. Your decisions are made based on what other people want, without always taking the time to consider what is best for you.

We all want to believe that the good guy is rewarded for his deeds, justice is always served, and the bad guy always gets his just desserts in the end. But there we go assuming that abuse is rational again. Hell, if this were a fair and orderly existence then abuse would cease to exist at all.

If we could make such fairy tales come true then the victims of abuse would not be the ones left struggling with the after effects. They would all go on to live happy and successful lives. The perpetrators would face justice and pay for their crimes.

You want to live in an orderly universe but there doesn't need to be a reason for abuse, not one that you could understand anyhow. Maybe your abuser has told you that you deserved to be mistreated, if not through words then through deeds. Maybe you are just telling yourself that. Abuse doesn't make sense, so you grab onto whatever does.

Survivors come pre-wired for guilt and shame.

You were the one who was left with the secret shame of a crime you didn't even commit. You were left with the guilt. You weren't born with negative feelings about yourself, but children as young as three can show signs of shame. And those feelings can run mighty deep.

If the world were fair, you would have had the things that you deserved all along, the things every human being deserves: dignity, respect, safety... but we didn't. It is hard to feel loved and accepted when someone is always find-ing fault with you. Once you accept that you are unworthy of being loved it isn't too far of a jump for the mind to make to also see you as being worthy of abuse. Funny how that works, isn't it?

(Pssst. Your abusers already knew this, they were just hoping that you never figured it out.)

Guilt can play a positive role in your life. It can keep you from harming others or stepping outside of your moral compass. When you step outside of your definition of what makes a good person, guilt can help you correct it. Guilt and shame are close cousins, so close that people often mistake one for the oth-er, but shame is the ugly cousin.

If you are still trapped in cycles of guilt and shame then you are stuck doing penance for the sins of others. We can't correct something that never belonged to us in the first place.

When my mother was sexually abused as a child, there was no escape. Angry, frightened, and with no other options, she said, "I wish they were dead." Both of the men who molested her did die soon after. Even fifty years later that little girl feels somewhat responsible for the deaths of her abusers. That guilt was not hers to bear, nor the guilt from the acts those people committed upon a small child. She still feels responsible for something she had no control over.

Loving someone and approving of their actions are sometimes two totally dif-ferent things, or at least they are supposed to be. In a rational world you can love someone fully and still wholly disapprove of a certain action they have taken at the same time. They are in fact two separate and distinct states.

When love is conditional and you fail to meet those conditions on a regular basis, then guilt for your own abuse kind of makes sense in a sick and strange way. Some people can recite their flaws as if they were rehearsing lines for a play. They dig through every shortcoming, pick at every scab, and poke at the open wounds.

After your brain has been rewired even disappointment can be read as personal rejection. You actually start to believe that good little girls deserve to be loved, but bad girls (whatever the definition of "bad" may have been at that moment) are no longer loveable.

You believed you were denied love because you were not worthy of it. Love was for good girls, not for girls like you. Those pathways in your brain were first walked by the earliest abusers in your life. They were deepened with every unhealthy relationship that followed.

Abuse is not an action as much as a reaction. In the bully's world, if they become angry and hit you, resulting in a broken hand, the fault is clear: the person who *made* them strike out is responsible. There is only one problem, nobody MADE them do anything. It was their choice all along.

They may have reacted to something that you did, but that reaction was their responsibility. This was not the only response available to them. They could have chosen to do something less destructive, like walk off their anger or call a friend and vent. They could have chosen to write it down or deal with it in therapy. They even could have chosen to just let it go, and offered love and acceptance instead.

But they didn't.

An abuser person views the world in terms of what it can offer them, and decisions are based on what the individual wants without regard to what is best for the other people involved. While you may have heard of glass houses, bullies live in a houses made of mirrors. Everywhere they look they see themselves. They blame you for the things that they do. Their true natures are constantly being reflected back to them by others.

"I win, you lose."

A relationship where your needs become secondary to the needs and even the wants of your partner is not really a relationship at all. But it is close enough to keep you hoping.

"You win, I lose."

The tough guys are right. You aren't entitled to jack shit in this life. Nobody will hand you anything without expecting something in return, but you don't deserve to be treated like shit either. You were not abused because you deserved it. It was not for your own good. You did not ask for it, and the need was not implied. Hold out for the love that you deserve.

The legal system in the United States is heavily based on the concept that one is innocent until proven guilty. Once guilt is decided the punishment follows. We start thinking that life works on the same system, but it doesn't.

Punishment is supposed to be designed on some level to induce shame for an offense. There is nothing wrong with taking responsibility for your actions; in fact, it brings with it a certain liberation. When followed by a commitment to correcting the problem you have the recipe for success.

Before you own guilt though, you need to consider the source. Who is responsible for your abuse? The person who did the damage, of course.

Abuse is not our sin to bear. You can't make somebody abuse you against their will. The person who molested you, the parent who demeaned you, the lover who hit you...they all had a choice before them, and they chose to use it to do harm. Whether they recognized it as a choice or not is their problem. It was their decision, and they chose poorly. Whether they accept it or not it is still their responsibility.

Let them have it.

If the relief of our guilt is dependent upon the actions of another person then we could very well be in a permanent state of shame. Their anger belongs to them, their actions belong to them, and their choices belong to them. Your responsibility does not lie with your abuser or their actions. It lies within your own body and your own choices.

Let them have it!

Almost everyone suffers from guilt at some point or another, but it was never meant to be a lifestyle.

Make the choice to be free from the guilt and shame that has burdened you. Even if you did make a decision that somehow led to abuse, that doesn't make it your responsibility. The abuser had a choice as well, and they chose to harm you. They were the ones in control of the situation, and as long as you allow guilt and shame to reside in yourself then they are still the ones in control.

Ask anybody who has had an unhealthy relationship in their past if they would go back once they have escaped. Their answer is likely to be not only "no," but "hell no." Unhealthy relationships are a prison, a dark, gray place that sucks the life out of you. Once you have escaped the chaos you would do anything to avoid going back.

Nothing helps you appreciate freedom like a cage.

Maya Angelou, the woman known worldwide for her words, once stopped using them entirely. She endured years of guilt thinking that her words alone had made the man who raped her die. After she named him, he had been murdered. An act she had nothing to do with, but she punished herself as if she had. She thought that her words had brought this fate, so she refused to speak at all.

Our voice is part of our Survivor Spirit.

The case has been tried, the jury has rendered a verdict, and we are doing the time when we weren't responsible for the crime. Victims don't need anyone else to make them feel guilty about things; they do a pretty good job on their own.

Silence does not help anybody.

When I saw the hurt in the Big People's eyes what I tried to tell my secrets, I thought I had created that. I thought that I had hurt them, and that their reaction was my fault. I didn't want to cause anybody pain so I learned not to talk about my abuse. I was almost 30 before I learned how to talk about it again. I protected the abusers without even meaning to.

Many Survivors never tell of their abuse at all and their secrets have been there for a very long time. Maya Angelou has since used her voice to change the world, but imagine for a moment if she hadn't.

You deserve better than an abusive relationship. We all do. Society doesn't want to talk about us. They will have a few fundraisers and throw a bake sale or two, and most people agree that abuse should not happen. Then when it comes time to actually do something about it everyone starts mumbling and staring at their feet.

Calling the police on the abusive husband next door or turning in the neglectful mother down the road in is not the easiest choice, but it is often the right one. If more people chose to hold the abusers responsible for their actions, if we offered fewer excuses and more alternatives, then perhaps the cycle of abuse really would stop.

There is something better. A balanced center, life lived in a constant flow from inside to outside and back again. It isn't that you want to be superior in your relationships, only an equal. What is best for the individual is a consideration, but so is what is best for the other parties involved.

A true "win-win" relationship.

Your love is a gift that is all too often wasted on someone who doesn't deserve it, but there are people out there who do deserve it...so find them. Those people will not be a part of your life until you believe without a doubt that you do deserve them. Until you stop broadcasting your old self-image, that of a beggar on the streets willing to accept whatever scraps you are given, people are going to keep offering you leftovers. When you love and value yourself it is much easier for other people to love and value you in return.

What you deserve now is peace.

You deserve happiness now.

You deserve healing now.

You deserve to know that you are safe now.

You deserve to know that you are loved now.

Love cannot be bought, sold, or taken; it can only be given. It can't be bribed or repaid either. It is your gift to give, and it is nobody's to take. It can't be forced. It can't be beaten into submission. It can't be stolen like a thief in the night. It can't be begged for or borrowed either.

My father's bride was right. Relationships are about choosing to meet certain needs in exchange for having certain needs of your own met in return. Happy relationships are out there, with people who love one another and treat each other in loving ways. They do exist.

The simple knowledge that you deserved better can change everything....

Perhaps you have heard of healthy relationships, even witnessed a few interactions that left you wondering if there really was something more to them that you were missing. Did you dare to dream for just a moment?

Stop letting anyone else determine what sort of love you are worthy of. Don't

216

let anyone else define love for you either, not even me. What do I know? I am, after all, just another fool in love with love.

Dreams are not the same thing as fantasy. In fantasy we try to force reality into a mold we have already created. When we dream we create new realities and mold ourselves to fit them. So dare to dream of a new kind of love. After years of chaos, sanity has taken on a surreal quality. In reality love can be quiet and comfortable, a positive feeling of respect and tenderness for the other person. Sometimes love is just...there.

Sometimes the idea of a relationship where two people just exist can seem scary, but it's really nice once you get used to it. I'm not trying to sell you anything. The last thing you need is another fairy tale, we've all seen how they really turn out.

Time after time the castles came crashing down from the sky and Prince Charming turned out to be another Toad. The last thing you need is the hope of something else that doesn't exist, but healthy relationships really do exist. You just have to program your mind to accept it when it comes along.

But you are good with fantasies when you want to believe them, so dream now for just a moment of a fantasy world where love isn't about controlling one another but simply loving and being loved.

It's okay to dream again, it really is.

Don't we all deserve...

> *A love where you exist in a partnership but still maintain an identity separate from it.*
>
> *A love that leaves you free to have your own hobbies and interests, and your own friends and support systems.*
>
> *A love that is based in reality, on what is happening here and now, not what will be "someday, when..."*
>
> *A love where you are encouraged to develop yourself within the relationship as well as outside of it.*
>
> *A love where you enjoy time spent alone as well as with others.*
>
> *A love where the partners are secure in their roles even when they differ from the norm.*

A love where two people can just come together as equals and share their lives.

A love where problems are acknowledged and dealt with in constructive ways.

A love where communication is honest, clear, and without expectation.

A love where partners take responsibility for getting their needs met.

A love where interactions are based on an underlying affection felt for one another.

A love where sex is a free choice between two loving people.

A love where partners' moods are reasonably stable and independent of one another.

A love where two people come together and work toward solutions.

A love where change doesn't have to be a threat.

A love where there is trust.

A love where your thoughts and feelings are safe.

A love where partners seek to understand one another even when they disagree.

A love where there is no need to protect yourself or hide your true self away.

A love where there is plenty of room for both people to grow and change.

A love where individuality is encouraged and even celebrated.

A love that gains its security from your own confidence and strengths.

A love where neither partner is dependent upon the other.

A love you receive simply because you are you.

Roll Call

Angela Shelton
Actress
Incest Survivor

Clara Bow
Actress
Incest Survivor

Deelish
Reality TV Star
Rape Survivor

Rita Hayworth
Actress
Incest Survivor

Suzanne Somers
Actress
Domestic Violence Survivor

Promise me you'll survive. That you won't give up, no matter what happens, no matter how hopeless. Promise me now, Rose, and never let go of that promise.

~Jack Dawson – Titanic

Letting Go Of The Remains

My daughter Brooke and I have collected a great deal of Titanic memorabilia over the years and have been to the Titanic Artifact Exhibit In Las Vegas, Nevada twice. One of those trips was to observe the 100th anniversary of the sinking of the Titanic.

Simply put, we are obsessed.

One woman suggested that we were on the Titanic when it sank in some past life, and this may explain our fascination. I know nothing about past lives, but in this life the Titanic has touched us both deeply. So of course we have seen the movie dozens of times. And we still cry every single time.

We still read every book we can find on the subject, and it's a lot of work to tell the facts from the fantasy. We have long known that the famous love story portrayed in the movie between pampered socialite Rose and the mysterious adventurer Jack was pure movie magic. Romantic? Sure. Inspirational? Definitely. One of the greatest movies ever made? Quite possibly.

Right up until the end…

Who could forget the lovers' final moments together? Rose is alive when the rescue boat finally comes for her, but just barely. Debris from the grand ship is all around them, and so many, many bodies. Rose tries to awaken Jack. She calls his name, she tries to rouse him…

Jack is gone.

In that moment, Rose has to make a decision, and she makes it. She lets go. He disappears into the icy depths and she goes on with her life.

I've never quite forgiven her for that. I don't know what I expected Rose to do. She couldn't have gone through her life dragging a corpse around behind her, could she?

Every single time that I watch the movie I still secretly hope that they find a way to save Jack. There was plenty of room in my imagination for a happy ending. She could have pulled him to safety and found a way to warm him. They could have given him whiskey and a blanket and found he was still alive. Stranger things have happened...

It didn't happen. Jack still died. Rose still let go.

When the movie first came out I was still married to my ex-husband. I remember the end of my first marriage, realizing that if I didn't leave I was going to die. Not that he would kill me, but that I would no longer be able to find a reason to go on. The things that went on in that home were slowly sucking the life out of me. I could see the light in my children's eyes dying too.

I've held on to a lot of relationships long after I should've let go. They weren't corpses just yet, but they might as well have been.

Once I understood the difference between a victim and a Survivor it changed the way I saw everything in life. The ending of Titanic has never changed, it still sinks, thousands of people still die, and Rose lets go every single time.

Titanic didn't change, but I did.

All of those years I had held a grudge against Rose for giving up so easily. In my mind, she was a quitter.

The hard part wasn't the going on, it was the letting go.

It usually is.

Rose was a Survivor. If she had held on, they both would have died. She didn't have time to mourn what she was leaving behind. She could not survive and keep holding on. She let go because she had no other choice.

Rose didn't give up; she fought on.

Unless you have found a way to bend space and time, you are stuck with the past you have. You can't wish it away, worry it away, deny it away, or avoid it. It is there and nothing is going to change that.

Go ahead, just try to change the past. I'll wait.

...

How long have you been dragging your own corpses around behind you?

It's hard to tread water with all of that baggage you know. We carry negative emotions around with us long after the abuse is over, dragging them around like corpses.

Regret, shame, and guilt all stem from past experiences. Sometimes those memories are there for a reason, as a way of learning from past mistakes, but they were never meant to be a permanent state of mind. We all have circum-stances in our lives that we wish we could go back and change, no doubt about it.

There will be times in life when you will make poor decisions, when you will do things you shouldn't, when you are left wish-ing you had turned right instead of left. Wishing you hadn't worn that skirt that night.

Give it ten minutes, ten years, or ten lifetimes. Barring the invention of a memory eraser, you are stuck with your past as it happened. It's not fair, but it's the stone-cold truth.

No matter who did what to you, what's done is done, and nobody else is going to fix the dam-age for you.

You had control over your actions but not those of your abuser. Your responsibility stops where the other per-son's starts.

Let go.

All of the bitterness in the world isn't going to change a single damn thing. Waste all of the time you want, it isn't going to have much of an effect on their life. The only life that will be destroyed is yours.

The abuser is responsible for the abuse, but you are responsible for every step you have taken since then. I know how unfair it is that someone else left a mess, but it is still there. If you don't clean it up, nobody else will. The sooner you figure that out, the better.

We like to focus on the problem, and yes, it is very easy to do, but focusing your energy on something only feeds it.

If you want to fix your problems you have to determine responsibility for them first. You knew there was a catch, didn't you?

Yes. I am talking about forgiveness. Please don't move along just yet.

Well-meaning, too-much-helping-type people are so quick to encourage you to forgive and forget your abuse, and that has kept a lot of Survivors scared for a long time. Our pain has been a very private one, not something that's easy for others to understand.

Maybe there's even a part of us that is afraid that forgiving the abuse is the same thing as forgetting about it. We were betrayed by people who were supposed to love us. Sometimes forgiving them feels a lot like betraying ourselves. Forgiveness is so much easier said than done.

What are you supposed to forgive, exactly? Do we forgive the past wounds or the present scars? The acts themselves? The effect they had on your life? The fact that they keep doing it no matter how deeply it hurts?

Feed your problems until they burst, but don't be surprised when they take over your whole life.

All problems large or small are fixed the same way: by focusing on the solution.

Some of our abusers are still hurting us today.

It can be difficult knowing that the harmful people in your past have gone on with their lives. For the most part your pain has little or no effect on them today. They've gone on, and the greatest revenge of all is for you to move on with your own life.

Holding on to past hurts to protect you from being harmed in the future is pretty common, but it's still doesn't work.

It helps if you stop thinking of forgiveness as relieving someone else of responsibility. Forgiveness is also giving responsibility where it is due. They don't have to deserve it. They don't have to ask for it either.

You aren't forgiving them for them, silly. When you blame others, you are giving them control over your life. You are allowing them to direct your course. Relieve yourself of your burdens.

Let those corpses go.

The word forgiveness also has a second, less understood definition: *to stop blaming.* You can forgive someone AND allow them to retain responsibility for their own actions. We have a right to know what belongs to us, and to protect it, but we have a responsibility to know what belongs to the other person too.

People have been shifting blame since the beginning of time and will likely continue doing so until the end. In the Christian Bible you will find the creation story of man followed shortly by the very first blame game ever played. Adam blamed Eve, Eve blamed the snake, and no doubt the snake slithered off muttering that the devil made him do it.

From there, we've become a society of victims. Nobody wants to take responsibility for anything anymore. Then again, why should they? We can sue other people for our own stupidity. There is little reason to accept responsibility when someone else can do it for us.

Accepting personal responsibility is a dying art in our modern society. If you need any proof, just look around. Talk shows are filled with people blaming others for their circumstances, but so are prisons, and so are courtrooms. As long as we see ourselves as a culture of doormats, destined to be victims one way or the other, nothing is going to change.

> Your abusers can and will go on with their lives, and you have to give yourself permission to go on with yours too.
>
> It isn't right, it isn't fair, but there isn't a damn thing you can do about it.

When someone wants to avoid the consequences of their actions, the easiest way to do so is to point the finger at someone else. If a girl wearing a short skirt is to blame for the actions of the date-rapist, then the rapist has no responsibility of his own. If the child is responsible for the abuse he received from his parents, then the parents have no responsibility of their own.

Don't confuse pity with love, or rescuing with aiding.

Nothing you can do will save another person who is hell-bent on self-destruction. The more you try to save them, the less responsible they have to be, and it just makes more responsibility fall on you. You will keep giving, they will keep taking, and eventually they will take you down the path of destruction with them. Sound like a few relationships you've had?

Of course abusers want you to take the blame; it's easier than taking responsibility for themselves. If there is a lesson to be learned from your abuse then by all means learn it. If there is something in there that will keep you from being abused in the future, or to help another abuse victim recover, then keep it.

Throw the rest of that junk away.

If you can't use it to better your life, then give it back to its rightful owner. Blame only serves one function: to keep you stuck. Relieving yourself of responsibility for the actions of others while still finding the strength to accept responsibility for your own actions is not easy, but you can't move on without it.

My friend Susan told me long ago that the worst thing you can do for someone that you love is to deny them the consequences of their own actions. When you constantly bail them out, make excuses for them, fix their mistakes, and otherwise take responsibility for them, you are assuring that they will never have a need to take responsibility for themselves.

If you are still stuck, it is not because someone else is holding you back; it is because you haven't made the decision to move forward. Like the concept of victimhood, blame is passive. Blame ensures that no matter what happens it will always be someone else's fault.

Responsibility, on the other hand, is an active concept. It shows that you too are part of the process and therefore have the power to remedy it.

Go ahead. Let go.

Roll Call

Dog the Bounty Hunter
Reality TV Star
Child Abuse Survivor

Drew Barrymore
Actress
Child Abuse Survivor

Eleanor Roosevelt
Former First Lady US
Child Abuse Survivor

Greg Luganis
Olympic Swimmer
Abuse Survivor

Kate Winslet
Actress
Bullying Survivor

Naomi Judd
Singer
Child Sexual Abuse Survivor

"For some reason we see divorce as a signal of failure, despite the fact that each of us has a right and an obligation to rectify any other mistake we make in life."

~ Dr. Joyce Brothers

Abuse, Faith, And The D-Word

After the first draft of this book was released there was one thing that nearly every Survivor that read the book asked me: Why didn't I talk about religion and abuse?

To be honest, I was afraid to.

Abusers like religion. It suits them just fine. A whole book full of rules they can use to justify their control over their targets! They can even back it up with spiritual teachings when pressed.

It shouldn't be surprising to learn that those raised in homes where religion was used as a source of control over the family often have the same codependent traits as those raised by alcoholics.

Those controlled by religion share many of the same traits that victims of abuse display, even when no excessive physical punishment was present. Excessive control in any form can be damaging to those on the receiving end, no matter what is used to justify that control.

I wasn't always the fairly goth mommy that my children know now. There are pictures out there of me looking just like every other mom in the neighborhood. I became a born-again Christian in my early twenties. I was the girl with the Bible always tucked under her arm. By my mid-thirties I had seen enough hurt and pain come from religion to last me a lifetime and I walked away.

For years before that I only met with Christian counselors, I only read Christian self-help, and only sought Christian counsel, just like I was taught to do. I believed everything they ever told me and did my best to live the life required of me, but it just never seemed to be enough. It wasn't just the Bible I was supposed to follow but the individual person's interpretation of it.

Nearly every Christian I knew had a habit of saying one thing and doing another. They talked about love in church in Sunday but treated the people around them like inferiors. They talked of God's all encompassing power, but seemed to think that he couldn't save the world without their input on how it should be done.

Those in the church knew about my abuse, but their answer was to just pray and trust God to take my sorrows away. God would fix me, they said, if I was faithful, if I tried hard enough, if I just...

"But from the beginning of the creation, God made them male and female.' For this reason a man shall leave his father and mother and be joined to his wife, and the two shall become one flesh; so then they are no longer two, but one flesh. Therefore what God has joined together, let not man separate."

~Mark 10:6-9

The church told me to be submissive to my husband, and I was. They told me to please him, and I tried. Oh, how I tried.

Submission... *shudders*

I still remember the day the pastor read Proverbs 31 to us and said that this was God's ideal woman, the goal to which we should all aspire...

"An excellent wife, who can find? For her worth is far above jewels. The heart of her husband trusts in her, and he will have no lack of gain. She does him good and not evil all the days of her life. She looks for wool and flax and works with her hands in delight.

She is like merchant ships; she brings her food from afar. She rises also while it is still night and gives food to her household and portions to her maidens. She considers a field and buys it; from her earnings she plants a vineyard.

She girds herself with strength and makes her arms strong. She senses that her gain is good; her lamp does not go out at night. She stretches out her hands to the distaff, and her hands grasp the spindle. She extends her hand to the poor, and she stretches out her hands to the needy. She is not afraid of the snow for her household, for all her household are clothed with scarlet. She makes coverings for herself; her clothing is fine linen and purple.

Her husband is known in the gates, when he sits among the elders of the land. She makes linen garments and sells them, and supplies belts to the tradesmen. Strength and dignity are her clothing, and she smiles at the future. She opens her mouth in wisdom, and the teaching of kindness is on her tongue.

She looks well to the ways of her household, and does not eat the bread of idleness. Her children rise up and bless her; her husband also, and he praises her, saying: "Many daughters have done nobly, but you excel them all."

Charm is deceitful and beauty is vain, but a woman who fears the LORD, she shall be praised. Give her the product of her hands, and let her works praise her in the gates."

With every syllable the pastor spoke, my heart sank just a little bit further. The women around me were all smiling and nodding and I just wanted to cry. My house was always a disaster zone. The kids called my utility room "laundry mountain." I was shite with money.

My hopes of reaching this unattainable goal were about a million to one. I was an example of everything a wife shouldn't be. There was no way I could earn anybody's love at so steep a price.

Some in the church even told me that my body did not belong to me, that it was my husband's to claim or ignore as he pleased.

I felt guilt about having sex, or even wanting it but it was the only affection I really understood. As his secret visits to the world of pornography increased, he lost interest in me entirely. I still wanted sex and he didn't, and that, too, was one of my failures as a Christian wife.

I prayed constantly. I even laid hands on my husband every night while he was sleeping. I asked God to help me be that perfect wife in Proverbs so that my husband would love me and stop pushing me away. If he had beaten me even once I would have left, but he didn't.

I didn't count pushing me against the wall, bruising me, punching holes in the walls, or using words and insults to wound deeper than any fist could ever go. He had to live through my breakdowns and freak-outs, too. It was chaos and our kids were in the middle.

There was nothing left unbroken between us but that final promise.

I thought my marriage was my cross to bear, punishment for all of the things I had done wrong in my life. I was slowly dying. I did things back then that I didn't even understand, and still don't.

Leaving a marriage was on the No-No list. Every Christian knew that. I had made a promise to God and there was no excuse for breaking it. I prayed for him to set me free...

> "So husbands ought also to love their own wives as their own bodies. He who loves his own wife loves himself."
>
> ~Ephesians 5:28

He asked me for a divorce on the day of our sixth anniversary. I didn't hesitate. It was time. We were just putting each other through hell. I was ready to be set free; I just needed his permission to do it. When my Christian friend found out about our pending divorce she tracked me down to tell me I had no right to leave. "It isn't like he beat you or anything," she said. No, I wasn't in great physical danger but my emotional safety was constantly in question.

In my Christian peer's eyes it just meant I needed to try harder. I couldn't get her to understand that there was nothing there to save. Trying to explain what it was like to be married to a man who was either raging or ignoring you fell on deaf ears.

It didn't matter how deeply he hurt my feelings as long as he didn't leave bruises. Many of my old Christian friends shunned me.

The Christians taught me about a God that can do anything, handle anything, a God that can create anything, a God that can see anything.

But I left my first marriage truly believing that God can't handle a simple divorce between two miserable adults.

Divorce is always a very sensitive issue when it comes to the church. I have an aunt that had to petition the Catholic Church for years to get permission to leave her extremely abusive husband. He could have killed her, but doctrine was more important than her safety.

A good Christian wife is supposed to be submissive, to give herself to her husband fully. The Bible neglects the advice on what to do when that marriage is abusive.

The church often leaves the victim with very few choices. You can stay in the relationship, placing yourself and your children in further danger, or you can leave and risk the rejection of your church, which is usually your support group as well.

The church had shunned me. I shunned them back. When my marriage crumbled, so did my faith. I was pissed off at the world and I wanted them to know it. I didn't start out trying to be "Goth," I really just like black. But the more my old Christians labeled me as such, the more I began to embrace it. A lot of those people will look at my outside now and avoid me, and you know what?

I think I did it on purpose.

Nobody can hurt me if they refuse to get close. I pushed them before they had a chance to reject me. If they don't get close, they can't hurt me. This is my armor. It protects me from those who are bound to reject me no matter what. We get it out of the way up front.

As Christian leader John Wimber once said, "God offends the mind to reveal the heart." The real Christians in my life know who I really was under the dark eyeliner and strange hair colors. They reminded me that to be Christian means to be like Christ. They just loved me because I was me.

I saw so little of Christ in the people I came to associate with the church. I wasn't trying to please God; I was trying to please those people.

Instead of escaping abuse I kept pushing myself harder and harder to please my spouse, the church, and ultimately, I hoped, God. The bar was set at perfection all the way around; but they didn't set it, I did.

I tried to please everyone, and even the smallest of failures left me devastated. Just more proof that I wasn't worthy of that fairy tale life I sometimes dreamed about, a life free of abuse.

During my years in the church I learned over and over that there was not much of a difference between abuse and some people's ideas of religion. I was already attracted to controlling types, so the people I was drawn to in the church were not necessarily the healthiest.

It was a long time before I was able to see that it wasn't God that had hurt me but the people in my life who represented him. Their Bible did not contain the same messages as mine. Their Jesus did not speak the same words as mine. They were there for the power and control and nothing more. Churches are a great place for faith, but they don't know shite about psychology.

If God is as big as they say he is then he doesn't need our help or anybody else's. What is between you and God is your own business and nobody else needs to get involved. He's a big boy. He can handle it.

I have heard similar stories from people of all faiths, people who have reached out for help and found condemnation. Instead of advising them to keep themselves safe they were told to try harder to please God, or to pray for their spouses, or to have more faith.

> 'Husbands, love your wives and do not be harsh with them.'
>
> ~Colossians 3:19

People from church offer prayers, empty advice, and the assurance that faith will see you through anything. But it's all empty, isn't it? It is excellent advice for the problems that face your average marriage but total crap for the victim of abuse. Their advice could be exactly what gets you hurt.

If faith has been used to control you in the past, it can be hard to move beyond the idea that God requires nothing short of full submission to those in authority over you. If they have used that authority to abuse you, they were not using it in God's name.

The church has been used to excuse abuse as long as it has existed, but any knowledgeable teacher will tell you that the majority of teachings in the Christian Bible are about love, not control. Jesus specifically commanded followers to care for the children, for family, for spouses, for friends, for neighbors, and even to show hospitality to strangers. Above all the Bible taught us to love each other as Jesus loved us.

WWJD isn't just a catchy saying; it is a commitment. Any person who chooses to call themselves Christian has promised to be like Christ. Even when Jesus drove the money changers out of the temple he remained calm enough to braid a whip. He didn't grab one from the nearest passerby; he took the time to make it. That is not a man who condones abuse. That is a man who condones control over oneself even in the face of burning anger.

Even those that caution against abuse have no idea what to do when followers ignore those commands. Within the Christian church, those who are brave enough to come forward with confessions of abuse are met with doubt and denial.

Sadly, many religions objectify women, reducing them to property. They excuse abuse as a husband's or a parent's right, and even duty. The women are often punished, but rarely, if ever, is anything done to the abuser. The abuse is minimized or excused. Victims are ostracized. It isn't right, but it happens all of the time.

Denial. Repentance. Forgiveness. Continuance.

Not once in all of the years I sought counsel did a single spiritual leader identify my past experiences as abuse. The word was never even used.

> Husbands, love your wives, just as Christ loved the church and gave himself up for her.
>
> ~Ephesians 5:25

While some faiths make the concession for physical abuse, they gloss over verbal and emotional abuse completely. Some encourage submission to a spouse and make no distinction at all between submission and being a victim. So many who have escaped abuse have met with resistance and criticism from their religious peers and the leadership of the church.

Most of those people were just trying to help, but like me, they did not have the proper tools to recognize or cope with abuse. We all use the tools that we have at our disposal, but recovering from abuse doesn't require a hammer and nails. You are going to need to break out the power tools now and then.

Most pastors have some experience in family counseling, but they tend to approach it from the standpoint of keeping the family together. Quite often a spiritual counselor will ask both parties in a relationship to attend counseling sessions. That method works well for basic therapy, but when your partner is abusive this approach can be very dangerous.

Couples counseling requires emotional honesty from both partners and a safe place in which to express those emotions. Emotional honesty is not safe when the abuser is present–a lesson that many victims have already learned the hard way.

Exposing your most vulnerable self to an abuser in public can lead to the worst retaliation in private. Bullies are used to being on stage and they play their parts well. Any resistance on the part of a victim can be played off as an unwillingness to work with their partner. The counselor can be sucked in just as easily as the victim was.

Spiritual counselors are in the business of saving marriages, but they don't always stop to ask themselves if a marriage *should* be saved in the first place.

There are options for those who are not yet ready to consider divorce for spiritual reasons though.

I have known a few Survivors who found their own ways to honor both their faith and church doctrine. They have stayed legally married despite years of physical separation, or have decided not to remarry and continue to honor their first marriage after having obtained a legal divorce.

These choices may not be popular, but they reach the intended goal. They protect the Survivor and put some distance between them and their abuser. You were commanded to keep your promises, but so was your spouse.

If it really is an issue then don't worry about the actual divorce until you are ready, if you ever are. If you can't do it because of your faith then at least get yourself somewhere safe. You don't have to file for divorce to leave the relationship physically. Learn to place yourself at a safe distance from bullies and set some healthy boundaries for yourself.

The church does not outright teach that abuse is something you must accept, but in the legalistic mind of the abuse Survivor it can easily become so. When you find yourself in the position of either accepting abuse in the name of faith or walking away for your own safety, it is a hard barrier to cross. Especially when you fear that hell might be waiting on the other side.

After my divorce I spent a lot of time studying the major religions of the world, and even a few of the minor ones, on a quest to discover if there was any agreement among them. I thought it was an impossible goal, but it turns out that there is one common belief shared among nearly every religion I have ever studied.

The Dalai Lama expressed it most succinctly when he said, "Every religion emphasizes human improvement, love, respect for others, sharing other people's suffering. On these lines every religion had more or less the same viewpoint and the same goal."

It is known as the *ethic of reciprocity*, or *the golden rule*. Some call it karma while others call it the threefold rule. Either way, it all means the same thing.

> *What thou avoidest suffering thyself seek not to impose on others.*
>
> ~Ancient Greek Philosophy

> "Blessed is he who preferreth his brother before himself."
>
> ~Baha'i

> "One who, while himself seeking happiness, oppresses with violence other beings who also desire happiness, will not attain happiness hereafter."
>
> ~Buddhism

> "Do unto others as you would have them do unto you"
>
> ~Christianity

> "Never impose on others what you would not choose for yourself."
>
> ~Confucianism

> "That man who regards all creatures as his own self, and behaves towards them as towards his own self, laying aside the rod of chastisement and completely subjugating his wrath, succeeds in attaining to happiness."
>
> ~Hinduism

> "That which you want for yourself, seek for mankind."
>
> ~Islam

> "Thou shalt not take vengeance, nor bear any grudge against the children of thy people, but thou shalt love thy neighbour as

thyself: I am the LORD."

~*Judaism*

"The sage has no interest of his own, but takes the interests of the people as his own. He is kind to the kind; he is also kind to the unkind: for Virtue is kind. He is faithful to the faithful; he is also faithful to the unfaithful: for Virtue is faithful."

~*Taoism*

"If no harm is done, do as you will"

~*Wiccan Rede*

"And, in the end, the love you take is equal to the love you make."

~*The Beatles*

How we treat others comes back to us. Apply that to yourself, but apply it to your abuser as well. Get yourself out of the way of their karma or it's going to keep coming, and you are going to keep paying for it. If you are in the wrong, then that is on your conscience and your conscience alone. That's between you and God.

I was always taught that the whole point of human creation was to allow us our own free will. Nobody can force you to comply with God's will. Nobody else can define it for you either. Religion used to control others is still abuse.

> Do you not know that your body is a temple of the Holy Spirit, who is in you, whom you have received from God? You are not your own; you were bought at a price. Therefore honor God with your body.
>
> ~1 Corinthians 6:19-20

We still need faith though. We need faith in something and someone better than ourselves, someone who can handle the things that we can't. Many abuse Survivors credit their spirituality for helping them heal. If your faith is important to you then hold on to it. Don't let anybody take it from you, but don't let it keep you in misery either.

Keep yourself safe first, for yourself, for your loved ones, and even for your God. If you believe that God loves all creatures, then why deny yourself that love?

There are people out there who are trained in advocacy for victims from all religions and all walks of life. They can help you with your specific beliefs far better than I. If you can't get the support that you need from your spiritual leaders then find someone who can offer it.

"Til death do you part" is a noble promise, but not if it is your marriage that is killing you.

⬥⬥⬥

Victims of Domestic Violence

Bai Jing
Chinese Actress
Murder Victim

Laci Peterson (and child)
Wife of Scott Peterson
Murder Victim

Nancy Benoit (and son)
Wife of Wrestler Chris Benoit
Murder Victims

Nicole Brown Simpson
Exwife of OJ Simpson
Murder Victim

Phil Hartman
Actor/Comedian
Murder Victim

"I once had a feeling, and when it was there it was as if it had always been a part of me. But when that feeling left me I felt as if it had been nothing but a dream all along. Later, my feeling returned to me and it was as if it had never left me at all."

~Unknown

An Emotional World

I am an excessively emotional drama queen, but I am sociopath too. I am both a kind and loving person and a cold-hearted bitch. I am a good person. I am a bad person. I am everything in between. I've never really understood how all of those people could exist inside of one body but, according to others, those personalities are all there.

I don't have a multiple personality disorder, but I do feel that way when I try to live up to all of the different expectations others have of me. What I have felt were a million emotions, each one simultaneously vying for my immediate attention. While one person was telling me not to be too emotional, the next was saying that I didn't have enough of whatever it was I was supposed to have. Dozens of stations bleeding through the television of my mind, and someone else always seemed to have control of the remote.

Survivors walk emotional tightropes a great deal of the time, as if there is a right way and a wrong way to respond to certain events. We aren't talking about scientific theory or historic documentation here, we are talking about feelings.

Some abusers weren't content with just controlling our bodies or our lives. Even our minds were their playgrounds.

If we express our feelings we never really know how we will be punished, only that we will be, with name calling, insults, hurtful teasing and threats. Perhaps we will be ignored. Perhaps we will be chastised. Perhaps they will just tell us that we are just plain wrong.

So, we learn to stuff our feelings down deep inside where they are safe. Sometimes we push them so far away that we lose track of them entirely. We replace those "bad" feelings with ones that are more acceptable to the bullies in our lives, but they have nothing at all to do with who we are or what we need.

These fake feelings exist only on the surface. Surfaces can be scratched, and sometimes when under enough pressure they can rupture entirely. It is controlling your way to an emotionally out-of-control life.

There are many indirect ways to cope with your emotions, but unaddressed feelings are like a powder keg. All it takes is an ignition source, and it doesn't matter who is in the way once the explosion happens. You may strike out at strangers. You may take it out on yourself. You blow up at your children, your spouse, or your coworkers. You become depressed. You become self-destructive.

After years of being told not only what to feel but how to feel it, I learned to shut down emotionally. When my emotions threatened to engulf me I just denied they existed at all. I sometimes cut or injured myself just to numb the deep pain I was feeling. For many years I thought I was the only one who did it. This was long before cutting was "fashionable."

I shut out the parts of life I couldn't deal with and hyper-focused on what I thought I could handle. Physical pain I could handle. Keeping my focus on anything distracted me from the things in my head that I couldn't avoid. Injuring myself was better than hurting others, but I still felt guilty. I was still ashamed.

I would stuff until I could stuff no more, and then I would break.

All of those built-up emotions would come pouring out of me at once, and I had no idea what to do with them. If there was nobody else around to punish, I punished myself. I tried to outrun it. I would literally push myself until I dropped.

I turned it into a way of life, and not a very satisfying one. I found many ways to numb myself over the years, ways that were far less noticeable to the outside world and far more acceptable to me. They sort of covered things up for awhile, but never for very long.

Self-destructive behavior is an effective distraction from the emotional pain that we are not yet ready to deal with. It will not work forever. As more distractions from the chaos are needed your problems multiply and things start falling apart.

Your emotions are supposed to serve you, but when they are in charge, chaos is always the result. We try to steer our emotions in the direction we think they ought to go, but they boil just below the surface, delayed but never denied.

Those emotions are still there whether you allow yourself to feel them or not. All it takes is a moment when your defenses are weakened and they come pouring out. When you are tired, or hungry, or under stress, your strength lets go. Before you know it, you find yourself yelling at someone who doesn't deserve it, making small issues into large ones, or crying with little or no provocation.

> The proper response to "I feel" is not "you shouldn't feel that way." The proper response to "I want" is not "no you don't." The proper response to "I believe" is not "this is why you are wrong."
>
> ⊜
>
> There are no right and wrong answers.

What a mess.

Now we have added present feelings of guilt and frustration, anger and shame. That pile of emotions just keeps growing into a tower, into a mountain range. The feelings and emotions will wait as long as they need to but eventually they will be dealt with or lead to your destruction. We become workaholics, people pleasers, constant worriers. It doesn't matter how we are destroyed, only that we are.

Some of us cut or injure ourselves outright, but drugs, alcohol, and promiscuity all play their part in our self-destruction. You find more ways to tone it down: sex...food...fantasies...

Instead of dealing with your emotions you stuff them and try to make them "right." You may even learn to deny them totally.

If we lived in an emotionally healthy society we would all be taught that emotions are tools, and tools are meant to be used. They sometimes require training in order to be used properly, but they are nothing to be afraid of.

When you feel physical pain it is an alert from your body that you have a problem that needs to be addressed. You may need rest, medication, or even a visit to the doctor, but ignoring or minimizing physical pain often leads to injuring yourself even further. What could have been a quick fix with an antibiotic can quickly, if ignored, become a lengthy hospital stay.

Many people have been taught that it is wrong to be angry, sad, or hurt, but those internal indicators that something is wrong are there for a reason. Emotions may be easier to ignore than physical pain, but the consequences of not dealing with them can be just as dangerous.

Feelings are tools that serve to keep you aware of the world around you. Functioning as part of your survival instincts, they protect you when you are in danger, alert you to injury, and help you form bonds with others for both protection and companionship. They tell you a great many things about your circumstances if dealt with directly.

There is no such thing as a wrong feeling. All feelings are valid. All feelings belong to you. You ignore them at your own peril. When you don't trust your emotions, you don't trust yourself.

> Emotions can be painful, but they can also be life-giving. Allow yourself to experience them fully as they come..
>
> ⊜
>
> They give you the capacity to love and to be loved in return. They are what can bring you to tears, yes, but they are also responsible for what brings you laughter.

Experiencing the good emotions also means sometimes experiencing the bad, and that's what really scares us. Learn whatever lessons those feelings are trying to teach you so you can grow through them and past them.

It doesn't matter if you need to laugh or cry as long as you find a healthy way to do so. You can be angry or you can be joyful. Don't hide from your emotions find healthy ways to acknowledge them and release them.

For some that release can be found in a hobby or physical activity that they enjoy. For others it can be more of an intellectual pursuit. You may find that you need support and encouragement from a trusted friend, or you may find that you just need to be alone.

Many see my discomfort with the physical discipline of children as a lack of strength. On the contrary, I think the real display of strength is NOT hitting someone in anger. If my answer to emotional upsets is striking out and hurting others then I am just continuing the cycle.

We can do a lot of damage acting on our feelings, but we can do a lot of good if we so choose.

Power struggles with my children are a waste of time. We have found far more constructive ways to communicate than screaming about proper adult and child roles in the home, enforcing rock-hard rules, or telling them what to think and how to feel.

My children are human beings. They have wants, needs, and rights just as much as I do. I try not to stray from that. Sometimes I do, but my children are well aware of their rights as human beings and so am I.

If I do not want it done to me I refuse to do it to my children. It's that simple.

In teaching my children to recognize their emotions and express them constructively, I broke all of the parenting rules. For this I am often be labeled as a "politically correct" parent, and it is assumed that my children have run wild.

> Stop ignoring your feelings. They are there to bring your attention to a need in your life.
>
> It makes no difference if your emotions are positive or negative; both types are there for a purpose. There is a whole range of human emotion to experience.

I know I am supposed to be doing things differently, but there is no defense in my mind for being a bully. Anybody who knows them will tell you that they are some of the most considerate children you will ever meet, until you try to force them to do something they feel is wrong. They do try to leave the world a better place than they found it, but they refuse to be victims while doing it.

If you expect a child to be honest with you, be honest with them. If you don't want your children calling each other names, refrain from calling them names. Do not hit children that you don't want to hit you in return. We all screw up sometimes. Our tempers flare. Our mouths run out of control. We say things we don't mean.

We can do better.

We will all make mistakes, but a simple apology followed by a sincere attempt to correct it goes a long way.

If I tell my children how they should feel, or act, or be, they will never learn to do those things for themselves.

I am a big believer in rules, but not the solid unquestionable legalism of my past. Emotions do not comply with laws. Emotions flow and change depending on the circumstances, how those situations have impacted our lives in the past, and how they will affect our lives in the future. I didn't make my children's decisions for them; I expected them to make good decisions for themselves.

As a teenager, some of my most self destructive times were when I was dealing with difficult emotions: after a breakup, being teased and bullied at school, feeling misunderstood in my home life. I didn't always know what to do with all of those feelings, so I turned them inward.

I knew that someday all of those things would happen to my children someday, there was little that I could do to prevent it. So I taught them to deal with their most difficult times before they happened.

We talk about the decisions they are making in their lives and how they will affect their futures. We talk about the good decisions they have made and why they bettered their lives or the lives of others. We talk about the decisions that led to unpleasant consequences and what lessons they have learned. It has been an odd experiment in parenting from the outside, but I was not raising victims, I was raising Survivors.

If you are having trouble finding the good memories.

Go out and make some new ones. While you are at it, why not make them good ones?

I have the only daughter I know who deals with break-ups by building dollhouses and planting gardens. I can't say that she has avoided any of the pain that the teen years can bring, but she sure has handled them a hell of a lot better than I ever did.

She knows that she is the only one who is truly responsible for her feelings. You can create with the same passion and energy with which you destroy, if you focus it. Use that energy to fuel your passions and you will find a whole new life waiting.

Find your passions and enhance them with those emotions. Put it into your cooking, your scrapbooking, or your volunteer work. Write it, paint it, sculpt it, photograph it, or sketch it. Try capturing your emotions in different ways and see what feels best. Put it into creating something worthwhile. There is a great deal of tension built up underneath some of our oldest feelings. Only by staying with the emotions involved can you deal with and eventually resolve them. You have to acknowledge the pressure before you can relieve it. I know how frightening that may sound, but like many steps in the process it gets easier with time.

Your emotions belong to you. Only you can name them, only you can feel them, and only you are responsible for them. Emotions can be frightening when you aren't able to handle them properly. You can't let them roam around at will; that's just inviting trouble. You have to contain them at first, like the wild animals they are. Contain them, soothe them, and then redirect their attentions to more constructive pursuits.

Stop waiting until you explode and express yourself in ways that are likely to result in a negative outcome. Stop fighting your emotions and open yourself up to the lessons they offer.

Instead of allowing my children to flail like I did, I tried to teach them the things that I didn't know all of those years ago, lessons that I had to learn the hard way.

There are healthy ways of dealing with your feelings, but it takes some practice...

Recognize your emotions.

If you haven't been listening to them for a long time then you may not even know where to start. Anger may be masking fear, fear may be masking sorrow, and sorrow may be masking shame. Pull off those masks and see what lies underneath.

Name your emotions.

Are you angry today? Or is that anger really just irritation? It could be rage that is making you feel the way you do, but it could also be sadness or fear pretending to be anger. Expand your emotional vocabulary and learn to name each emotion as it comes using the proper feeling and the proper degree. The clerk at the store may be irritating, but does it really need to cross into fury? Probably not.

Accept your emotions for what they are.

Just a fact...your emotions send you important signals about what is going on in your life, and you owe it to yourself to listen to them. They are a weather report on the kingdom of you.

Figure out what your emotions are trying to tell you.

If your emotions function as some sort of alert, then what are they trying to alert you to? Are they trying to tell you that a certain person or situation is unsafe? Are they trying to tell you that someone has just crossed your personal boundaries? Are they trying to tell you that some need is going unmet? Listen first, and then learn.

Trust your emotions.

As Survivors, you often push emotions aside while looking for what you may consider a sane solution. Instead of getting yourself to safety when you are uncomfortable you tell yourself not to be silly. When someone crosses your personal boundaries and you feel violated, you tell yourself that it really wasn't that big of a deal, so you should just let it go. When it comes to your attention that your needs are going unmet, you fear you are just being selfish. You discount your feelings and you say you have no right to feel them, but those feelings are tools, and the more you use them the more accurate they become.

Deal with emotions before they become a problem.

Emotions should be addressed and dealt with as soon as possible after the fact. Sometimes just being honest about your feelings can release a large part of your stress, but you aren't always in a position to deal with emotions right away. If this is the case then make a note in your mind and promise yourself that you will deal with it at "X" time. Make sure to do so as soon as you possibly can; this is one date you really should keep. The longer you put it off, the harder it is to connect with that initial feeling.

Life is so very short. Live, love, laugh...but whatever you do, FEEL.

Roll Call

Ella Fitzgerald
Singer
Abuse Survivor

Fran Drescher
Actress
Rape Survivor

Gabrielle Union
Actress
Rape Survivor

Helen Mirren
Actress
Rape Survivor

Kelly McGillis
Actress
Rape Survivor

Teri Hatcher
Actress
Incest Survivor

"Any problem, big or small, within a family, always seems to start with bad communication. Someone isn't listening."

~Emma Thompson

Just Say What You Mean

Communication should be the simplest thing in the world. One person speaks, the other listens, it is understood, and all needs are met. But it never seems to happen that way, does it?

Your methods are only effective if the message is sent and received accurately. What you don't say can sometimes be just as important as what you do say.

There is far more to communication than just opening up your mouth and seeing what comes out. How you say it, when you say it, why you say it, and who you say it to all play a part. Communication is complicated business.

You don't have to take a college course on communication to enter into a relationship, but you do need to understand the basics if you plan on being involved with other human beings.

If you can't communicate, you can't participate fully in any type of relationship.

There are so many different types of communication in this world but there are three basic types used to confuse and befuddle relationships the world over: passive, aggressive, and of course the favorite of both victims and abusers alike, the good old passive-aggressive playbook.

They are all very different means to an end, but they have one thing in common...they usually just make things worse.

It's like purchasing a piece of property where your neighbor makes use of your yard whenever they wish. At first it isn't so bad. They plant flowers, then they plant trees, and soon they are chaining their dog up on your property.

If you are a passive communicator, you ignore it and tell yourself that it really isn't a bother but you always seem to stop short of action.

Instead of saying anything you just watch them take it over, until one day you wake up to find they have placed a fence right up against your house.

The problem with passive communication is that you wait so long to take action that you end up being just as much at fault as your neighbor.

Your friends and family would have to be mind readers to understand the messages you are trying to send. At first it doesn't seem like a big deal, so you don't want to make a fuss. People take and take, and you keep giving. It would have been a lot easier if you had just clarified the property lines in the first place, but you avoided yourself right into an even bigger mess.

> Passive communication is like turning yourself into a giant doormat and inviting anyone and everyone to wipe their feet on you.
>
> Rights that aren't asserted tend to waste away in both your own mind and the mind of the abuser.

Did you get what you wanted here? No, because while you are out looking at your property your neighbor called the police on you for trespassing and you are the one making phone calls to raise bail.

Passive behavior is exactly what it says it is: taking a passive role in your own life. You fail to respect your own rights and feel as if you don't have a right to ask for things you want. You hold other people responsible for things that only you can remedy. Favorite tools of the trade for getting needs met: guilt and pity.

Those who use passive behavior tend to feel as if their rights are consistently violated. They aren't; they just aren't detectable for the average person. Boundary disputes are destined to happen when there are no real boundaries in the first place.

The passive person doesn't really feel they have the right to speak up. As the abuser violates more and more of their rights, they fade away into the mists of time. Rights that aren't asserted tend to waste away in both your own mind and the mind of the abuser. The abuser gets their needs met at your expense, and it works, for them.

If you don't stand up for yourself then you will be the world's doormat.

If your intention in communication is to avoid conflict or discomfort then there isn't much of a point in talking at all. Conflict is still a part of healthy relationships; a much smaller part than we are used to, but it does happen.

Conflict is a part of life, but there are limits.

Nobody in, nobody out, and life has suddenly become all about you.

Aggressive people have an inflated sense of entitlement. They don't ask, they demand. The world owes them, so they take what they want. You get your own needs met at someone else's expense.

Directing the lives of others brings with it an illusion of control, but it is only an illusion. You avoid responsibility for things that you have control over and hold other people responsible for things that only you can remedy. You take the lead in the communication process but only at the expense of others. Favored tools of the trade for getting needs met: fear, intimidation, and threats.

And now, you are the neighbor. That property next door to you was vacant for years. Nobody was using it until you came along. It wasn't even being taken care of. In reality you are doing them a favor, taking a burden off of their shoulders if you will, and don't you deserve it after all that you have been through?

Aggressive people attempt to get bigger by making other people smaller. They insult, pick, and tease. It puts other people on the defense, and the walls go up. If both parties are taking an aggressive stance then nobody is really listening to anything being said because they are so busy defending themselves.

If your communication is intended to control others or to hurt them then they will eventually stop communicating entirely. There will still be words, and even full conversations. If you really pay attention though, nobody is saying anything. They are dancing around on the surface, but it never goes any deeper.

If you can't trust someone with your true self, you stop sharing it all together.

Now, let's switch back to being the homeowner for a while, the one who was arrested for trespassing on their own property. How likely is it that your wants and needs are going to change because your neighbor is trying to force you? It may feel good to be the one in control, but resentment builds when you are not. You dig your heels in and fight.

In an attempt to balance ourselves out we adopted a bit of this extreme and a bit of that extreme. Neither is effective, but that doesn't stop people from clinging to those old habits.

It might seem then like the best alternative is to combine these communication styles. Actually, sometimes that is even worse.

When you are passive-aggressive you attempt to get your needs met through the most indirect means possible. You build up secret resentment for unspoken needs that nobody even knew existed in the first place. They are not expressed outright, just implied. Doors are slammed, feet are stomped, and catty remarks are made under the breath. You tell everybody BUT the person you are angry with. You may apologize on the outside, but deep down you still feel like you got screwed. Problems are danced around instead of addressed.

> Aggressive behavior violates the rights of other people. Now that doormat has been replaced by a brick wall.
>
> While it may feel better to be the one wiping your feet at the door than being the doormat, it once again places the control of your life in the hands of another.

Your method of control is chaos.

If you are passive-aggressive, you invite the neighbor to use your land then blame them for taking you up on the offer. One day you don't mind, the next you expect something in return. Then you want to know why they never come see you anymore. You move the fence back and forth depending on your moods. Everybody is confused.

There certainly are times when you must be more aggressive than others, such as when defending yourself against an assailant, but visiting your elderly grandmother in the hospital requires a more passive approach. If you get those two confused a lot, problems will arise.

There isn't even an illusion of control with passive-aggressive people. There are no real boundaries, just implied ones. They are adults that act like children, controlling while appearing to be helpless, manipulating others into doing what they want them to do, and getting needs met through indirect means.

The worst part is, we all do it. How anybody ever expects to get their message across while actively trying to cloud that same message is beyond me.

You think you have sent the message but you've only confused thing further. It doesn't solve the problem. It doesn't even clarify it. It is just more complications.

Though most people tend to have a single dominant style that leads their communication efforts, we often move between the three different styles depending on the circumstances. Some people are passive with strangers and dominant with those they are more familiar with. Some push total strangers around, while being treated poorly in their own homes.

If we would all learn to say what we mean and mean what we say, the need for therapy would decline across the nation. Divorce rates would drop, families would function, and our nation would be stronger as a whole. It would almost be too easy. When you were hungry you would simply say, "I am hungry," instead of "A burger sure does sound good right now." Instead of saying, "I don't care," you would say "I really do care, and this is exactly what I want right now." Or how about "That hurt my feelings," instead of "Why do you always have to go there in front of my parents?" Life would be a little more boring, but at least we could all understand one another.

In the beginning when two people truly trust one another the communication is at its best. Both lines are open. Everyone is participating. Then over time a bit of that trust is naturally lost. Hurts and insults begin to add up and they get more difficult to get over. Communication is replaced with all-out battle.

We need to abandon those amazingly useless conversations we have like, "I don't want you to do it *now*. I wanted you to do it *then*. I really just *want you to want to* do it without me having to ask."

There is nothing wrong with wanting them to want to do things with you, but they don't. You can either find a hobby that you both enjoy, find a close friend to do those things with you, or you can choose to go alone. You cannot and will not ever, ever, ever make them want something that they genuinely do not want.

You can con them of course (passive), or you can force them (aggressive), and you can even manipulate them (passive-aggressive), but you will never win them over until you answer the one question that is burning bright in their minds.

"What's in it for me?"

Show them how their happiness will be achieved by helping you get what you want and you will have a willing partner.

Control is often a key factor in communication. The underlying goal is to build a specific image, to illicit a certain response, or to obtain information. Both parties are trying to get their needs met, both are trying to be heard.

When you come to someone saying, "This is what I want," their brain can't help but ask "What's in it for me?" Will it make them feel good? Will it meet their needs in some way? Will it further their own happiness?

The moment someone's defenses go up you have lost them. You can still walk away from the conversation feeling as if you came out on top, but winning the battle can cost you the war. When it comes to their pleasure, or your pain, the answer is usually obvious: "Me."

> Assertive communication maintains the rights of both parties whenever possible. It does not require a clear winner and a clear loser.
>
> ⊜
>
> Acceptance, respect, personal responsibility, boundaries, and the power of choice are all building blocks to the ultimate goal of an assertive self.

It's okay to need things and even to want them, and it is okay to ask for them directly. Before you approach any situation make sure you know what your goal is, then stop and ask yourself what the other person wants. It isn't giving in or being weak; it is just accepting the facts. People would rather do something willingly than be forced. If you can remember that, you will be better off than most in this lifetime.

You also get the added benefit of avoiding the passive-aggressive temper tantrum - when they go with you, but make sure that you are miserable the entire time. Or when you ask them what's wrong they say "nothing," but they sure don't act like nothing is bothering them.

If you can find a way to reconcile the two without either party feeling as if they have lost then you have both won. If you want them to go to the movies with you, don't tell them what it means to you. Take the time to explain what they will get out of it. If you can peak their interest, offer them something that they truly want, they will be engaged as well.

Ask them to accommodate you now and then, but if it is a regular pattern in your relationship then there may be deeper issues. If all they ever want to do is stay home, and all you want to do is go out, then there is obviously a gap there. How big is that gap? Is it a few cracks in an otherwise smooth sidewalk, or are we talking about the Grand Canyon?

Humans spend far more time trying to control others than trying to better their own lives. Only one of these pursuits will be productive.

The people you share your life with are not responsible for reading your mind and knowing that you have unmet needs. If you have a need, find a way to meet it that leaves your dignity and the other person's intact.

Saying what you mean - and meaning what you say - is a freedom and a responsibility.

Know your weaknesses as well as your strengths. Know your partner's as well. Instead of trying to change those things, utilize them. If you are good with the money and they are the better cook, then use that knowledge to make you both stronger. If you know they don't like large social gatherings and you do then compromise, but remember that you are pushing them into an area they are not comfortable with.

> The goal of assertive communication is to actually communicate.
>
> ⬚
>
> You know, saying exactly what you mean. Shocking I know.

My ex spent years trying to turn me into a good little housewife, and that was that last thing in the world that I was meant to be. He married the wrong woman and I married the wrong man, but we were both too stubborn to admit that for a long time..

Don't exploit another's weaknesses, balance them out. Accept yourself and others at face value. Allow them to have their differences without trying to categorize them and figure out how to use them to the advantage of the relationship. Helping yourself is good, helping others is better, but finding a way to help as many people as possible is always best.

Ed and I have nothing close to a traditional family, but we are willing to get creative to make it work. I am so not a housewife, and he knows that. We threw traditional out the window in favor of what actually works for us.

You don't need to fit people into a black-and-white world anymore. You don't need to have the right feelings, or the right thoughts, or even the right words to be worthy of love. You just need to BE.

You can allow them to BE too. Speak honestly, and in a way that the other person can easily hear and understand. I am all for creativity, but if the message is lost then the audience is lost as well.

The bigger person is not free of faults; they just know how to accept them gracefully. If you are guilty of wrongdoing, admit it. Other people will respect you for taking responsibility for your actions, and you will respect yourself all the more. Sometimes you will make mistakes. Don't slip into defending them, just accept them. Other people are big enough to take responsibility for their own actions as well, so let them.

That, too, is part of being assertive.

If you can find a way to communicate that leaves both people feeling as if their needs have been met, you will find far more willing partners in future efforts. Your goal of being heard is important to you, but if you plan on involving other people then they are coming to the table with their own agenda. They need to be heard just as much as you do.

Communication is not a battle. It doesn't matter who won or who lost; the goal of communication is not to conquer - but to connect.

Roll Call

Dave Pelzer
Author
Abuse Survivor

Dorie VanStone
Author
Abuse Survivor

Halle Berry
Actress/Model
Abuse Survivor

Jill Scott
Singer
Child Sexual Abuse Survivor

Mo'Nique
Actress/Comedian
Childhood Sexual Abuse Survivor

Ricki Lake
Actress, Talk Show Host
Child Sexual Abuse Survivor

*And this is one of
the major questions
of our lives: how
we keep boundar-
ies, what permis-
sion we have to
cross boundaries,
and how we do so.*

~A. B. Yehoshua

Boundaries: Walls And Fences

Even my Girl Scout troop understood that we should always try to leave a person, place, or thing better off than it was when we found it and they were in elementary school.

If you find a place lacking in love, or joy, or passion, then fill it with such

There are nearly seven billion people in this world, and still no two people share the exact same characteristics. That is not an accident.

We have a right to pursue happiness if we so choose, but it comes with a responsibility that we do not claim that happiness at the price of another's misery.

People who have been hurt sometimes build high walls around themselves in order to enforce their personal limits. That invisible fortress protects them at first, but it can so quickly become their prison. Walls keep out those who might harm us, but they also keep us isolated from those that care. Being safe can also be very lonely.

When someone wants to keep dangerous or potentially harmful people away from a piece of property they don't resort to razor wire and concrete walls when picket fences will do the job just as nicely. A fence is there to protect you and whatever belongs to you, but it does not isolate you from the world. People can still see in, you can still see out, and fences even have gates, allowing you to venture past them when the need arises. That's what a relationship is: venturing outside.

Boundaries tell you where your property ends and another person's property begins. Boundaries tell you where *you* begin and where *you* end.

In the physical world property limits are usually marked, perhaps by a fence, a survey marker, or landscaping. It's nice and simple. Even the law requires you to respect them in most cases, as long as the lines are clear.

There is one basic kind of boundary in the real estate world, a simple dividing line between here and there. Those you deem safe can pass through while those you feel threatened by are kept out. A clear line between what you own and what you do not.

Body, mind, and spirit create a human being and when joined together, a whole person. Wholeness is not possible in an abusive relationship because abuse keeps us fractured. Humans have different types of limits that can vary depending on the person and the situation. The first and most obvious are your physical boundaries...

"All human beings are born free and equal in dignity and rights. They are endowed with reason and conscience and should act towards one another in a spirit of brotherhood."

~Article 1 of the United Nations Universal Declaration of Human Rights

Physical boundaries are the most concrete, but you have a right to set your own emotional space as well. You have a right to your feelings, and you have a right to express them in an appropriate manner. You have a right to set your emotional boundaries firmly with those who can cause you harm.

Personal limits let us know that someone is crossing over into our territory. People have their spaces, too. They aren't visible, they aren't even tangible, but they are there. Since you can't put up "No Trespassing" signs around yourself marking your boundaries clearly can be very difficult, but without markers how will someone know when they have gone somewhere they don't belong?

In the abuser's world boundaries are always open to interpretation. What they did not own today they may quite possibly own tomorrow.

A victim has been taught the exact opposite of healthy boundaries, especially if the abuse came in sexual form. Abuse is a violation of your personal limits in the most intimate of ways. Boundaries that have been ignored, violated, kicked around, and manipulated never have a chance to grow stronger.

So the victim develops personal limits that move here and there in the name of survival. They are sometimes as rigid as stone and others as soft and pliable as clay. You say "yes" when you really want to say "no." You take on too much responsibility. You let other people direct your life. You neglect your own needs.

Once your boundaries have been stripped it can be very hard to know where to begin rebuilding them. What belongs to you, what belongs to your lover, what belongs to your parents, what belongs to your children. It is very difficult to set limits when they are bound to be ignored.

Sometimes we expect people to just know where our limits are and to honor them. Unclear boundaries can be coerced, pushed, moved, and even destroyed. We can't expect someone to honor boundaries that we can't even keep straight, but somehow we do.

When you combine people who have no clear idea of where their personal boundaries lie with those who feel that everything is their own personal domain, you often end up with abuse. Abusers do what it takes to get what they want. Victims do what it takes to survive.

Chaos ensues.

The lines between two people can so easily become blurred in even the healthiest of relationships. Given enough time it can become almost impossible to determine where the other person ends and you begin. When your boundaries are ignored your Self is ignored, and you lose it for the sake of the relationship.

Sometimes to correct our out-of-control course we turn to the opposite extreme. We try to control too much. We set expectations for other people and then get angry when they don't comply. We think we are being assertive when really we have just become a bully in a different form.

Chaos still.

There is a better way.

Let's say, for example, that your father is a drunk who violates your boundaries by continuing to drink in your presence. What can you do about it?

If you are uncomfortable with drunken people, you can't walk into every bar you pass and demand that everyone there stop drinking. That isn't a boundary. That is control.

Trying to tell your father to stop drinking is going to meet with the same level of success. It is his body, his life, and his choice. Any solution to your problem that involves changing him will fail before it even begins.

Boundaries are the exact opposite of telling someone else what to do. Your choices in any matter are always limited to what you can control: *yourself*. What you can do is choose to not go into situations where alcohol is present anymore. You can choose to remove yourself. That is a boundary for you. You are in full control of your actions and reactions.

Once your boundary has been communicated clearly, it is your job to enforce it. If you continue to remove yourself when your father is drinking, he will soon learn that sobriety is a requirement for being around you and it is up to him to choose.

You have a right to decide who may touch you and who may not.

You have the right to decide how much or how little they touch you, and where they may do so.

You have the right to say yes, and you have the right to say no.

You have the right to change your mind.

You have the right to define your own personal space.

And you have the right to have your boundaries respected.

In sharing your boundaries with others you need not be confrontational. Just communicate them firmly and clearly. More words only cause confusion.

It can be as simple as explaining that you are limiting your exposure to alcohol, so in the future when someone chooses to drink you will leave. Neither party is telling the other what to do. Both people have a choice.

If (blank) occurs, then I will (blank).

You are the only one who knows where your comfort level is. It is up to you to figure out how to communicate those limits to others and to enforce them when they are ignored. It is up to you to remove yourself, but your control over the situation stops where the other person starts.

Your boundaries can certainly be flexible, and you might even feel comfortable enough with some people to relax your limits almost entirely, but it should always be a choice. If you did it to relieve some sort of outside pressure or in order to get something from someone then you are still allowing others to control your life.

What are *you* going to do about the situation? Pay attention to your personal comfort bubble. Notice how it contracts and expands when around certain people? Those are clues...

Pay attention to them.

In healthy relationships boundaries are expressed and respected by both parties. They are communicated in a way that leaves everyone knowing exactly what to expect if the actions continue. The same dynamic exists between parents and children. By teaching my children to recognize healthy boundaries now I hope to give them a head start in the adult world.

We all make mistakes. We all cross lines we shouldn't. It happens. Just fix it.

When you have crossed into someone else's territory try not to defend, try not to tell them how they should feel, or act, or be. Those are control tactics that eventually lead to rebellion.

Respecting their boundaries shows them how to respect yours.

You can choose not to be around him when he is drinking.

You can refuse to visit his home but leave your own door open.

You can explain to him that there is no alcohol allowed in your home.

Or, if nothing else works, you can limit your contact with him altogether.

The way to show other people how you want to be treated is by treating them that way first. For every human right you have been given there is a responsibility that comes with it.

You can walk all over other people if you choose, but consistently violating the rights of others tells them that they don't have to respect yours either. If someone continues to ignore your personal boundaries then perhaps it is time to strengthen them. The most basic right that human beings should have is the right to live their lives.

So, what are *you* going to do about it?

Roll Call

Erin Merryn
Author
Child Sexual Abuse

George Orwell
Author
Child Abuse

Martin Moran
Author
Child Sexual Abuse

Mary Wollestonecraft
Author
Child Abuse

Rudyard Kipling
Author
Child Abuse

Theo Fleury
NFL Star
Child Sexual Abuse

"Using the power of decision gives you the capacity to get past any excuse, to change any and every part of your life in an instant."

~Tony Robbins

Decisions, Decisions...

The Queen of Bad Decisions: We've all met her. It's almost as if she wants to have her life declared a Federal Disaster Area. This is no act of God; this is a lack of rational decision making at its finest.

The Queen couldn't help it that her boyfriend skipped town with her car, her money, and her best friend. How was she to know?

A quick background check may have been her first clue. Listening to what her friends and family told her would have helped, as well. How about asking a few more questions and paying attention to the answers?

Everybody tries to tell her that he's a jerk, but she thinks she knows something that the others don't. They try to tell her not to buy that car or get that puppy or rent that house but it's almost as if she actually craves the challenge. And then, she wants to know why these things "just" happen to her.

We've all known her, even worse...we have all been her.

Raises hand

We step out there and repeat the same mistakes anyway, still wondering where in life we keep going wrong. Silly humans.

Of course you don't want to see the red flags; that would require action. You would have to make a decision. And decisions aren't easy for Survivors.

The drama can overwhelm the strongest of relationships.

When you ask victims what they want, be that for dinner or for the rest of their lives, their answer is so often "I don't know." And they honestly don't. Deciding where to eat lunch, choosing a new outfit, picking a movie, and even sorting out simple likes and dislikes can be overwhelming when you haven't had the proper practice. So why are we surprised that we have the same sorts of problems with the bigger decisions.

What were we thinking?

Most of the time we really weren't. What's most important to the victim is what benefits them right now: what will keep their lover happy, what will keep their mother quiet, what will keep them safe.

Healthy people can be frightening when you aren't one of them. Secrets are easy to keep as long as the other person is kept at a distance. It's only upon closer inspection that many of our cracks are visible, so we learned to push away anyone who got too close. Anyone who looks too long is bound to see.

The truth is I've never been very good at decision making at all. Friends and family would watch me from a distance shaking their heads in disbelief. Each decision was a spectacular disaster of a different nature. I couldn't have told you why I pushed away anything that seemed to be too good. I just did.

> People don't leave the Queens life out of disloyalty, they leave out of exhaustion. When all of the evidence is there and someone still refuses to see it, there is little you can do.
>
> ⊜
>
> Watching her make the same mistakes over and other but never expecting the same results can be exhausting, but in some strange way drama works for her.

I had this irrepressible need to screw everything up. I pushed healthy people away and pulled the unhealthy ones close. Having someone whole and healthy in my life was just too much contrast. The more healthy they were the more broken I felt beside them.

It wasn't that I couldn't find nice guys out there; it was more that I didn't want to keep them. When I did find someone relatively healthy, somewhere in the back of my mind there were alarm bells going off.

"Abort! Abort! This guy isn't broken enough!"

When I'd tried to make good decisions I'd fallen flat on my face so many times. You get used to that status after awhile. You sabotage your own relationships or find people who will sabotage them for you.

I thought that the ability to make good decisions had somehow passed me by. Anyone I was attracted to back then was probably the exact opposite of what I needed. I could walk into a party filled with 100 nice guys and one jackass and find the jackass every single time. I was looking for the guy that I thought I deserved.

What you seek, you shall find. When you see yourself as damaged goods, you command bargain basement values.

"25% off our already low, low prices!"

You enter into relationships already stacking the odds against yourself. "This could go wrong and that could go wrong, or what about...." Constantly looking for signs of infidelity. Accusing them of cheating outright. Pulling them too close, pushing them too far away. Asking them to leave and then begging them to stay. Yeah. There just might be some intimacy issues there.

If seeing the real person behind the mask is a threat to the relationship then…

NEWSFLASH.

"It isn't really a relationship."

What you are trying to prevent from happening is exactly what is supposed to happen, by the way. The reality is supposed to show through.

I left a lot of relationships in my life that I would love to have truly participated in, to have been there while it was happening-instead of being worried about the future or lost in the past.

The more someone was willing to give me, the less I was willing to take. I learned at a very young age that there is always a price. Everybody is going to expect something in return eventually, and I had so very little to offer. I was taught to call healthy relationships "boring," or "whipped," or "tied down."

If the love I had been given in the past had been a bit perverse, or disconnected, or painful, then who was I to change patterns dating back to ancient history?

Bargain basement prices slashed even further.

My entire life showed this same pattern. Jobs, friendships, promises. I knew it, but that didn't mean I could stop it. Pulling them close but not too close. Pushing them away, then being crushed when they went too far.

Keeping secrets from each other. Hiding failures. Leading double lives. Just about the time things started going well, I always seemed to find a way to screw things up. Eventually they all found out I was flawed.

I wanted to make everybody happy, and that is what I lived for but my dependence upon their approval kept me frozen for half of my life. Even if ten people approved, I focused on that one person who didn't, and tried to find ways to make them happy.

Sometimes, I still do.

When you are dependent upon others for your self-image, it never really has a chance to form. You begin every relationship the same way: determined to preserve its pristine condition. You will be the ever-giving partner, and they will be your one and only soul mate. You try to become someone loveable and in the process you lose yourself.

It is easy to become used to having someone else in the driver's seat, but eventually you will lose all sense of direction when it comes to yourself. What you ultimately sacrifice through that training of your brain towards the pleasures of others is your concept of "me."

You can tell people exactly what your partner likes, down to colors, textures, and preferred temperatures, because that is the information you have been rewarded for knowing. Knowing what you want is usually met with the opposite reaction, so you go where the rewards are.

> You won't always know when you are making a decision that will turn out badly, but will know without a doubt when it is the right thing to do, and that is usually your first clue.
>
> ⊜
>
> The least we can do for ourselves, and for those who are affected by our choices, is try to make decisions that will better our lives instead of complicate them.

You show them the very best of yourself and save the worst for after the veils come down, but they always come down sooner than we expect; the reality comes through. If false advertising were illegal in relationships, the judges of the world would never want for work (not like they do, as it is).

Whether it has been done through force, manipulation, or guilt, when your own choices have been derailed by the control of another person you fail to learn the proper steps to making your own decisions. When you have lived with unhealthy people, your decision-making abilities have often been interfered with.

Imagine that you are making a choice, say, between the red ball and the blue ball, and you are drawn to the red ball, it may be your first choice. You are holding it when someone comes along and says, "The red ball is the dumbest choice you could make. Look at it. It is loud and obnoxious. It will never bounce as high as the blue ball. You are just wasting your time."

So, instead you reach for the blue ball and someone else says, "The blue ball is a horrible choice. Someone has marked it all up, and it is far too full of air. It will probably burst...but it is your decision."

Then a chorus of voices fill your head. "Hurry up. We haven't got all day. Just make your mind up already!" Now either choice you make is incorrect, and you stand there frozen between the two of them.

There isn't a lot of pressure involved in choosing a ball, but many of your decisions are made the same way every day when living with a bully–what types of food you eat, what types of clothes you wear, who you are and are not allowed to associate with.

We are supposed to learn about one another, accept one another, and get to know each other on deeper and deeper levels as the relationship progresses, not hide more and more.

Change will happen.

We can mourn it, or we can roll with it. That's that growth thing that people are always talking about.

Eventually it is easier to just let them make all of your decisions for you.

We learned to just go with the flow. We aren't always given the time to make good decisions, so we make the ones that serve us best right now. It's a Survivor thing.

You have wants, needs, and desires, no matter how repressed they may be. Knowing what those things are is crucial in finding out who you really are.

More than just a habit, abuse becomes a lifestyle. You lose touch with yourself and you focus more and more on pleasing the people who fulfill that need for sameness. If you are content allowing others to direct your course while you keep getting left with the responsibility, then nobody will stop you. As a matter of fact, they would probably prefer it continue.

There was supposed to be a little voice inside of our head that warned when we were about to make a poor decision, but it was short-circuited because our survival depended on keeping someone else happy. The people who are making the decisions in the victim's life rarely have to live with the consequences.

Too often the future repercussions of our decisions are too far away to be concerned with. We will always end up dealing with the consequences sooner or later. Putting it off only makes it that much more difficult.

As you are trained to be easier to control by an abuser, you are also made easier to control for the next person that comes along. You leave abusive childhoods to enter into abusive marriages. You go from one abusive partner to the next. You find abusive religious practices or social groups that also continue that sameness.

In abusive homes, making mistakes made our lives miserable. We learned to avoid them at all costs, even if it meant doing nothing at all. Staying very still and not risking error is sometimes the easiest way to avoid notice, so we get very good at it. We develop a strange sort of perfectionism. If we are confident in a skill it easily becomes an obsession - but if the confidence isn't there, the action can stop entirely.

Mistakes will be made. Bad decisions hurt us and other people. They begin chain reactions that can alter the histories of entire civilizations, but they usually aren't that big of a deal. How do you know if it is a bad decision? You don't.

I have made a lot of bad decisions. I brought three children into a horrible marriage with no way to support them. When I was struggling with depression after my son was born, a doctor actually told me that I had no business having children and should get sterilized. I have genetic health problems. My ex and his family criticized me constantly. My own family threatened to remove my children from my care because I struggled with the basics.

The only thing that came naturally to me was the love part, I didn't know how to cook, or clean, or even take care of myself, let alone three kids. People saw the places I failed, but it was the more private side of my parenting that eventually came through. I wanted to be a good parent, so I took classes, read parenting books, and constantly sought out advice.

I spent a lot of time thinking about the long-term consequences of my parenting, and I started doing things very differently than most.

Skills build with practice. One good decision leads to another.

I'm glad that I didn't raise perfect children. That was never my goal. Awards, grades, and public recognition mean nothing when you have no happiness to back them up.

Doing your homework is more important in adulthood than it ever was as a child. This is your life. Your life affects others. The decisions you make today will determine where you find yourself tomorrow. The more good decisions you make, the better the quality your life will be. It's okay to make mistakes. It means you are learning.

Every mistake you make is one more step on the journey to perfection. You will never have a perfect life but as long as you are moving forward you are still in the game.

When you make a bad decision, learn from it and try to figure out where you went wrong, but let it go. Don't kick yourself around. If you keep dwelling on it, you are bound to repeat it.

> There is more than one step to making a good decision, hence some of our past fiascoes.
>
> ⊜
>
> We chose what felt intensely important to our happiness at the time and weren't ready for the long-term consequences.

I taught my kids how to see their mistakes as stepping-stones, because I knew they would need it. I didn't know that it would actually change me, though. One day someone was teasing me and remarked, "Since when has Ayngel ever made a good decision in her life?" I just stood there, unable to defend myself, unable to express my hurt.

My young son, not yet ten years old, stepped in and spoke up. "My mommy makes good decisions every single day." And he could actually name some of them. My son didn't see the me from the past. He saw the mother who put her children first, even when it meant pissing off the rest of the family.

I still make poor decisions on a daily basis. We all do. We choose soda over water. We choose fast food over nutrition. We choose television over exercise. We choose the cute guy when we should have chosen the stable one.

The only way to make good decisions is to practice. We can't always keep ourselves safe. There are people out there who will find their way through even the strongest of defenses. But my children can make better decisions, and choose safer alternatives than either of their parents were capable of in their youth.

When my children mess up, they admit it, and can usually tell me how they plan to fix it. When they wrong someone they make an effort to correct it.

Plenty of people told me in my younger days that my children would be my karma, that they would be worse than I ever dreamed of being but they are far from it.

One of Brooke's teachers described her to me as a quiet leader, being the oldest she has always been bossy but no more so than when she sees another living being suffering.

While the other boys were pushing kids down on the playground Justin's teachers said that my son was the one picking them up and dusting them off. He not only defended them, but helped them to the nurses office when needed.

Mystery, my youngest, wants to be a civil rights attorney, and volunteers to do fundraisers for youth groups that she doesn't even belong to. My step-daughter Jaid has plans to be a pilot in the military.

Despite my families dire predictions, to this day my kids will stand up for what is right over what is easy.

My kids make good decisions on a regular basis, and somehow they learned by watching my mistakes. I could have tried to cover them, I could have denied they existed, I could have insisted on that illusion of perfection that so many in my past had hid behind, but I didn't. I just admitted that I was imperfect and tried to fix the situation.

I have made some very good decisions, but I had to learn to trust those instincts again, to stop and make a conscious decision no matter who was pressuring me otherwise. There will always be outside pressure, but they don't have to live with the consequences, I do.

Good decisions take time. If someone is pressuring you to make a decision quickly, there is always a reason. Get feedback from other people before you act–people that you trust to make good decisions. People who make good choices live lives that reflect those decisions.

Before taking advice from anybody always ask yourself if you want to be where they are in life.

You will find that the same lessons keep presenting themselves over and over in your life. Until you learn from them you are doomed to repeat them. If you are afraid to ask for advice, there is a reason. If you have to silence your conscience to go forward then maybe you aren't moving forward at all.

Don't ignore the red flags. Stop, assess the situation, and proceed with caution.

Abuse has found many ways to pervert love and twist it around in our heads. Our intimacy issues will continue to surface in our relationships until we deal with them. We will push people away when they are good for us and pull them near when they are dangerous. It's what we do.

Intimacy has hurt us in the past, physically, emotionally, sexually. It is only natural to shy away from things that have caused you pain. Sometimes relationships will leave us hurting, but that hurt will heal. We will be stronger. It is difficult to allow those walls to come down after years of hiding behind them, but happiness requires risks. The reason those fears of intimacy are still there is because you formed a faulty emotional connection. To rewire that connection you need new experiences with strong emotions to connect them with. Why not make them good ones?

> "Guilt says I've done something wrong;
> Shame says there is something wrong with me.
> Guilt says I've made a mistake;
> Shame says I am a mistake.
> Guilt says what I did was not good;
> Shame says I am no good."
>
> ~Bradshaw

Stop trying to control everything. Just let it go.

Don't enter into relationships wondering if someone will screw it up; instead, enter them wondering where it will lead. As much as you want to believe that each relationship is the one, while you are busy planning your perfect family portrait, real life is passing you by.

Not only are you distracting yourself from important red flags, hints that the future of the relationship might not be as solid as you would like, you are missing the good stuff, the stuff that relationships are supposed to be about.

Everybody comes with baggage. The best any of us can do is look for someone who can at least compliment our own. Don't get all wrapped up in where things are going or how they are going to get there. Just take the time to enjoy the moments in your life.

Retrain your brain to make conscious decisions.
Identify the decision, and then figure out what you would like

the ultimate outcome to be.

Look at all of your options and weigh them out. Find the one that is the best fit for you.

If you can't find any other options, keep looking until you find them.

Gather as much information as you can before you commit to anything.

Read the fine print.

Ask yourself if you are ready to deal with the consequences of your decision beforehand.

Look at the worst-case scenario. Can you handle it?

What is your exit strategy if things go wrong? Is it feasible?

Living in the now stores up the good parts. It saves them for times in your life when you need to draw on them. Those are the things that will make you smile when your world is at its darkest.

Learning to let go and let relationships happen is hard for every Survivor. We've all faced hurt that we would rather not repeat, so we try to control it, manipulate it, and force our relationships into place so that we can keep them the same forever and ever.

Stop and smell the flowers. No, really. Actually do it.

Feel the summer sun on your skin, the cool sweetness of the ice cream on your tongue. Even when you are alone in your home you can make those moments.

When you find yourself reasonably content with life, stop what you are doing and recognize it. Set aside the past and the future just for now. Just feel your happiness for a few minutes and allow it to grow. Experience life going on around you. Learn to record the moment in your brain.

What a lovely day for an adventure, don't you think? It turns out that every day is. Don't wait for someone to join you to have them, but when they do, don't waste time worrying about what could happen, should happen, or possibly might happen. Just live it for a moment.

⚜

Roll Call

Catherine G. McCall
L.M.F.T. Author
Incest

Patricia Weaver Francisco
Author
Rape

Shari Karney
Author
Child Sexual Abuse

Stasi Eldredge
Author
Rape

Sue William Silverman
Author
Incest

"Strength does not come from physical capacity. It comes from an indomit- able will."

~Gandhi

Courage : Tough Enough

Women in my family are stubborn to be sure. My relatives have been known for their independent stubbornness since somewhere near the beginning of time. If you really want to motivate a Hilleary woman, tell her that a task is impossible and then get out of her way.

It isn't always a good thing though.

One day my mother called to tell me that she had to stay home from work because she "pulled something stupid." I stopped in my tracks. It is a phrase which has given me great cause for alarm over the years. In the past, it has meant she has broken bones, tried to lance a wound on the dog, cut her own hair, or taken on a full construction project. In this instance, a bad tooth and no insurance lead to a few shots of whiskey and a pair of pliers.

She wasn't sure if it was infection or the painkillers she'd taken that were making her feel funny, but she was a bit blurred around the edges.

It isn't just her.

My husband and I have caught my eighty-ish grandmother swinging a sledge-hammer that weighs almost as much as she does too many times to count. This is the woman who dropped a log trying to put it in the fireplace and it took the tip of her toe off. She just wrapped her foot, and put it in a dishpan so that she could get on with with her morning chores, dragging a dishpan full of blood behind her. I've seen that woman work with broken ankles and busted ribs, I have seen her work through pneumonia.

She is a tiny little powerhouse. My grandmother raised four kids and then when she was almost done raising her own kids, she took me on.

Me? I am the woman who once loaded a side-by-side refrigerator into the back of a truck by myself. It took a dolly, some straps, and only a few minor injuries to my back and knees, but I pulled it off.

One wrong move and I could've won a Darwin Award, but I didn't.

All you have ever had to do to motivate me in life is tell me that something couldn't be done. I learned from the best...

When I was a child, I did a lot of crazy things. Mom and Grandma used to look at me, shake their heads, and say, "We don't know where she gets it from..."

The funny thing is, they still do.

Five generations of fighters, five generations of determination, five generations of spirit. My children grew up watching me risk my health and safety in the pursuit of higher stubbornness. It turns out that they are pretty stubborn themselves.

Are the two connected? Stubbornness and being an abuse Survivor? Without a doubt.

I have seen the women in my family give and give until they could give no more, but they always seemed to keep going. There is a certain ferocity to their love that anybody who has ever messed with a family member can testify to. We can love with a passion that borders on insanity.

The women before me did the impossible. They were laughed at and ridiculed for leaving abusive husbands to raise children alone. They struggled for every dime. They went without a lot, just so their children could have better. They all made it. They did odd jobs to earn the money. They took on extra hours. They got through it.

But it was not easy.

My mother raised me without any outside financial support. Most of my clothes were second hand. We did a lot of our shopping at yard sales. We went without a lot, but never went without a roof over our heads and food in our bellies. She refused to rely on public assistance, which meant a lot of mayonnaise sandwiches after school but even if my mother had to send me to stay with my grandmother until she got back on her feet, I did not go without.

She has been in the military. She worked in construction, owned her own interior decorating business and was even mayor of our town for a short time. I told her that she was crazy for taking a job in politics in the first place, but she was determined to make a difference. Fierce, independent, and bold, she never took anything from a man that she could provide for herself.

Somewhere in her childhood my mother decided that being the oldest also meant she must be the strongest. Even when people offered her help, she pushed them away. I watched her work in one male-dominated industry after another, alongside men who viewed her not as an equal but almost as an intruder. She was a woman in a man's world, and getting about half of the pay.

You've lived in a black-and-white world for a very long time and the only way to balance one extreme is to head towards the other.

When the only two options are good and bad, if you aren't "good" you begin to think of yourself as bad. If you are not strong, then you must be weak.

Why can't you just BE?

Sometimes I think Survivors stick it out just to prove they can hack it.

When I was a kid, she drank like a man, and when someone pushed her long enough and hard enough she fought like a man, but in her intimate relationships she was often abused. It was a fact that she hid from me as best as she could, but children always seem to know.

My mother wanted to be loved, but too many people had told her there was nothing in her worthy of loving. So she tried to earn it. My mother wanted to be the one who could handle anything. Through one unhealthy relationship after another she struggled to change the things she couldn't change. I remember her telling me that she knew she couldn't fix the people in her life, but she couldn't stop trying either. There was this stubborn compulsion that drove her that even she couldn't fully explain.

Stubbornness always has a price.

There was a secret side to my mother that only I saw. She would take it until she just couldn't take any more. Then she would crack. There were times she cried so long and so hard that I was afraid to leave her alone for fear she would hurt herself.

When she emerged from her darkened room she never talked about it and I never asked. In contrast to the iron woman who ruled my day, this fragile and seemingly broken woman frightened me. Its rarity made it even worse.

I was well into my adulthood before I could accept that these two people really were the same person.

My mother's tough exterior was never real. She just convinced herself that people who are tough never got hurt. She expected herself to be able to handle everything that came her way, but everyone has moments of weakness.

I don't think she could forgive herself for hers. Not for a very long time.

Everyone else saw her take her hardships with her head held high. I was the one who would find her on her bed, butt in the air like a little kid, screaming into her pillow.

If my mother felt weak then I thought that I had to be strong. I tried to fill in for the absent male in her life by taking on all of the man stuff in the home.

I was splicing speaker lines and setting up stereo systems before I was in double digits. By my teens, I was running functional phone and cable lines. Fixing radios and televisions. Setting up entertainment systems. I learned how to fix broken electronics because somebody had to. There was a need in my family, and I stepped in to fill it.

I was just stubborn enough to teach myself.

I've heard my stubbornness described as both a compliment and an insult. It helps me reach goals. It helps me get things done. It keeps me from sinking into depression.

But it has also convinced me that I was safe in situations where I wasn't. It has also kept me in relationships that were hurting me. It has even kept me depressed far longer than necessary.

People either adapt to the life they have been given or die, but there is so much more to life than survival of the Darwinian sort.

Part of survival is knowing when to fight and when to get the hell out. Staying in a miserable relationship is one of the slowest forms of suicide there is.

We have all sorts of reasons for staying that have to do with keeping promises, sticking to our word, honoring our marriage, and pure, old-fashioned loyalty. Even when they have broken their vows over and over, we stay. Even when we are in danger, we stay.

Maybe we are just too stubborn for our own good?

Abuse is a power exchange. When one person has the bulk of the power, the other is automatically in a place of weakness. We can carry that idea of weakness with us for the rest of our lives. Some broadcast it as if it were a beacon, inviting anybody and everybody to join the party. Sometimes we do the exact opposite and overcompensate for the weakness we faced in our past by becoming whatever our idea of strong may be.

We find ourselves picking fights with others, puffing up at the first sign of trouble, showing off our strengths in competitive arenas, or exercising our sexual prowess.

That which is a weakness in the abusive home can so easily become one of your greatest strengths in the right situation. Stop avoiding them and enhance them.

◉

See where they take you.

It's only natural for someone to highlight their strengths, to want people to see the areas in which they excel, but we can take it to extremes. Putting ourselves in danger to prove a point isn't going to help anyone in the long run.

Survivors need to know when to quit.

Survivors spend their lives trying to prove to the world that they are tough enough. You will never outrun the ghosts that are chasing you. You can't drink them away, exercise them away, or hate them away.

You cannot live your life as a person split in half. Instead of looking at yourself as a bundle of weaknesses with a few strengths, see yourself as you really are: a person with some skills that have been developed and some that are still waiting to be.

My grandmother and Red the powerhouse, get along fantastically. They are both small, they are both feisty, and that's where the similarities seem to end, but there was something else I noticed about them that really sets them apart. Neither of them slows down long enough to get stuck.

They are two stubborn dames who took very different approaches to their freedom, but they got there. I adore them both, and hope some day to be half the woman that either of them are. They have set a mighty high bar.

My mother and I, we get stuck sometimes., but we know how to dig in and dig ourselves out when the time comes.

Survivors have little difficulty offering an almost sacrificial love to others, but you can't seem to save an ounce of that love and concern for yourself, can you? While your abusers struggle to maintain control of other people and situations, you struggle to maintain balance. But the only way to balance one extreme is to head towards the other.

Being hard on yourself will not banish weaknesses, it will only camouflage them. You push your strengths beyond their limits, constantly testing yourself. You don't rest when you are ill. You don't take medications when you need them. You push yourself to keep working long after your energy ran out. You stay in relationships long after they have lost their functionality. You put up with abuse.

The need to be tough enough may get you through some of the more difficult times you may face, but it can also make those tough times more frequent.

It can leave you looking for a challenge just to prove you are up to it. It can leave you feeling guilty each time you fail. In the end, it is just another way of destroying yourself, pushing yourself to the limits and then pushing the limits a bit more.

Strong people face hardships when they have to, but they don't go looking for them.

Once again we come to the idea of balance. Acknowledge your strengths with honor, for they are a gift, but honor your weaknesses as well, for they are what make you human. They are what make you unique. They are what make you, YOU.

Stop trying to prove to the world that you are tough enough, you have already proven it. You survived abuse.

Life is fragile, but you are not.

Roll Call

Armond DeGasperis
Child Author
Child Abuse

Elizabeth Loftus
Psychologist & Author
Child Sexual Abuse

Johannes Brahms
Composer
Child Sexual Abuse

Leslie Triber
Author/Poet
Abuse

Sugar Ray Leonard
Boxer
Child Sexual Abuse

You can't save others from themselves because those who make a perpetual muddle of their lives don't appreciate your interfering with the drama they've created. They want your poor-sweet-baby sympathy, but they don't want to change."

~Sue Grafton, T is for Trespass

Rescue Me

Somehow, I got the idea that it was my job to fix everybody else's problems. As much as I would like to blame it on my Wonder woman Underoos, it turns out that I came by it naturally.

It's just another family tradition.

My grandmother's life could be falling apart around her and yet she would drop everything for an offspring in need. There is nothing that she has that she would not offer to alleviate the pain of another. She has fed, sheltered and clothed total strangers.

My mother and daughter both show the same tendencies; in fact, most of the women in my family do. Some of us have rescuing in our blood. We rescued our parents. We rescued our siblings. We rescued our lovers.

My family has threatened to make me a photo board of all of the strays I've taken in over the years, just to remind me of some of the outcomes. These are not success stories in any sense; they were some of my hardest learned lessons.

Rescuers will rescue. It's what we do, and most likely what we have been doing our whole lives, going back over and over trying to correct the mistakes of the past. If we couldn't fix daddy then maybe we could fix our high school sweethearts. If we couldn't fix them then maybe we'd have more success with our spouse, our child, the kid next door or maybe the homeless guy down the street? We're always willing to martyr ourselves for love, but our success rates remain dismal.

And it happens that there are never a shortage of people out there who really do want to be rescued. They call you when their car breaks down. They call you when their bills are due. They call you when their lives are falling apart. (And there you go pinning on your superhero cape and heading off once again to save their day.) They seem to be attracted to our type of people: the rescuers.

It's like this invisible tattoo...

In the abusive relationship, we were expected to fix their problems, we were often blamed for their problems, and we were often expected to take responsibility for their problems.

Translation: Love means fixing other peoples problems.

Saving other people from themselves is exactly what we were trained to do. Always there to listen. Always ready with a solution. Always there with a helping hand. Always there to save the day.

It's not a matter of you can't save them all." You can't save a single one of them.

You can offer the tools, you can offer the education, you can even help them with the parts they can't do on their own... but you can't do it for them.

They take a few tottering steps forward and there you are, the proud parent coaxing them on. Then, without fail, they screw us over–when their husband leaves, when he moves back again, when he marries his girlfriend, when he comes home again...

We get our hopes up when they make a step in the right direction, but they come crashing back down when the promises come due. Don't kid yourself, people like us can't rescue without an emotional commitment. We get attached. We get involved.

It isn't a question of whether they are good people are not; they often are. It's not a question of whether they need our help or not; they often do. And it isn't about appreciation, or debts owed, or even meeting expectations.

As Survivors, we tend to invest ourselves in our relationships to a greater degree than most, but we've been trained to invest ourselves in the wrong relationships. All of our energy goes to the relationships that require the most attention, and often with the poorest returns.

If love were a bank account, we would always be in the red.

Sometimes we are far more committed to them changing than they are, and after we have invested our time and energy in them they still keep living their own lives. Funny how that happens.

They will either save themselves or they won't. You can support them, but the final decision is always their own. Sometimes strays are on their own for a reason.

We can offer them love for the first time in their lives, a stable relationship, and acceptance, but the moment they are faced with a crisis they will revert to what they've always known in the past.

If they've done it once you can bet money that they will do it again, and again, and again. As long as their ways keep working, they will keep using them. As long as you keep saving them, there is no reason for them to change. They will keep making messes and we will keep cleaning them up, and it will go on like that until someone refuses to play the game anymore.

They even stop trying to save themselves anymore. They just sit down and wait for someone else to come along. That someone is NOT *you*. They are very good at convincing you that a failure to save them from their messes on your part will lead to dire consequences that you are somehow responsible for. They will convince you that it's up to you to fix it, and if you don't, the world just might end.

What about our world? Will our world really cease its rotation just because they are upset with us? Probably not.

It's only when they have no other choice that they find someone else to keep their world turning. They find new girlfriends just as naïve as you once were. They find another mentor to get them through their unfortunate luck. They find other siblings to call at the first sign of crisis. They find other parents to bail them out of jail. Their chaos keeps churning with or without you.

Liars will lie. Cheaters will cheat. Thieves will steal. Abusers will abuse.

Rescuers will rescue.

Imagine if you could take back all of the time you have spent trying to fix other people, trying to fix your relationships, and trying to save the world, and reinvest it in your own future. Where would you have gone with your life? What would you have experienced?

We can't rescue them. Nobody can. You can waste a whole life trying to rescue this person or that, but the rewards are few and far between. You will give more than you will ever see given back.

And they will always *neeeed* you.

Yes. They will moan. Yes. They will whine. Yes. They will accuse you of being selfish. You don't think they are going to give up something they have worked so hard to gain without a fight, do you?

You will either help them avoid responsibility for their actions or help them help themselves. The choice is not theirs. It's yours. When you rescue and rescue and nothing ever changes, that's your clue that it is time to explore your options.

Yes. No. Maybe so. Make a conscious decision.

When we try to save others, we only reinforce their image of victimhood. Don't take ownership of the problem, put it right back in their hands. Show them that you have the faith in them to figure it out, and allow them to surprise you. If they stomp and whine and call you selfish then so be it.

If you want to transition from sucker to Survivor, you are going to need some magic words. Words that are supportive, but without commitment. Words that place their problem back in their hands but still say. "I have faith in you."

Words like...

"That's unfortunate, what are YOU going to do about it?"

"Wow! How are YOU going to handle that?"

"I have faith that YOU can handle this."

"Don't worry, I'm sure that YOU will figure something out."

You don't have to stop taking care of the people you love in order to meet your own needs. Healthy people think of themselves, but they also think of others. If what is best for us is best for others, then our decision is easy. If what is best for us may or may not be best for other people involved, then that takes a bit more consideration. Pros and cons must be weighed out. Compromises must be made.

Everyone must sometimes sacrifice their own wants to meet the needs of those they love.

But where do those sacrifices stop? If you go too far the other way, don't worry, you will know it. You will be the one that people are refusing to rescue anymore. Nobody else needs to save you. You are perfectly capable of being responsible for yourself.

A person with self-esteem is in touch with themselves and the world around them. It is not an excessive love, but a new, healthy way of seeing yourself. You can be aware of your weaknesses and still be confident in your strengths. You can still be firm with yourself when the situation calls for it, but you also have to be gentle when it is needed. Attempts to meet your own needs are not selfish, neither is saying no, protecting yourself, or making your own decisions.

The success of a relationship is not about the amount of control that you exercise over one another, it is about the amount of control each partner exercises over themselves.

When your true needs are met, you are free to both give and receive. In a healthy relationship nobody is scrambling to get their needs met in indirect ways.

You can't take care of anybody else if you can't take care of yourself.

Roll Call

Cheryl Burke
Dancing With the Stars
Child Sexual Abuse Survivor

John Peele
Disk Jockey
Rape Survivor

Laveranues Coles
Football Player
Child Sexual Abuse Survivor

Mata Hari
Famous Spy
Domestic Violence Survivor

Paula White
Evangelist, Author
Child Sexual Abuse Survivor

"We're never so vulnerable than when we trust someone–but paradoxically, if we cannot trust, neither can we find love or joy."

~ Walter Anderson

The First Rational Bank Of Trust

Trust is so easy to violate. When you trust other people, you offer them a place in your world, a piece of yourself. It would be nice if everybody respected and appreciated that gift. Sadly, some will not.

Human beings are flawed.

It turns out that other people are just as human as you are. The whole human race has some glitches we are still trying to work out. People strike out, people tell secrets, people cheat.

When you have been hurt, you tend to be on guard for any sign of betrayal. Those defenses go up, and they can stay up for a very long time.

I lived in a black-and-white world for a very long time, and sometimes I still do. Old habits die hard it seems. When I was loved and cared for, the world was a wonderful place, but the first sign of betrayal and all defense systems were "GO." I knew how to trust people fully and completely and totally, and I knew how to lock them out entirely. It was the in-between that I really struggled with.

My youngest child, Mystery, has always been the friendliest of my children. Living in a small town really made things difficult for her. When you know everybody it is hard to understand the concept of stranger. As a preschooler, she would start up conversations with total strangers, and before you knew it she'd wormed her way into their hearts and sometimes onto their laps.

Everyone was a friend in her eyes, and I didn't want to take that away from her, but I didn't want her to get too close to people who could harm her either. I struggled to find a way to explain it to her in a way her young mind would understand.

It finally came to me one day while the two of us were sitting on the floor counting the change in her piggy bank. We let the change fall through our fingers a few times as I told her how proud I was of her for saving up so much money. It wasn't exactly her college fund–just a few dollars in nickels and pennies, with the rare quarter here and there–but it was hers.

Because of her older siblings, she was more of a collector than a saver. It was hard for her to hold on to silver change, as being the youngest meant she had two older siblings who could con her into some sort of "four pennies are better than one quarter" trade.

I explained to her that trust is like a piggy bank. If someone does nice things for you, or is kind, it's like putting money into your piggy bank. If someone isn't nice to you when they lie to you, steal from you, or they hurt you in some way, they are taking money out of the bank.

When you first meet someone, the piggy bank is empty. As the friendship progresses and you continue to do nice things for one another, more deposits are added. Now and then, everyone is going to take a little bit away from your trust bank.

That's okay, it happens. As long as they find a way to rebuild that trust, the friendship will suffer no harm. What happens is someone keeps taking? Even with a small amount here and a small amount there, all of the trust will eventually run out.

While I did not want her to be suspicious of all strangers I wanted her to be aware of her trust levels with people on an individual level. By sitting on a strange man's lap, she was giving him trust that he had not yet earned. She had extended him credit, only it was a lot more than money she stood to lose if he turned out to be someone untrustworthy.

Some people will take the whole thing if you let them. They will even start stealing from remaining piggy banks in your life, from trust that belongs to other people, both now and in the future.

Trust can be rebuilt just like a savings account can, though it isn't nearly as easy. The only way to be safe is to allow the trust to build up slowly just like we do our savings. Don't give it away all at once. When you trust someone, you are always taking a risk. Sometimes the risk is worth it, but we can also lose it all.

None of us are immune to what is in our nature as human beings. You are imperfect. You make mistakes. You act selfishly. That doesn't necessarily make you a bad person, it just makes you a person. Sometimes even the best of friends will do something that hurts you. Everyone will say and do things that cause hurt or disappointment, but a time will likely come when you will disappoint others just as much as they have you.

Sometimes you do place unrealistic expectations on your friends and lovers. You expect them to be able to read your mind, or to act out of character, or to give up their needs in order to meet yours. If there is a very good reason for that request then perhaps an exception can be made. However, if you are pushing people to do something against their will, you are crossing into the territory of the bully.

Yeah, you.

There will be times when you do things you aren't particularly proud of, or you say something without thinking about the consequences, and sometimes you will outright betray the trust of others.

A penny here, a nickel there... over time those little withdrawals add up.

When an account starts running low, we can always recover. If they deserve credit based on past experiences, extend it.

But if the account consistently runs low, it's time to take a look at your overall investment in the relationship.

Is it helping you or hurting you?

You can focus on the problem (your human imperfections), or you can focus on the solution. You can make it right. If you want to set yourself apart from your abusers then this is where it happens. You can make mistakes; that is your right. You can fix them too, that should be your responsibility.

If you can't fix your mistakes, learn from them. Sometimes things will happen in life, trust will be damaged, but we can get past it.

Stop trying to place all of your trust in other people and save some for you. Trust your own judgment, and when it fails you, take some time to find out why. How can you give something to other people when you can't even give it to yourself? Trust yourself first, the rest will follow.

Toads have a way of manipulating your perceptions, and with their help you learn to not trust your own instincts. When you have expressed your doubts or fears in the past, you may have been told that the way you felt was not accurate. If you believe that something is wrong, but you do it anyway, your self-esteem is going to take a heavy hit.

Your gut instincts are there to protect you, but you have to have enough faith in them to hear what they are telling you. Over the years, you have learned to ignore the red flags that are supposed to alert you to unsafe people and situations. Learn to pay attention to them again.

Living with abuse can dampen our instincts, and eventually short-circuit them altogether.

The flags are there as an inner alarm bell, and it is up to you to listen. What has happened once will keep happening until you start seeing the patterns that are right in front of your face.

A person who lies to others, will eventually lie to you. People who cheat on exes eventually cheat on you. If someone resorts to name-calling and physical violence when angry with others then you can expect to find yourself in the same situation eventually. It's simple logic.

A world full of imperfect people is bound to let you down once in a while. We sometimes let that drain our faith in humanity, but we shouldn't.

When you are looking for someone to trust, what you often want is someone you can trust completely–someone who will keep your confidences, someone who will keep your best interests at heart, and someone who will stand beside you when you need him or her most. And of course, you want someone who would never, ever hurt you.

Do you have a right to expect others to respect the trust you have placed in them? To some degree, yes, but if you insist on your expectations being met at all times and in all circumstances then you are bound to find yourself frustrated. Like many things we have talked about so far, you have to put the picture in a new frame. You need to look at it in a different way. Trust is not black and white; there are many shades of gray in between. It isn't all-or-nothing. It just is.

We sometimes let our disappointment and frustrations with one person destroy our belief in the power of love as a whole, which is even worse.

You don't have to trust all people equally, nor do you have to trust one person at all times. You have the power to decide whom you will trust, and in what situations you will trust them. You can trust them with a little or you can trust them with a lot. You can even adjust that trust as the relationship progresses, allowing more or less as the person shows you more of their true self.

However, once a person has shown themselves to be untrustworthy, even to other people, it should be a red flag. It might not seem so bad when a friend keys her ex's car, but someday you could very well be the target of her anger. At that point, it's a little bit too late to plead the "How could they do this to me?" defense.

When you stop to think about the people you trust in your life, you will likely find that you trust some more than others in any given area. You may trust one friend to listen to your problems and keep your secrets safe, but find that person untrustworthy when it comes to financial matters. So tell him your secrets and stop loaning him money.

We aren't bankers, and we don't have to keep meticulous accounts (In fact, that is a great way to ruin a relationship).

What we can do is ask ourselves the most important question of all... are they really as invested in the relationship as we are?

You may trust another friend to offer you support and nurturing, while also being aware that she isn't very trustworthy when it comes to keeping secrets. That doesn't mean you can't call her on a Saturday night to come hang out. Just don't tell her anything you don't want to be public knowledge. The one person you should always be able to trust in this life is *you*.

Everyone will let you down at some point or another. They can't help it, humans are flawed. The whole race has some glitches we are still trying to work out. It turns out that other people are just as human as you are.

You can't trust the whole of the human race, but you don't need to.

Roll Call

Goldie Taylor
Journalist
Child Sexual Abuse

Janice Dickenson
Model
Child Abuse

Kara Dioguardi
Singer, former judge on American Idol
Child Sexual Abuse

Lara Logan
Journalist
Rape

Richard Nixon
Former President U.S.
Child Abuse

Avoid problems and you'll never be the one who overcame them.

~Richard Bach

How to Avoid Eating An Elephant

A dear friend of mine, known to the world as Red, called me one day to discuss the things that I left out of the first draft of this book. She puts up with exactly zero shit from anyone, least of all me, and this is why I adore her so.

They should base a superhero on her, seriously.

She has been an Olympic athlete, holds a record in women's weightlifting, and once played professional football in a short-lived women's football league. She also tended bars for a lifetime. Now, this is not a woman anyone would label as weak, at least none to my knowledge that have survived.

In my book, this woman is invincible. No medal left unearned, no competition left unconquered. She was the one who brought up the subject of the "Tough Enough" chapter. She asked me to write about how Survivors push themselves to be strong, with the ultimate goal of being the strongest.

She has pushed her body in ways that would make the average American blush with shame, but sometimes even she feels like there are common, everyday things that she can't handle. I feel the exact same way, so please know this chapter is fully written with my own hypocrisy in mind.

Yet, I knew what Red meant immediately when she said "I hate it when the telephone rings."

The answering machine is my friend. I chose to be a writer for a reason: because I wanted to live in a relatively quiet world where few unexpected things happen. It isn't possible; but I keep trying.

The telephone is always an unknown. Its presence unnerves me. I can't control when it will ring, and once it does there is a giant question mark hanging in the air. It could be good news. It could be bad news. It could be someone calling to sell us something or someone calling to collect money.

You learn to avoid answering the telephone based on the potential stress levels involved. You avoid answering the door, getting caught in large crowds, and traffic.

The more unpleasant the tasks, the more avoidance needed. Like those skeletons that need to be evicted from your closets, the dirtiest of deeds that need to be done, and those unpleasant confrontations that need to be had.

I still put off getting the mail as long as possible, especially when there are bills due. I know if I pick them up they will sit in my mind all day and all night. The further behind I get, the more the pressure builds. There are many factors in the mailbox that I can't control. So I sometimes push them out of my mind entirely.

They say that serial killers function by compartmentalizing their personalities. That term never fails to make me think of a glove box of a car. That's where you keep the stuff you need to access the most, the stuff you don't necessarily mind the rest of the world seeing. Okay, so maybe the occasional bottle of booze or joint makes it in there, but for the most part it's clean.

"The doting husband and loving father. Active in the community. Nice guy." That's the stuff that you want the world to know.

Serial killers don't usually hide bodies in the front seat. Into the trunk they go, like yesterday's garbage. In the dark. In the secret place. Personalities have a secret place too. No loving and doting here. This part of them is not for public consumption.

Those compartments work really well at first, but after a while the icky stuff leaks out. Dead bodies in the trunk begin to stink. No, we aren't serial killers– at least, one would hope not–but we have a lot of stink in our trunks, don't we?

We all have a dark and musty place inside of us, the place where our secrets dwell. That's where we put all of those things that we aren't sure what to do with.

It's amazing, the ways we come up with to bury the hurt parts of ourselves away: working too hard, working too little, shutting the world out, avoiding being alone. We have had to learn to live in a society that expects us to behave in certain ways. We have to function, at least on some level.

We tucked our own secrets away because we had to. That was the only way to survive. I've known cutters, addicts, and foodies. I have known a few sadists and masochists, too. All of them are seeking some sort of acceptance of their pain. The outside world doesn't understand, but their band-aid of choice appears to. It comforts them a bit. They feel like they are more accepting of themselves, at least until the guilt sets in.

Whatever happened to them came in the most horrible circumstances, from the most unthinkable places. And those people had to go on. They had to leave their dark secrets behind and live in a world that expected them to be fully functional. To do that, they had to compartmentalize.

> We shove a lot of the things we don't want to deal with into these hidden compartments in our lives.
>
> Things like the abuse we can't allow ourselves to see, the family problems we can't fix, and the bills we can't pay.
>
> Everyone from sinners to saints has it; some of us just use it more than others.

How could we have talked about our secrets? Who would have listened? The other people who were trying to ignore the problems just as hard as we were? Not likely. The problems stayed in there, festering, bubbling, churning.

When you've lived in an environment where you have been punished for addressing problems head-on, you learn to dance around them. Years later we are still avoiding the discussion of certain topics, hiding things from others, hiding things from ourselves. We are denying our weaknesses, denying the addictions that are ruining our lives, denying the gravity of our situations.

Then there are those bigger problems, like the need to confront a loved one with a serious issue, or the need to be honest - when lying would be so much easier. There are elephants in every living room, but we really don't like talking about them.

Survivors are famous for taking on the ills of the world then collapsing under the weight. Yes, it ties back into personal responsibility versus the responsibility of others, as well as setting boundaries and assertive communication.

It's that survival thing again. Everybody has their compartments in their brains. You deal with the things you can deal with and do your best to ignore the rest. If something happens to you that is so unbearable that you can't handle it at all, your mind actually protects itself. It compartmentalizes, blacks out, reprograms, splits off, and, in extreme cases, shatters entirely. They have to be addressed or the consequences will be permanent.

Our bodies have some incredible defenses. They can remove many foreign bodies from themselves if given enough time. A foreign body recognized, an enemy battled; that's what an infection is.

Why do we assume that infections are limited to our physical bodies alone? Our bodies get them, yes, but sometimes our souls do, too.

I spent years hiding in my home, refusing to answer the door or the telephone. I even avoided that overwhelmed feeling that took over when I was faced with something I wasn't ready to face.

Try as I may, I couldn't just spend my life avoiding everything. Those little stressors add up and become huge mountains on the verge of collapse.

People wonder how those who have survived sexual abuse could do the things they did. They didn't think about it any more than they absolutely had to. Over time, the abuse victim trains themselves to hide certain parts of their lives away from others and from themselves. It builds up and builds up, and eventually the whole pile comes crashing down.

When we have to deal with something, we do. Sometimes it means sucking it up and doing things that you don't want to do at all–difficult things, sometimes distasteful things–but didn't we learn that from abuse too? We do what we have to do to survive, even when it is unpleasant. You just...do it.

So, that's what we are still doing today: just doing it. We deal with life one crisis at a time, and put aside the things that can be put aside.

The more out of control one part of your life is in one are, the more control you may seek in another. You must become a master of the art of avoidance to continue ignoring abuse. That tired, old elephant is ever present in the room.

Sometimes we all get overwhelmed, and this is not a weakness, it is just a fact. Because of that black-and-white thinking, we tend to think that we have no choice but to take on everything at once. We don't. I'm still trying to learn that problems dealt with today are not allowed to become the monsters of tomorrow. Who knew that we didn't have to wait for a task to become unbearable before we tackled it? All along we were trying to maintain control, and that is exactly what we lost.

The difference between Red and I is that she actually answers the phone when it rings.

It sounds rather irresponsible, but avoiders can be some of the most over-responsible people you know: projects and contests and committees and protests, letters to editors and lawsuits and political causes. Sure, they are very responsible in some areas of their lives, because those passions are usually directed in the areas in which they feel most competent.

Some Survivors have developed their avoidance skills into an art form so intricate that they don't even realize they did it. It wasn't that they didn't have the money to pay the bills, they just didn't pay them. They could have done the housework; they just didn't. A washer, a dryer, and plenty of soap and water, yet Laundry Mountain still remains.

> Nothing in your life is going to change until you believe in you. The first step has to be yours and is yours alone.
>
> ◉
>
> Yes, other people will always be there to tell you exactly how you should travel, when you should leave, and where exactly your final destination should lie, but in the end your journey belongs only to you.

The problems feed and grow, and eventually take on a life of themselves. If we put them off until we have to deal with them, we can easily find ourselves overwhelmed.

The problem becomes so big that we can become stuck.

If you can't deal with the whole problem, try to deal with as much of it as you can. Take a step back. Deal with what you need to in order to get yourself in the right frame of mind. Don't let yourself get lost in busy work. If the problem will not become an elephant over night then let it rest and tend to the ones that will.

Sometimes I still have to step back and ask myself, "How does one eat an elephant?"

One bite at a time, my dear, one bite at a time.

Bullying Survivors

Jessica Alba
Actress
Bullying Survivor

Tom Cruise
Actor
Bullying Survivor

Michael Phelps
Olympic Gold Medalist
Bullying Survivor

Tyra Banks
Model/Actress
Bullying Survivor

Chris Rock
Actor/Comedian
Bullying Survivor

"Sometimes you just need to find a safe place to fall, and then let go. "

~Linda Poindexter

Finding Your Safe Space

I've spent a very long time living as an on-again, off-again recluse.

I've had panic attacks for most of my life; I just didn't know they were called that. I would be standing in the grocery store with a cart full of food and three hungry children when that feeling would grip me. My heart would begin to race, and I could feel the sweat popping out of my pores. My eyes would dart around, searching for the nearest clear path to the door. I didn't want to freak out the people around me and I didn't want to scare my children, so I would stand there as straight-faced as possible, praying that the woman in front of me with a cart full of items with no prices would just get out of my way so I could leave the store.

I just couldn't breathe.

I didn't know what it was or why, only that I had to get out of the situation I was in or bad things were going to happen. It took awhile to figure out that the attacks in the store were linked to spending money. We were always struggling and had three different things that money needed to be spent on. I knew that I would be in trouble no matter where I spent it, that I would have to justify every purchase. Waves of guilt would flood over me, and that overwhelming sense that I was a BAD GIRL.

No matter where I was or what I was doing, I had an incredible urge to hide.

I had similar experiences as far back as I can remember. When the adults in the home were arguing, even when it was only about politics and religion, and their voices got loud, it scared me. I was a small child, so I learned to tuck myself away in the oddest of places, such as under kitchen counters, behind doors, or in the spaces between walls and couches. Sometimes I would be missing for hours while they searched the house for me, only to find me asleep beneath the kitchen sink.

When I got too old to hide inside of the house, I found places outside to comfort me. I always had a secret hideout of some sort as a child, be it a clearing in a thicket of bushes, an abandoned trailer, a church that was left unlocked, or an old abandoned car. I found places at home, and places at school, and even a few places in public places that worked in a pinch.

During my first marriage I was once again reduced to hiding in closets and under bathroom counters when things got bad. Together we were volatile at times. I could only handle so much of the arguing and confusion before my mind would just shut down, so I regressed to my childhood coping strategies.

I hid.

What a grown man thought about finding his wife tucked into the space under the bathroom vanity, he never said. It was my problem, and he expected me to deal with it. He didn't believe in psychology, so discussing my panic attacks with him was out of the question. I couldn't always hide from danger physically, so I eventually learned to hide emotionally, pulling so far inside of myself that nobody could hurt me.

It was another trick I had learned as a child, like a turtle with its shell. I think all Survivors develop a safe place to go inside of their heads during the abuse. Some go as far as developing multiple personalities, but the rest of us learn to tightly compartmentalize our feelings, to tuck certain things away and keep them safe.

My panic attacks are most likely to happen when I feel the control over my life being pulled from me, which is why security lines are the bane of my existence.

I have only flown a few times in my life, and it had been many years since the last time, so everything post September 11 was new to me. I was already out of sorts. There were too many things to do at once, way too much input, and then my my eyes locked with Agent "Walrus the Hutt."

Anxiety is visible to those who are looking for it; TSA Agent W. T. Hutt was looking for it, but it wasn't her job to determine the source. If someone in the middle of a panic attack also happens to be wearing a belt they just bought on sale that looks like weaponry, well...

This was not a wardrobe choice I had considered thoroughly. Apparently belts with plastic bullets aren't a good idea when one flies. Duly noted. A conclusion I clearly should come to about an hour before I actually did.

Instead, Agent Hutt clued me in to the little known fact that there is no distinction between the identification of a terrorist with a bomb and a mom having a panic attack. I was really nervous before we got to the airport. It got worse from there.

If the only safe space you have is inside of your head then you will use it. Sometimes that is the case when you are living with abusers. Your property isn't really yours. Your room isn't really yours. Your belongings are not yours. Your body is not yours. They controlled your money. They controlled your outside relationships. They controlled how long you wore your hair.

Sometimes you literally had nowhere to hide that they could not touch you. Your mind really was all you had left.

She had seen my belt, and there was no escaping. She immediately pointed to me and motioned the other agents over. I watched them handle my computer, my underwear, my exercise equipment.

What I really thought was, "Those are my things. MY things." "My things. "Mine!" I started to say something out loud when my daughter elbowed me in the gut. She knows when to tell mom to quit.

After determining that the belt was not a danger, they allowed me to keep it, but it was placed on the no fly list.

They marched me through *America's Friendliest Airport®* barefoot with my daughter panicking behind me, watching as they swabbed my exercise ball looking for explosives. I began muttering things about being an American and remembering when that used to mean something, way back when there used to be rights before it became clear to me that I was making thing worse. I handed the offending belt over to my friend Matt, gathered the rest of my things, and we ran to catch our flight, which had already departed by then.

It was humiliating, but it wasn't their fault exactly.

I don't always think things through. It's not like I can deny it. My brain has always worked in very different ways than the average person. I have been diagnosed with Attention Deficit Hyperactivity Disorder (minus the "hyper" part), Bipolar Depression (high-functioning), Dissociative Disorder, and Borderline Personality. Basically, I'm not normal and never will be.

But that isn't as bad as it sounds.

I know I don't take the time to think sometimes, so whenever possible I try to give myself as much time as I need to make a good decision.

When I don't, bored TSA agents notice. It would have been nice to avoid the whole ordeal, but where there are lessons to be learned I try to learn them.

I will avoid large airports in the future, and when I can't I will do my best to dress as inoffensively and plastic bullet-free as possible. It's the least I can do for my country.

Sometimes my adrenaline overload gets me into trouble. My family has obviously learned to keep me in check and I've learned to listen to them. They know when I am more likely to panic, and they help me stay calm. They know my limits, and I trust them.

Even the bravest of soldiers must seek sanctuary for a time, a place to keep their thoughts peaceful, where the outside world can't reach them while they recover from their injuries.

Your sanctuary is a consecrated place, your shelter from danger and hardship.

They aren't always there though, and unexpected adrenaline rushes happen. Jerky people happen. Regressing into a yelling match with a stranger isn't a good thing in my book, so I do try to avoid it. I have acted in the heat of the moment and most of the time those actions were irrational and counterproductive.

It means I have to recognize my own cues without a support system.

One day, as I was trying to calm myself, I became aware of the way I was rocking and hugging myself. It was the very same thing I did when my children were little. They would come to me crying, and without hesitation I would pull them into my lap and soothe them. I didn't try to reason with them, there was no use. I didn't try to correct them either.

No value judgments, advice, or scolding, just comfort.

I was nurturing myself just as I would a child and that was exactly what I needed at that moment in time. Once my mind is centered, I can approach the situation rationally again, but before that I'm just wasting my time and everybody else's.

Instead of fighting my panic attacks, I learned to let them go. It isn't the time to solve the problem, or worry about the future, or anything else. It is just time to re-center, to find a place to be alone–in my vehicle, a bathroom stall, even a private alley behind someone's garage to sit it out–somewhere that I feel safe. If I feel like crying, I do. If I feel like cussing, I do that. I do whatever it takes to get my head back into thinking mode.

Then I count my blessings, every single one of them, until I can't find any more. Then I list them again. Or, as I often tell others in the middle of a panic attack, "Tell me the good stuff. Just keep telling me the good stuff."

Yes, there will always be days when you feel weak, but that isn't the time to strike out at others. Instead, take yourself away from the world for some time, and rebuild your strength. It's okay, it will still be turning when you get back, I promise.

It isn't who we are or what has happened to us that will determine our futures, but how well we learn from our pasts. We don't have to let panic attacks rule our lives.

You can keep pushing for longer than most people could imagine, but eventually you will pay for it: more panic attacks, worsened PTSD and ADHD symptoms, and it could lead to permanent disability.

We will all feel overwhelmed at times, and if you have already aggravated your adrenals through years of abuse then you will wear down faster, and it can take longer to recover than a healthy person would. Sometimes it is one big thing that breaks us, but most of the time it is many little things building up, one on top of another.

Abuse Survivors tend to take on too much. They keep saying yes long after they should have said no. They keep taking on more responsibilities long after they felt like crumbling. They push their bodies long past what they can handle. Eventually all of that excess pressure is going to go somewhere. When too much is flying at you it can overwhelm you emotionally.

Come up with a list of things you can do if you find yourself down in the pit. This list should preferably be stored where you can see it every day. It should range from small things that only take a minute to complete, to bigger things like your favorite hobby, or even a much-loved vacation destination. When you feel yourself heading south, pick out an item that appeals to you and take some time to reset yourself.

Create a *Yay Me!* file. You don't have to show anyone else this file, it is just for you. Fill this file with anything that makes you feel good about being you, such as cards and letters from friends, nice comments you have received, awards you have won, and souvenirs of events you participated in that added to your life in some way. It doesn't matter what goes into your file as long as it motivates you to remain positive.

You should have at least one place where you can go to relax, somewhere you can shut out the world and just regenerate. That can be a special place outdoors, a special room, or if you are in a very small house then it may even be your bathroom or a spot behind your shed. It doesn't matter where it is as long as you can access it when you need to.

Panic attacks happen. Remain in control and get yourself calm as quickly as possible. When we feel overwhelmed it is easy to become self-destructive, to make poor decisions, to leap without looking.

Find out what need is going unfulfilled at the moment and allow yourself to fulfill it.

Stop whatever it is you are doing, put whoever it is you are caretaking for aside for a while, and take time out to reset yourself.

My safe place is my bedroom. My bedding is aimed at comfort, with soft textures and relaxing colors. Over the years I have filled my room with items that make me happy, even if they don't make sense to anybody else. I have one full wall covered with letters and small gifts from friends and family, photographs of my friends, a few rocks from my kids, troll dolls, reminders of my accomplishments, several keepsakes from my wedding, and a few other things that are special to me for no real reason. They're the things that remind me of the love and support I have in my life.

My bedroom is that place for me, and your bathroom might be that place for you.

Wherever you set up your sanctuary, find things that make you smile and place them where you can see them. Add affirmations, positive quotes, or whatever you need to create a loving atmosphere. Candles with your favorite scents, your favorite music, and even a book you enjoy should all be nearby. Make it mean something to you. Whatever it is that makes you happy, try to surround yourself with it.

Whatever your safe space is, make it your own and spend time in there whenever you can, even if it is for only fifteen minutes. The closer you can come to keeping yourself balanced, the less likely those scales are going to tip and leave you feeling overwhelmed. Having a safe place is important for almost everyone, but especially for Survivors. Make it your place of renewal.

You can't take care of anyone else unless you take care of yourself.

Roll Call

Carrie Otis
Model
Rape Survivor

Iyanla Vanzant
Motivational Speaker
Child Sexual Abuse Survivor

Toni Childs
Musician
Abuse Survivor

Dave Mustaine
Musician
Child Abuse Survivor

Carlos Santana
Musician
Child Sexual Abuse Survivor

"Every day above ground is a good day."

~Flora Klein

Every Day Above Ground

I stopped telling people I was born in Germany when the other kids at school started calling me a Nazi. I didn't know what a Nazi was exactly, but I could tell that it was bad. When I asked my mother about the subject, she introduced me to the story of Anne Frank. I still remember the growing horror within me at the thought that I could possibly be one of these people.

Imagine my relief when I discovered that being born in Germany did not make me anything one way or the other and had nothing whatsoever to do with the Nazi party.

The true depths of the Survivor Spirit were tested to their limits during World War II and the years that followed. When we think of what life must have been like for those who were deemed less than human under Hitler's rule, it is almost unfathomable.

Nazi officials sought out more economic and efficient means of wiping out large groups of people and somehow succeeded. Entire families were wiped out in a single day, using some of the most inhumane means imaginable.

An estimated 6 million Jews were sent to horrific deaths as a result of the National Socialist Party's ideology along with 1 million Soviets, 1.5 million political prisoners, and hundreds of thousands of "undesirables."

No matter how bad my life got, I would always think of people like Anne Frank and remind myself how truly blessed I was. The abuses that I have seen seem to matter so very little when compared to the suffering that others have seen. If she could remain positive hidden away in an attic while death and desolation surrounded her on all sides, then I told myself that I could make it through my own childhood.

Her story gave me strength as a child, and it still does today.

Despite the Nazi party's best efforts to suffocate the very spirit of humanity, the Survivor Spirit still found a way. After two years in hiding, Anne Frank and her family were sent to the gas chambers, and in the end only her father survived. Her father was the one that found her journal among the rubble of his life, and it was that one man who found a way to broadcast his daughter's voice to the world.

Another young girl perhaps less well known than Anne Frank went on to share her voice with the world in very different way.

Florence Klein was imprisoned at Ravensbruck concentration camp. Her mother and grandmother were taken to the gas chambers immediately. When Flora's mother saw what was about to happen she leaned down to whisper to her young daughter, "Survive and God will bless you."

So, the girl did exactly as her mother had told her; she kept going.

Her training as a beautician made her an asset to an officer wife and is probably what kept her alive while so many she knew and loved died. But Flora had some other skills at her disposal that were even more important.

Abuse is always about power and control. The Nazi's had the power, and they had the control, but they made the same mistake every abuser in history has ever made. They underestimated the power of the human spirit.

They certainly misjudged young Flora Klein. Flora was eventually liberated from the concentration camp and immigrated to Israel where she got married to another holocaust Survivor. They were dirt poor and struggled to survive. Her husband walked out on her shortly after their child was born. A little boy that she named Chaim Witz.

> *"Israel was a new country, only a year older than I was, and its existence was still very much in question. But I was unaware of all that. It was always such a part of my daily routine that I wasn't able to separate it from any other aspect*

of my experience. For example, I remember that my dad, Yechiel (or Feri)Witz – who was physically imposing, at least six foot five – would come in on the weekends with his machine gun and put it on the kitchen table. The front lines were fifty miles away, and everybody, every male and most females, was in the army. There were no exemptions. If you lived there, you were in the army.

The gun on the table was one of the few things I remember about my father, because he wasn't around very much..."

~Chaim "Eugene" Klein-Simmons

Flora's Survivor Spirit told her that it was time to start a new life in the United States, so she and her son immigrated to America where Chaim changed his name to the much easier to pronounce Eugene Klein.

Gene's mother often told him that "Every day above ground is a good day," and he still lives by that principle today. His mother had seen what life was like without the freedoms her son had in the U.S. and she encouraged him to make full use of them.

Gene was born to be a Survivor. He adapted to American life quite well, never forgetting his first visit to a supermarket which he said "...was like a city of food, with streets going in different directions."

Gene dedicated himself to his studies, learning to speak several languages including English, German, Hungarian, and Hebrew. He was especially fond of the American dream, the idea that anyone can attain success if they work hard enough for it.

As an adult, he worked for a time as a sixth-grade teacher, and an assistant to an editor of *Vogue*. His talent for business was undeniable but there was this little band that he started with some friends.

Despite his humble beginnings, as of 2011, Gene's net worth was about 300 million dollars.

Among his credits you will also find bassist, singer, songwriter, actor, producer, and above all, entrepreneur. I have no doubt that future generations will find statues of him and think he was worshiped worldwide. He certainly has left a huge mark on the world.

Today Chaim Klein's face is instantly recognizable even if his former name is not. Now known as Gene Simmons, Flora Klein's son has built one of the most recognizable brands in the world. Well known for his blood spitting and pyrotechnic stage theatrics, his band KISS has sold more than 100 million albums worldwide and has over 3,000 unique product licenses.

Gene has been at the top of his game for nearly 40 years, and isn't slowing down yet. And who does this giant of a man credit with his success? His tiny, little mother.

Flora Klein tested the Survivor Spirit to the limits, and triumphed over the darkness. People worldwide have heard her story and responded with admiration and support. Flora even has her own Facebook fan page called Flora's Army, of which I am a proud member. How could you not want to stand as close as possible to someone who emanates such a vibrant light?

Gene Simmons credits his mother for teaching him to be the man he is today, but I suspect he learned far more from her than even he realizes. He has used those lessons to build a strong home life, an impressive career, and like his mother, he is every bit a Survivor.

> My mother is probably the wisest person I've ever known. She's not schooled, she's not well read. But she has a philosophy of life that makes well-read people seem like morons.
>
> ~Gene Simmons

He grew up knowing that his mother was a powerhouse and somehow picked up the resiliency traits that kept her going all of those years ago. She carried those traits out of the darkness with her and she passed them on to the next generation.

Funny how we do that, isn't it?

Coping is a learned skill, just like anything else. People who cope with one trauma successfully are better prepared to deal with the next. What we can learn from Gene Simmons and his feisty little mother Flora, is that Post Traumatic Growth Syndrome can even be passed down from one generation to the next.

A lot of people experience trauma, but not everyone handles it in the same ways. Some, it seems, come out stronger.

They often talk of Post Traumatic Stress Disorder, but how often does anybody talk about Post Traumatic Growth Syndrome?

While some people will wither and die as a result of their experiences, others will go on to find a greater appreciation for life. Their priorities change. They report deeper and more intimate relationships and a greater sense of personal strength. They weren't just changed by trauma, somehow they were made better by it.

Surely they were simply born strong?

Oddly, this doesn't seem to be the case. Sometimes the best coping skills leave the least room for growth. It isn't our experiences but our struggles to overcome them that make us stronger.

It isn't the trauma that changes us as much as the challenges that we face in the aftermath. It isn't what we deal with, but how well we deal with it that matters.

Like the story of two sisters that had grown up in an abusive home. Their father was an alcoholic who sometimes flew into fits of rage. The youngest sister, predictably, went on to be just like their father and faced many hardships in her life: alcoholism, addiction, divorce, and estrangement from her children.

The older sister was the opposite of her sibling in every way. She went on to see great success, both personally and professionally, had risen to the top of her field, and found much contentment in her life. One day a reporter came to interview the sisters.

She asked both of them the same question: "Why do you think things turned out the way they did for you?"

Neither sister hesitated when they responded,

"My father was an alcoholic. What else could I do?"

What else can you do?

Victim or Survivor, the choice is yours.

Some of the darkest times in humanity's history have brought forth Survivors who not only resumed their former lives but went on to be very successful. In the years that followed their abuse, they found stronger marriages and families, successful businesses, and financial prosperity. They used skills formed in the darkness to light the way to their futures.

How did they do it?

By being open and willing to learn from life, and the lessons that present themselves. Grieving and acceptance of the past are crucial to handling stresses and traumas in the future. Don't be afraid to look closely at your experiences. Sometimes there is sorrow in there, but where there is pain there is always growth.

What is the one quality that Survivors have that victims lack? Resiliency. Not only do Survivors bounce back, they come back stronger than before and if done right, it's extremely contagious.

Gene Simmon's mother taught him that mankind can be capable of unimaginable inhumanity, but that there will always be good in the world.

Your job is to find it.

It is those who are most open to growth experiences that have them. Abuse in our past can help us focusing on having healthier relationships in the present with our spouses, our children, and everyone else. Sometimes abuse directs us to a support system or makes us see the strength we already have on our own. Sometimes we simply grow.

> It's in the history books, the Holocaust. It's just a phrase. And the truth is it happened yesterday. It happened to my mother. I never met my grandmothers or my grandfathers. They were all wiped up in the gas chambers of Nazi Germany.
>
> ~Gene Simmons

Maybe it has made you more aware of the kindness that you offer to others. Perhaps it pushed you into a vocation that you would not have sought out otherwise. Maybe it has made you intolerant of abuse and more willing to help other people escape. It can even lead you down spiritual paths you would have never traveled on your own, driving you to success.

Stop looking at your past as a negative, and admit that it isn't going to change. Look beyond the shadows and find the lessons that can be learned. Find the lessons that can make your life better, and the ones that can change the world. Build your resiliency traits when times are good, so they are there when you need them. Feed your Survivor Spirit and it will grow.

Somewhere in your life the world warped. Things that should not have happened to you did. If your world was warped, your perceptions became warped as well. Through abuse a separate world developed within us all, a dark place where secret things are stored.

What happened to you will never be okay, but it will never go away either. The sheer determination to survive in our darkest circumstances often translates to something far more positive in the light.

Before you can set off on a new path, you have to be willing to see it. Perhaps that's why it is so important to find a solid support system. Burdens are always easier to manage with some help.

So often people credit their spirituality for getting them through their most difficult times, but many also credit their hardship for strengthening their faith. The two go hand in hand. Those with healthy social support systems are better equipped to handle trauma.

What doesn't kill you makes you stronger.

All groaning aside, it is true, but only if you allow it to bring you strength.

Survivors are more aware of oppression than most, and tend to have a strong desire to alleviate it. Problem solving and peacekeeping skills that were developed under fire become valuable in work and social settings. Skills that were honed under abuse and neglect can be used in nearly every area of your life once you are aware of them.

Survivors survive. It's what they do.

Choosing whether to go on with malice or with dignity is something we will all face. The same is true of every single Survivor who has come before you. The same is true of you.

Every Survivor needs a higher purpose. It differs from person to person, and even situation to situation, but your passion is what gives you the strength to keep going. Whatever it is, find it and never let go.

I love my children more than life itself. I wanted to make the world a better place for my children, and in the beginning they were all the purpose that I needed. Every time I looked at them I knew that I had to change something. I didn't want them growing up seeing the things I had seen or hearing the things that I heard. So I figured out what changes needed to be made, and I struggled to make them.

To grow stronger, you must use the strengths you have been given whatever they may be. As you use them, they will grow stronger. Some people don't have children to put their efforts toward, but it doesn't matter. If you need to make changes in your life for your cat, then do it. Your starting-off point is often small, but the journey of a thousand miles always begins with a single step.

Now there are times when I am able to help someone else, and I almost feel like it did happen for a reason, that my experiences have been turned into something positive. It gave me that sense of purpose that I needed to keep going. Just getting this book finished is another step on that path. I already have several more projects in the works.

When it is too dark to keep going, look ahead.

Survival is a journey, not a destination. Where we are going changes constantly, but the goal is the same. Find whatever it is that will give you the drive to get up in the morning, and then get up. Do it today, and then tomorrow, and then the day after that.

The Survivor Spirit can be a gentle whisper in your ear, or it can be a wild creature. It can warn you of dangers real, or imagined, and spur you on to action.

⊜

You might find it snapping and snarling at the first hint of a threat. You might find it telling you to just be still and wait.

Listen...

Some will continue on along the path of victimhood their whole lives, always at the mercy of circumstances beyond their control, functioning from one crisis to the next, one disastrous relationship to the next, one bad environment to the next. It's what they do, and you can't fault them for that.

You are a Survivor. You were meant to move on.

Some families have lived with generation after generation of abuse, but few have taken the steps necessary to end that cycle. For each family member who heals and commits to ending the cycle of abuse, how many more continue that cycle? They pass it on to their children, and to their children's children, and...

But good things can be passed on to our children too.

Know that you really do deserve better and do not let anything get in the way of that. You will work through fears. You will work through tears. You will break yourself down into little pieces and put yourself back together again over and over.

It will be worth it.

It always is.

Why should you heal? Because you deserve it. Because those who come after you deserve it too. You will pass that legacy on to a new generation, so choose wisely.

I know without a doubt that I would not appreciate the sunny days in my life nearly as much if I had not experienced so much rain. I do not regret my experiences. There is no reason to. Each of them led me to where I am today.

Author, Speaker, Survivor, Dreamer... and the possibilities from here are endless.

Anybody can become a victim, but some continue those habits long after the actual abuse is over. Bad things just seem to keep happening to them, Lord knows why. They become perpetual victims of circumstance, buried alive in the wrongs that have been done to them.

Once you learn to see the world through the eyes of a victim, you are just waiting to be buried.

Victims are stuck, and by God, they are going to remain stuck. They haven't found their Survivor Spirit, and until they do they will stay right where they are. It is their life to do with as they please. Sometimes all you can do is get out of their way.

If you are still in an abusive relationship, keep yourself safe, keep yourself alert, and above all keep yourself alive. The time will come when freedom is possible. When that happens, do not hesitate. Once you are free however, don't stop there.

Survivors go on living, and that in and of itself takes courage. It takes courage to remove yourself from abuse. It takes courage to make a commitment to healing. Being a victim sucks, but as it turns out, being a Survivor isn't all that bad. Abuse taught you traits that have contributed to your survival and can even help you thrive.

Your Survivor Spirit has kept you alive this long and it is far too stubborn to give up now.

It is always on the look out for red flags, reasons to be on guard. With sensitivities toward certain situations honed to a razor-sharp edge, it quite often acts on its own. Sometimes you react without fully understanding why you did it, as if some invisible switch was flipped in your brain. Its reflexes are instantaneous.

It is a learned response.

Being aware of your strengths and weaknesses can sometimes mean the difference between life and death. Next time you get your hair done, stop and think about that for a moment. Who could have guessed that Flora Klein's hairdressing skills could be what may someday keep her alive?

You only develop the survival skills you need by using them. The more they are used, the stronger they become. PTSD is frequently talked about, but there is another less-known residual after-effect among abuse Survivors known as Post-Traumatic Growth.

To find out if you have PTGS, check the list of symptoms below...

Optimism

When someone has lost everything, they are in a better position to appreciate what they do have. As soon as you let go of hope, the darkness in your life becomes permanent. You have seen the dark side of life, but that doesn't mean that the light ceased to exist. Knowing that the sun will come up again makes the darkness easier to handle. The sun will come up tomorrow...I promise.

Resourcefulness

One thing found over and over in studies of Survivors is that they admittedly used whatever resources they had at their disposal, and they were always on the lookout for more.

Coping Skills

If all it takes to ruin your day is the wrong coffee, then you are going to have a lot of crummy days. That is your choice, but please keep it to yourself. Bad things happen to everybody. The world keeps spinning, with you or without you. Learn to cope with it or get left behind.

Tenacity

Victims give up. Survivors just don't have it in them. Like a dog with its teeth locked upon a big, juicy steak, Survivors take hold and refuse to let go. Why does it seem like so many Survivors are so successful in their given fields? It isn't because they fell into their success; they just refused to give up until they got there.

Creativity

In a survival situation, creativity is often the difference between those who make it out alive and those who don't. You can't explore all of the possibilities in life until you open your mind up to them. Just remember the Neanderthals, those who fail to adapt creatively often fail to survive.

Risk-Taking

Change is always a risk. Nobody can promise you that all of your efforts will be successful in life. Some plans will be epic disasters, but now and then one will work. You never know until you try. The Survivor knows that failure is just another bump in the road to ultimate success.

You have met a lot of Survivors throughout this book, and a few people who did not survive their abuse, but there are far more out there than I have listed here.

One in five people.

Whether you will be a victim your whole life or a Survivor depends on how far and how fast you move, if you even get moving at all.

Victims. Survivors. Thrivers.

Survivors have moved beyond victimhood, beyond feeling sorry for themselves, beyond allowing others to take responsibility for their paths, beyond allowing their self-doubts to rule their lives. Survivors keep moving.

You can use your experiences to hold you back, or you can use them to push you forward. You have already developed at least some ability to recover from hardship.

Those resiliency skills are already there, now use them.

...

If you would like to learn more about PTGS, the American Psychological Association has developed a Post-Traumatic Growth Inventory that can be taken on their website (http://cust-cf.apa.org/ptgi/). The assessment covers several different areas that can be affected by trauma: your relationships with others, openness to new possibilities, personal strength levels, changes in spirituality, and how appreciative you are of life in general.

> "Everything can be taken from a man or a woman but one thing, the last of human freedoms to choose one's attitude in any given set of circumstances, to choose one's own way."
>
> ~Viktor E. Frankl

Throughout the inventory you will find questions about the positive effects the trauma may have had on your life. As you make your way through it, you will begin to see that abuse has taught you to appreciate life and all of the experiences it has to offer in often unrecognized ways. You will learn to view your hardships in a very different light.

Learn to greater appreciate yourself and others, to value yourself and the gift of life more deeply. Things beyond your control can sometimes knock you down, but that doesn't make you a victim. That only happens once you get stuck. What you do after your abuse is what really makes the difference. Survivors refuse to stay down. They get back up. And they keep getting up as many times as it takes.

Resiliency = Bouncing Back

Holocaust Survivors

Bettina Le Beau
Actress

Cornelia "Corrie" ten Boom
Evangelist, Author

Curt Lowens
Actor

Imre Kertész
Author

Otto Frank
Father of Anne Frank, Activist

Descendants of Holocaust Survivors

Billy Joel
(Father)

Mila Kunis
(Grandparents)

Natalie Portman
(Grandparents)

Richmond, Patricia, Alexis, and David Arquette
(Mother)

Shia LaBeouf
(Grandfather)

*"You've got to be-
lieve you can be a
standup before you
can be a standup.
You have to believe
you can act before
you can act. You
have to believe you
can be an astronaut
before you can be
an astronaut.
You've got to be-
lieve."*

~Eddie Izzard

You Have Got To Believe

Reach out and touch the spiritual for just a moment. Faith is what feeds the Survivor Spirit. It's always there when you go looking for it. Spirituality isn't about rules, or dogma, or conformity. It is just about faith.

After my first marriage ended in disaster, I lost my faith in religion. I lost my faith in men. I lost my faith in love, in marriage, and in life.

I never meant to give it up. It wasn't as if this had been a conscious decision. I tried to fight it but there was no ammunition left to fight with. I've met a lot of Toads in my life, and sometimes just trusting a male is a very difficult thing for me.

It took two men to help me get my faith back, one of them I married, and the other just makes me laugh. And both of them happened to be named Eddie.

I met my very own Eddie less than three months after the separation, and just a few weeks after the rape. I kept telling him that he didn't want me, but he insisted that he did. He isn't one to give up once he has set his mind to something, and I've never really understood why he chose me.

I'm smart he says, and I make him laugh. I challenge him, and my skin is soft. He says I'm still sexy, and introduces me to pretty girls as the love of his life.

After ten years of marriage, we still fall asleep holding hands most nights.

We had to figure out a lot of things together those first few years, and sometimes it seems we were apart more than we were together. I was terrified of being caged again, and anything even resembling those old bars sent me into a panic.

He has never raised a hand to me, but when he was drinking he was a very different man. There was a fight one day and both tempers flared. He locked me out of the house, and when I shut the door behind me it automatically locked him out so he kicked it in.

I called the cop to come calm him down and the next thing I know my husband was facing Domestic Violence charges. It wasn't intentional on either of our parts, but by the time we realized how deep we were, it was far too late. He couldn't come to the house or even drive by.

I was angry with him, but I hadn't meant to have him arrested. Somehow my grand plan to avoid abuse in my life had backfired. It was late, late that night and insomnia and I were getting better acquainted.

I was lying on the sofa, trying to figure out what to do next while mindlessly flipping through the channels. I came across this odd character wearing makeup and heels while talking about taking over countries with the cunning use of flags.

From that moment on, British actor and philosopher in the guise of comedian, Eddie Izzard, was my obsession. I think it had a lot to do with his feminine appearance a first. Here was a man who unashamedly ran around in dresses and makeup, but dated women and those things softened him. They sort of made him okay.

I have always been a big fan of comedy, but this was the first time I realized that laughter really did heal. I have been a rabid Izzardite ever since. The next time I saw his show on cable, I recorded it. I played that video until the tape nearly rotted off of the spools. He made me laugh when I needed it most.

I have been fighting depression medication free ever since.

Even if I had decided to swear of men for the rest of my life, Eddie Izzard didn't really fall unto any cold, hard categories. He was soft enough that he didn't intimidate me, but at the same time he was all man. That was really all that it took. He was a man, but he was a safe man.

Once assaulted for his preference for feminine style dress, Eddie endured bullying as far back as grammar school for his many differences. He is now loved the world over, and he didn't even have to give up the lingerie to do it.

The word victim never once came into play in his documentary, *Believe*. Doors were slammed in his face over and over again, but he just kept finding new doors to knock on. It inspired me to keep knocking. When someone told him that he wasn't talented enough, he just tried harder. So when that happened to me, I just tried harder, too. He refused to let someone else define his reality.

Ironically, perhaps, this happened at a time at time I was trying so hard to be normal.

If this guy could stand up in front of the world and say "Here I am, take more or leave me," then what was stopping me?

Without Eddie Izzard, Boshemia would not exist. By the time his documentary, came out I had already decided to write Sister, Survivor, and I had at least a basic idea of what it would be about. I didn't know if I could actually write a whole book and, even if I could, I still had no idea why somebody would want to read it.

There is no secret formula, or magic What has happened in your past isn't nearly as important as what will happen in your future. Today–right now, in fact–is the beginning of that future.

What will happen, where it will lead, and who will share that path with you is all entirely up to you.

But I did it anyhow.

I didn't know how, and I didn't know when, but I knew it was possible, and that was all that mattered. If he could do it, then I knew I could.

I had to keep *Believe* on repeat at times just to keep me going. I might not have had enough faith for myself, but Eddie had enough faith for both of us, so I borrowed a little bit of it. Within a year, like Eddie, I also had a role in a documentary.

My own Ed inspired me in very different ways. I had stopped believing in love, but he refused to let me give up. It didn't matter how many times I slammed the door in his face, he came back the next day. He sobered up cold turkey the night of his arrest, and for eighteen months he kept coming back to prove it to me.

He gave me the freedom to discover that relationships are not total depend-ence, but they aren't total independence either.

There is another type of "dependence" that is far healthier. Professionals call it "interdependence." This is a place where you are a part of a relationship but you are not consumed by it, where you can allow others to do things for you, but also know how to seek out and find happiness within yourself.

When you are interdependent you are wholly part of your relationship but you still maintain a separate self. Wanting something for yourself now and then doesn't take away from the relationship, it adds to it. Everybody wants to be the focus of the relationship now and then. Before someone can enter into a truly healthy relationship they must first experience independence.

An interdependent relationship is about balance. It requires two self-ac-tualized people. A self-balanced person has surpassed the chaos of scrambling to have their needs met by others and put that energy into meeting them on their own.

While I was going through my darkest times, my Darth Edsilius refused to leave my side. He encouraged me to get better, and he encouraged me to *be* better. And he promises me that I will meet Eddie Izzard someday-when I have earned it.

Eddie Izzard taught me to Believe, and my Eddie simply believed in me. He offered me love even when I couldn't accept it. He didn't understand why I pulled away from him sometimes, or why silly things seemed to set me off. He never understood my startle reflex or my difficulties in letting people get close. In fact, there were a lot of things about me he didn't understand and still doesn't, even ten years later.

It didn't matter.

He has allowed me to teach him so much over the years, he has

taught me even more. He chose to love me, and because he loved me, he listened when I told him that I dreamed of being a writer. So he stood in the shadows and watched me become one.

I didn't know where to begin, so I had to find people who did, people I could relate to and learn from: Batman, Gene Simmons, Eddie Izzard. As soon as I was ready to learn, each of them had something to teach me. As different as we all were, we all had something in common. We all share a Survivor Spirit.

Each of the things that have happened in my life have made me who I am today. Those things all became a part of me. The good and the bad combined to teach me the lessons I now share with others. They weren't easy lessons, but I needed each of them to get here.

No matter how bad things may have been in my past, I wouldn't change them for the world. I am a strong and independent woman today because of those experiences.

You should know by now that you can't get rid of the bad without getting rid of the good that came with it. Sometimes life is glorious, and sometimes life just sucks. It doesn't matter how painful the lessons were at the time, you still learned them. You got through them.

You deserve to come to a point in your life where the day no longer begins with forcing yourself out of bed, dragging yourself through the day, doing your best to get through it, and going to bed hoping that tomorrow will be better. Lather, rinse, repeat.

That is not life.

Walk your path for yourself, and walk it with nothing less than your full self. When you choose to BELIEVE that something better awaits you, tomorrow really can be different than all of the days before it. You deserve a life that is not just a routine but an adventure.

Growth so often comes from those places you least expect it.

Because I have seen the dark, I can now more fully appreciate the light. I try not to let myself forget that. Both of them have to exist to have a full picture of the life before you.

Because of the unhappiness in my past, I can appreciate the happiness I have found today. I can only recognize those unhealthy patterns because I have lived with them. I can understand interdependence because I have seen its alternatives in my life. I have been hurt, and because I know what that feels like I am committed to instead being a positive force in the lives of others as often as possible. Sometimes I fail miserably, but the journey isn't over just yet.

The dream of being treated with respect and dignity within my personal relationships used to be the real fairy tale, but not anymore. I had a lot of great teachers along the way.

My mother, Roxy Wilson-Theodore, my grandmother Phyllis Hilleary Johnson, my great-grandmother, Minnie Marie Edwards-Hilleary-Van Voorhees. They were my very first. I am proud to be descended from them, to have their blood running through my veins.

Those that came before me taught me to put one foot in front of the other. To keep going no matter how bad things got. I watched them muddle their way through the dark parts of their lives on nothing more than blind faith. I watched them come out the other side victorious.

Every family member that escaped the cycle encouraged me further.

You belong to a different kind of family now, a safe family, a family with some of the strongest roots you will ever encounter. While your secrets have separated you from so many others, they are what connect you to the family of Survivors. Many have come fore you – both women and men. If you aren't sure that you have the strength of your own to use, it's okay, you can borrow some of ours for a while.

Sometimes I still feel like my world is crashing down around me, like I just don't have whatever it is that they had. Sometimes I just don't think I can take another damned step. But I do.

> We are men. We are women. We are young, and we are old. We've all lived our own unique stories. On the surface, it hardly seems we have anything in common at all, but we are a family.
>
> ⊜
>
> We are here with you in spirit always. We are Survivors.

Lucky for you, genetics isn't the only way to get it.

Upon first glance, it hardly seems we have anything in common at all, but we are a family joined not by blood, but by spirit. We have never met, you and I, but we are part of a family just the same. We share something far more intimate than blood or genes. We have secrets.

We are men. We are women. We are young, and we are old. We've all lived our own unique stories. We have our own backgrounds and cultures. Skin color makes no difference, nor does economic status. On the surface, it hardly seems we have anything in common at all, but we are a family. We are here with you in spirit always.

I've been an avid reader for most of my life, and finishing a book for me has always been like finishing a great journey.

This time we end where we usually start, with a new beginning.

Learning does not stop when you hit a magic age or milestone, that process continues throughout your lifetime. There is still so much beauty and wonder to experience in life that nobody should be in too big of a hurry to get there.

Life is a journey, not a destination.

Thank you for allowing me to be your tour guide for a short time. Perhaps our paths will meet again?

Until then, be well my friend, be well.

BoSHEMIA

For more information please visit www.BoshemiasBohemia.com.

More Survivors...

Donnie McClurkin
Singer and Preacher
Child Sexual Abuse Survivor

Joelle Moses
Singer
Child Sexual Abuse Survivor

KEM
Singer
Child Sexual Abuse Survivor

Rahsaan Patterson
R&B Singer
Child Sexual Abuse Survivor

Tami Roman
Reality TV Star
Rape Survivor

"The beginning of wisdom is to call things by their right names"

~Chinese Proverb

Calling Abuse What It Is...

Dr. Irene Matiatos from DrIrene.com has graciously given me permission to share the list she has complied of the many forms that abuse can take. If you recognize more than a few of these signs in your past, then it is time to start calling it exactly what it is.

Does Your Partner...

Ignore your feelings?

Disrespect you?

Ridicule or insult you, then tell you it's a joke, or that you have no sense of humor?

Ridicule your beliefs, religion, race, heritage, or class?

Withhold approval, appreciation, or affection?

Give you the silent treatment?

Walk away without answering you?

Criticize you, call you names, yell at you?

Humiliate you privately or in public?

Roll his or her eyes when you talk?

Give you a hard time about socializing with your friends or family?

Make you socialize (and keep up appearances) even when you don't feel well?

Seem to make sure that what you really want is exactly what you won't get?

Tell you that you are too sensitive?

Hurt you, especially when you are down?

Seem energized by fighting, while fighting exhausts you?

Have unpredictable mood swings, alternating from good to bad for no apparent reason?

Present a wonderful face to the world and is well liked by outsiders?

"Twist" your words, somehow turning what you said against you?

Try to control decisions, money, even the way you style your hair or wear your clothes?

Complain about how badly you treat him or her?

Threaten to leave, or threaten to throw you out?

Say things that make you feel good, but do things that make you feel bad?

Ever left you stranded?

Ever threaten to hurt you or your family?

Ever hit or push you, even "accidentally"?

Seem to stir up trouble just when you seem to be getting closer to each other?

Abuse something you love: a pet, a child, an object?

Compliment you enough to keep you happy, yet criticize you enough to keep you insecure?

Promise to never do something hurtful again?

Harass you about imagined affairs?

Manipulate you with lies and contradictions?

Destroy furniture, punch holes in walls, break appliances?

Drive like a road-rage junkie?

Act immature and selfish, yet accuse you of those behaviors?

Question your every move and motive, somehow questioning your competence?

Interrupt you; hear but not really listen?

Make you feel like you can't win? Damned if you do, damned if you don't?

Use drugs and/or alcohol? Are things worse then?

Incite you to rage, which is "proof" that you are to blame?

Try to convince you he or she is "right" while you are "wrong"?

Frequently say things that are later denied or accuse you of misunderstanding?

Treat you like a sex object, or as though sex should be provided on demand regardless of how you feel?

Your situation is critical if the following applies to you...

You express your opinions less and less freely.

You find yourself walking on eggshells, careful of when and how to say something.

You long for that softer, more vulnerable part of your partner to emerge.

You find yourself making excuses for your partner's behavior.

You feel emotionally unsafe.

You feel it's somehow not okay to talk with others about your relationship.

You hope things will change, especially through your love and understanding.

You find yourself doubting your memory or sense of reality.

You doubt your own judgment.

You doubt your abilities.

You feel vulnerable and insecure.

You are becoming increasingly depressed.

You feel increasingly trapped and powerless.

You have been or are afraid of your partner.

Your partner has physically hurt you, even once.

A Few Facts...

- On average, one in four girls will experience sexual abuse before the age of eighteen, as will one in seven boys.
- One in four women will experience domestic violence at some point in her life.
- Women experience about 4.8 million physical assaults and rapes by an intimate partner every year. (National Center for Injury Prevention and Control)
- We can now count the time between acts of violence in the U.S. in mere seconds.
- In the year 2000, 1,247 women lost their lives to violence by an intimate partner, but so did 440 men.
- The FBI's "Uniform Crime Report" routinely lists domestic violence as the leading cause of injury to women ages 15 to 44.
- It is believed that as many as sixty percent of abuse cases go unreported.

Keep Yourself Safe

If you are still in an abusive relationship, there are people waiting to help you now. In the back of this book you will find a list of resources, but don't wait. Call for help today.

1-800-799-SAFE (7233)

Boshemia's Bohemia

The personal website of Ayngel "Boshemia" Overson personal thoughts and articles for abuse Survivors. Advocacy, awareness, and inspiration.

www.boshemiasbohemia.com

Articles on Squidoo

More articles on Survivors and abuse written by the Ayngel "Boshemia" Overson.

www.squidoo.com/lensmasters/boshemia

ChildHelp USA National Child Abuse Hotline

Crisis intervention and professional counseling on child abuse, offers referrals to local service groups that offer child abuse counseling. 24 hours, seven days a week

1-800-4-A-CHILD (4-2-24453)

www.childhelp.org

Covenant House

Crisis line for youth, teens, and families. Gives callers locally based referrals throughout the United States. Provides help for youth and parents regarding drugs, abuse, homelessness, runaway children, and message relays. Operates 24 hours, seven days a week.

1-800-999-9999

www.covenanthouse.org

Dr. Irene's Verbal Abuse Site!

This site offers a moderated forum called Trubbles Catbox, and a wealth of articles on abuse. Excellent support and education system.

www.drirene.com

The National Center on Elder Abuse (NCEA)

Directed by the U.S. Administration on Aging, is committed to helping national, state, and local partners in the field be fully prepared to ensure that older Americans will live with dignity, integrity, independence, and without abuse, neglect, and exploitation. 1-800-677-1116

www.ncea.aoa.gov

The National Domestic Violence Hotline

24 hours, seven days a week, available in 170 languages this hotline provides crisis intervention, information and referral to victims of domestic violence, perpetrators, friends and families. Created by Congress as part of the Violence Against Women Act: currently funded by the Family Violence Prevention and Service Act. 1-800-799-SAFE (7233)

www.ndvh.org

RAINN

Rape, Abuse & Incest National Network.

The Rape, Abuse & Incest National Network is the nation's largest anti-sexual assault organization. Free, confidential services; educates the public about sexual assault; and leads national efforts to prevent sexual assault, improve services to victims and ensure that rapists are brought to justice. Hotline: 1-800-656-HOPE (4673)

www.rainn.org

The Wind Beneath My Wings, Thank You To...

Three years ago I started with a blank page, and an idea and a little bit of hope. Today I am ready to turn that book over to you. Before I do that however, I want to take a moment to say thank you to the people who propped me up along the way.

In no particular order or significance, cuz I love you all:

First of all to my Darth Edsilius, I adore you. Thank you for not only giving me my wings, but teaching me how to use them.

To Brooke, Justin, Mystery, and Jaid. You are my life. You are my reason for being. You are the reason for everything. To my family who saw me laugh, cry, scream, and threatening to give up more times than I care to admit. I finally finished the book! To Potterworld!

And then we have Sir Matthew Wint, my BFFTWGE and official world's best minion. Nobody will ever read this book as many times as he has, and I thank him sincerely. The student has become the master.

To Red. You are a true inspiration. Thank you for gifting the world with your talents, and with a Matt.

To my dearest Elizabeth, who consistently took time out of her own life to see me through this project from beginning to end. From editing to artwork to just allowing me to vent. A most sincere thank you for being a part of my world and allowing me to be a part of yours.

To Miss Kristen who came into my life just when I needed her most, and I thank you for everything. You were an awesome proofreader and editor.

Back to high school, To Mrs. Knick, who taught me to get it right or die trying. To Mrs. Barber who told me to keep writing. To Mrs. Sandefeur for years and years of friendship and support. To Miss Jennifer, I miss you so much. R.I.P.

My dear sweet Sugar can not be forgotten, nor can my mother or any of the amazing women in my life. This book is my thank you to them. I have been privileged to sit at their feet.

Aunt Barb and Uncle Larry, thanks for being there even when you thought I was crazy, and thank you for giving me a Derick to share that life with.

Derick, Dude. You know. Man, you know. I love you man.

To Aunt Tammy, my first and best mentor and hero. My Amway kit wasn't a total waste. Thanks for all of the rallies!

To Uncle Rob my writing mentor, I finally did something with it.

To Carol, you are an amazing woman who ruined your sons on other women for the rest of their lives. But above all you taught them love by example, thank you.

Aunt Connie and Uncle Jim, thank you for showing me God's Love every day of your life. My faith is only here because of people like you.

And to that end, thank you to Pastor Mark and Skitter Jones, and Steve and Tammy Lowrance. You have been my angels in this journey more times than you know. You kept reminding me that God had bigger plans for me, and when others shunned me because of their faith, you loved me because of yours. Thank you.

To Dawn the best step-mom a girl could ever ask for. And to my amazing siblings, thank you for sharing your love with me. I have always and will always love you and be thankful to be a part of your family. Daddy. I did it. You are always here in my heart and always have been . I miss you.

To Shane. This is still isn't the book I wanted you to see, but I am working on it.

The San Miguel Resource Center has been my life line for many years now. I still call them when I don't know what else to do, and they almost always have an answer for me too. If they don't they find one. Angela, you are amazing. All of you are. Such a blessing to see phenomenal women in action every day.

To my small but loyal local fan group: Albi, Chelle, Patty, Jessica, Valarie, Sue, Dewey & Linda, Donnie & Shelly, Betty, Josh, Tanya, Maggie and the many others I can't name individually. Thank you for believing in me.

And a special thank you to Susan Graybeal, you've come a long way baby. From high school dreaming to where you are today it has truly been a pleasure to watch your writing career bloom. Thank you for your friendship, and thank you for your encouragement. Thank you for being a Survivor too.

And to all of my Squidoo friends for encouraging me to do this in the first place. Correen, Bambi, Ramkitten, Holley, Alex, and the whole gang. I know I have a lot more to list, but there are so many! And I thank Seth Godin for giving me the venue and the inspiration in the first place.

A very special thank you is reserved for the Reel Thing Film Crew. Suzan and Casey, I love you guys so much. Jim, I'm going to miss working with you. Judith, Michelle, all of you. It has been a wonderful adventure. I look forward to many more together.

If your name isn't in this list, please do not think I have forgotten you. If I listed everybody who helped me get this book out it really would be a mile and a half long. You have not been forgotten. If you have been a part of my life for even a short time, know that you have inspired me in some way. I carry all of those lessons with me, and share then when I can. Thank you for inspiring me...   Now, on to the next book.

Thank you for everything.

Ayngel

Boshemia lives in Southwestern Colorado with her husband
Ed and four children. Two dogs and a cat rule her home.
Born to be a gypsy rubber tramp, Boshemia loves hot baths,
warm hugs, cool days and cold drinks. She prefers volunteer
work to the buffer life and prefers dogs to cats, fantasy novels
to reality television, and sincerity over status any day.

To contact Ayngel please use her website **BoshemiasBohemia.com**
(or @boshemia on Twitter)

Watch for Boshemia's upcoming memoir,

"The Adventures of Invisible Girl"

www.ingramcontent.com/pod-product-compliance
Lightning Source LLC
Chambersburg PA
CBHW060834280326
41934CB00007B/779